Trial by Treatment

Trial by Treatment

PUNISHING ILLNESS
IN AN AGE OF
CRIMINAL LEGAL REFORM

Mary Ellen Stitt

THE UNIVERSITY OF CHICAGO PRESS
CHICAGO AND LONDON

The University of Chicago Press, Chicago 60637
The University of Chicago Press, Ltd., London
© 2025 by The University of Chicago
All rights reserved. No part of this book may be used or reproduced in any manner whatsoever without written permission, except in the case of brief quotations in critical articles and reviews. For more information, contact the University of Chicago Press, 1427 E. 60th St., Chicago, IL 60637.
Published 2025
Printed in the United States of America

34 33 32 31 30 29 28 27 26 25   1 2 3 4 5

ISBN-13: 978-0-226-84040-6 (cloth)
ISBN-13: 978-0-226-84042-0 (paper)
ISBN-13: 978-0-226-84041-3 (e-book)
DOI: https://doi.org/10.7208/chicago/9780226840413.001.0001

Library of Congress Cataloging-in-Publication Data

Names: Stitt, Mary Ellen author
Title: Trial by treatment : punishing illness in an age of criminal legal reform / Mary Ellen Stitt.
Description: Chicago : The University of Chicago Press, 2025. | Includes bibliographical references and index.
Identifiers: LCCN 2024038173 | ISBN 9780226840413 ebook | ISBN 9780226840420 paperback | ISBN 9780226840406 cloth
Subjects: LCSH: Alternatives to imprisonment—United States | Alternatives to imprisonment—United States—Public opinion | Criminal justice, Administration of—United States | Offenders with mental disabilities—Rehabilitation—United States | Pre-trial intervention—United States
Classification: LCC HV9276.5 .S75 2025 | DDC 364.6/80973—dc23/eng/20241031
LC record available at https://lccn.loc.gov/2024038173

♾ This paper meets the requirements of ANSI/NISO Z39.48-1992 (Permanence of Paper).

Contents

Introduction: Punishing Illness · 1

Part I: Legitimation

CHAPTER ONE

Rescuing Legitimacy

Treatment-Based Reforms in the Criminal Legal System · 19

CHAPTER TWO

Extending Control

Diversion and the Interventionist Courtroom · 37

Part II: Assimilation

CHAPTER THREE

Managing Risk

The Design of Mandated Care · 55

CHAPTER FOUR

Coercing Care

Therapist-Enforcers and Client-Defendants in the Therapeutic Space · 73

Part III: Obfuscation

CHAPTER FIVE
Sorting People
Adjudication by Social Structure · 91

CHAPTER SIX
Punishing Treatment
The Costs of Diversion · 107

Conclusion · 125

Acknowledgments · 143
Methodological Appendix A · 147
Methodological Appendix B · 171
Methodological Appendix C · 179
Notes · 181
Index · 239

[INTRODUCTION]

Punishing Illness

On a muggy October day, George was walking under a highway overpass when a passing police car pulled over. Within minutes, an officer found heroin, cocaine, and a needle on the ground nearby and arrested the elderly Black man on three counts of possession. Hours later George found himself in the county jail on a five thousand dollar bond that he couldn't afford to pay. After a difficult month behind bars, George was offered the option to enter a diversion program that could get him out of jail that same day and keep his record clear. If he went into drug treatment, he was told, the prosecutor would drop all charges against him. He accepted without thinking twice, grateful to be free again.

Once in his assigned outpatient treatment program, though, George ran into a new set of troubles. The staff told him he would be sent back to jail if his drug tests kept coming back positive, but he had been using heroin for well over a decade and found himself too sick to function when he tried to stop. He had to pay for testing and get across town for regular treatment sessions, but he couldn't find the money for the fees or the bus fare. Already struggling to meet the daily demands of survival on his meager disability checks, George was desperate to get out of a legal entanglement that was making his life even more unmanageable. Instead, he felt himself pulled in deeper as he failed over and over to meet program requirements and his counselors increased the frequency of sessions and drug testing in response. He began to see it as only a matter of time before they put him back behind bars. As he reflected despairingly, "I'm a free-ranging animal. That's a method of farming where an animal look like it's free but it's actually not free.... And one day somebody gonna eat his ass."

George had been caught off guard by his experience in the diversion program. The program's leaders shared a goal with reform advocates around the country: to move vulnerable people out of the legal system and into supportive community mental health treatment that could address the root causes of their involvement in that system.[1] They used national best practices, employed only therapists with graduate degrees, and boasted an astonishingly low rearrest rate of under 4 percent among their graduates.[2] And yet George was watching more and more of the other people in his program get "eaten." More than half of them were kicked out and sent back to court, where many faced additional penalties for failing to finish treatment. Finally, afraid that he would end up back in jail if he reported to the program with another positive drug test, George went on the run.

Programs promising treatment as an alternative to punishment have become a central strategy for criminal legal reformers across the United States, where people with substance use or other mental disorders now constitute a majority of those held in US jails and prisons.[3] Hundreds of thousands of people are now diverted into mental health treatment by the criminal courts every year,[4] and hundreds of millions of public dollars are poured into these diversion efforts.[5] Advocacy groups and elected officials across the political spectrum are pointing to diversion programs as a crucial strategy to improve health and reduce the broad reach of the penal system,[6] and candidates for elected office around the country are placing them at the center of their political platforms.[7]

But the research in this book indicates that we have largely misunderstood the impacts of treatment-based alternatives to traditional punishment. In practice, those alternatives help to maintain the criminalization of illness and even intensify punitive interventions into the lives of the most vulnerable.

The promise of diversion into treatment, I found, leads policymakers, prosecutors, and judges to draw even more people like George into the court system rather than letting them go free. But the treatment those people then receive is fundamentally shaped by the legal institution. Treatment providers are asked to exercise standard forms of coercive control over their court-mandated clients, warping the therapeutic relationship. The clients most in need of services are often unable to meet that control—because they are too ill to appear at appointments and pass drug tests, too poor to pay for program fees and transportation, and too frightened to keep coming in to the program to ask for mercy—and are thus removed from treatment and returned to court, where they often face harsher punishments than they would have if they had never been diverted. Taken together, these findings illustrate a process of *institutional entrenchment* by which reforms can strengthen—rather than transforming—established patterns of action.

Punishing Illness

Punishment has become a primary response to mental illness in the United States. The vast majority of people suffering from mental health conditions are not receiving any treatment.[8] Instead, many are finding themselves behind bars. On any given day, most of the people held in prisons and jails meet the current medical criteria for mental disorders, whose boundaries are contested but which are often defined as "alterations in thinking, mood, or behavior (or some combination thereof) associated with distress and/or impaired functioning."[9] One of the most common among these is substance use disorder—referred to colloquially as addiction—a chronic brain disorder defined diagnostically by the functional impairment and suffering it produces.[10] As of 2010, an estimated 65 percent of incarcerated people suffered from substance use disorders.[11] Those disorders often co-occur with other forms of mental illness, and a recent national survey found that people with co-occurring disorders are *eleven times* more likely to be arrested than those without.[12]

A few threads of public policy have intertwined to draw punishment to the forefront of state responses to mental disorder. One is enforcement against drug use. People with substance use disorders are more likely than others to be found in possession of illegal drugs, as are people with other mental illnesses, who often use nonprescribed substances to self-medicate.[13] Rates of arrest for simple drug possession surged following the declaration of the "war on drugs" in the 1970s, and police now make more arrests for that offense than for any other—despite widespread reform efforts such as marijuana legalization.[14] Those arrests tend to lead to long entanglements with the court and carceral systems, since drug possession remains a felony offense in most states and can carry significant prison time.[15]

Social services have also been rolled back in the United States, leaving millions of people with mental disorders in poverty even as the policing of poor people has intensified.[16] People with symptomatic mental illness often struggle to find work, and government support is limited.[17] Subsidized housing waiting lists are years long, public mental healthcare is severely underfunded and often hard to access, and welfare benefits are frequently contingent on employment.[18] Even when services are available, individuals with more severe health conditions can struggle to manage the complex tasks necessary to receive them.[19] Owing to these holes in the social safety net, people with mental disorders are heavily overrepresented among the poor and unhoused.[20] At the same time, policing and punishment of those groups has increased. Most cities have now banned behaviors associated with homelessness—sleeping in parks or sitting on sidewalks, for instance—and local and state efforts to expand prohibitions on those behaviors are ongoing.[21] The most common reasons for arrest among people with histories of psychiatric illness, according to one large study, are "public order" offenses that are often associated with homelessness.[22] Around the country, millions of people are swept into the legal system every year on minor charges stemming from economic desperation.[23]

It is hard to overstate the negative impacts of punishing illness. A large body of research has now shown that incarceration is detrimental to people's long-term mental and physical health.[24] Criminal sanctions also increase social and economic precarity—itself a risk factor for mental illness[25]—by reducing employment, wealth, housing stability, and access to social services.[26] Even police contact that does not result in criminal charges can have serious consequences. Arrest records can trigger employment discrimination and penalties such as eviction from public housing,[27] and interactions with police can also end in violence: As many as one out of every four police killings is of a person with a psychiatric disorder.[28] The punishment of illness also amplifies social inequality. People who are poor, Black, Latine, and/or Native are less likely to receive the treatment they need, and they are far more likely to be swept up by police enforcement against behaviors often associated with mental illness.[29] Because of the long-lasting negative consequences of exposure to state punishment, scholars and advocates point to the criminal legal governance of mental health as a key site for the reproduction of economic and racial inequalities.[30]

Reform

After decades of precipitous growth in the US prison system—which is now the largest in the world[31]—we may be entering a new era.[32] Public support for mass incarceration and the war on drugs has waned.[33] Advocacy groups across the political spectrum are pointing to the injustice and fiscal waste of punishing people with mental illness for victimless behaviors. On the political left, social movements have drawn the criminalization of mental illness to the forefront of public conversations and called for new, nonpunitive government responses.[34] Progressive urban centers around the country have elected prosecutors who promise to reduce punishment for minor offenses.[35] On the right, conservative groups are pushing for reforms designed to reduce the astronomical financial costs of incarceration.[36] A devastating two-decade rise in opioid overdose deaths also had a disproportionate impact on White users and increased conservative support for treating drug use as a public health concern rather than as a crime.[37] And a wide range of advocates and policymakers see nonviolent offenses, such as drug possession and other behaviors that often stem from mental illness, as low-hanging fruit for reform.[38]

As pressure for change mounts, few criminal legal reforms have garnered broader support than diversion programs that promise mental healthcare as an alternative to punishment. These programs can operate at a variety of stages in the criminal court system. Judges can assign people to treatment in lieu of pretrial detention, for instance; prosecutors can divert them into programs with the promise that they will drop the criminal charges against them when they complete them; and judges can work with prosecutors and others to supervise treatment in the form of drug courts or other specialty courts, either before or after conviction. These different forms of diversion differ in their consequences for legal cases. They resemble each other in their basic structure: They ask people to meet certain requirements, monitor their compliance over time, and subject people who don't meet the requirements to more legal sanctions.[39] Together, they have become so widespread that a criminal legal mandate is now the *most common* form of referral into drug treatment in the United States.[40]

Among these programs, the gold standard for many advocates is *pretrial diversion* run by prosecutors, because it promises to let people avoid criminal convictions altogether.[41] Under this model—which is now in use in the vast majority of US cities[42]—prosecutors agree to drop all of the criminal charges against people if they complete therapeutic programs. Although most programs don't limit eligibility to people with diagnosable mental disorders,[43] they are widely championed as alternatives to punishing illness: Advocates frame pretrial diversion as an effective intervention for "offenders with alcohol, substance abuse, mental health, or co-occurring disorders."[44] Program directors, judges, and prosecutors frequently told me that they saw mental health conditions—usually substance use disorders—as the underlying issue to be addressed for almost everyone entering diversion.[45] And my national survey of diversion programs indicates that participants are typically assigned to some form of mental or behavioral health treatment.[46]

Despite the enthusiastic advocacy for pretrial diversion and its ubiquity in court systems around the country, we have had very little information about its operations or impacts. By its nature, it is doubly shrouded from view. On one hand, it operates under the umbrella of the therapeutic institution, which promises clients confidentiality and guards that confidentiality closely. On the other, it operates within the criminal court system, which is notoriously unwilling to let the public see its central decision-making processes, including charging, diversion, and plea negotiations. Diverted defendants also disappear from court records, and their legal trajectories are not tracked in administrative data. In addition, there are usually no laws dictating how the treatment programs must operate or what criteria they should use to decide whether someone should be freed or sent back to court. Programs use their own discretion, and they are not obligated to make information about their operations public.

In the absence of concrete information, a few key misunderstandings have taken hold. First, both advocates and researchers tend to assume that diversion is a one-to-one substitute for traditional sanctions like incarceration, so that it can only reduce people's exposure to criminal punishment. In this book, I show that the reality is more complicated. Certainly, diversion programs can offer legal decision-makers a viable alternative to more punitive measures. But around the country, the promise of diversion into court-mandated treatment has become a central pillar of arguments in favor of criminalizing victimless behaviors such as drug use. And once in place, that promise encourages legal professionals to pull *more* people into the court system, extending criminal legal control to people who would otherwise have walked free.

Second, diversion is widely understood as a clean exit from the court system. As a recent ACLU report declares, for instance, "Diversion is an effective way to redirect people with mental health needs and substance use issues *out* of the criminal legal system and into supportive community treatment."[47] But in fact, legal supervision continues after people are diverted into treatment. Treatment providers are asked to monitor their court-mandated clients closely and to enforce strict performance requirements—usually including attendance at mandatory appointments, payment of fees, and regular drug testing—and to send them back to court if they fail to meet them. Their clients' keen awareness that they could be returned to court at any moment profoundly shapes the treatment itself. Cognizant of their therapists' dual roles as enforcers, people tend to interact with them guardedly, in exchanges warped by fear.

Far from operating as exits from the legal system for everyone, diversion programs ultimately take on the courts' duties of judging and sorting people for punishment, giving them new form as they do. In the treatment setting, punishment is allocated largely along lines of social inequality. For people who are relatively healthy and well-resourced, the standard diversion requirements are usually just an inconvenience. They pay their fees, pass their drug tests, and arrive punctually in their cars at each treatment session. They have their cases dismissed on time. For those with severe substance use disorders or other mental illnesses, those who are too poor to pay their fees or get transportation, and those who are too afraid of the legal system to ask for help when things go wrong, meeting the same program requirements can be a Herculean task. Mandated treatment program completion rates often hover around 50 percent, and the participants who don't finish are overwhelmingly those who are poor, Black, or severely ill. Those people are returned to court, where they often face *harsher* punishments than they would have if they had never entered a diversion program at all.

The idea that reform can amplify the processes it promises to change is not a new one. Social theorists such as Michel Foucault, David Rothman, and Stanley Cohen have famously documented that phenomenon at several key junctures in the past.[48] As Rothman put it, well-intentioned reforms can take existing problems "to new, more ominous heights."[49] Contemporary activists such as Mariame Kaba similarly warn against "reformist reforms," or policies that promise meaningful change in the criminal legal system but in practice only increase the power of that system.[50] But exactly what differentiates the reforms these theorists describe from the rest remains unclear.[51] Certainly, plenty of reforms *have* delivered on their promises. Legislative changes reducing felony offenses to misdemeanors or expanding access to parole, for instance, have tended to reduce the reach of the criminal legal system without noticeable unintended consequences.[52] Why and how do some well-intentioned efforts produce meaningful change, while others take old problems to new heights? As criminologist Thomas Blomberg has observed, we do not yet understand the meaning of a cycle of reform wherein the best intentions often lead to undesired outcomes. Until we do, we will continue to repeat it.[53]

This book makes a close analysis of that cycle in a key contemporary site, showing in granular detail how reform that promises transformation can come to shore up established social structures instead. Despite everyone's best intentions, when new tools—new programs, new resources, or new forms of discretion—are placed into the hands of the same institutional actors, those tools become incorporated into long-established patterns of action and help to perpetuate those patterns in new and less visible ways. In doing so, they further entrench the power of the adopting institutions in the social world.

Research Site and Methods

To document the hidden processes that constitute diversion, I spent several years collecting—and often fighting hard for access to—various forms of data. I conducted ethnographic fieldwork inside a mandated treatment program, in trainings for diversion practitioners, and in courtrooms. I interviewed prosecutors, judges, diversion directors, defense attorneys, treatment providers, and people who had been through diversion. I fielded a vignette-based experiment with working prosecutors and conducted a national survey of diversion programs. I also collected thousands of pages of court dockets, state legislative documents, and administrative data from diversion programs and prosecutors' offices around the country. Finally, I triangulated among these data to analyze the operations of pretrial diversion and its consequences. Below, I outline each of these data collection efforts in more detail. A full account of each one can be found in the methodological appendices at the back of this book.

THE TREATMENT ENVIRONMENT

To understand how diversion operates in practice, I first spent nine months going through a program alongside mandated participants. I chose a pretrial diversion program that used standard best practices, such as employing entirely master's-level therapists,[54] whose eligibility and program requirements were common in programs around the country,[55] and that was located in a city in the South, the region with the highest imprisonment rates in the United States and one that has put significant resources toward pretrial diversion in efforts to reduce those rates.[56] I attended and participated fully in all of the treatment sessions the program offered. Therapists also encouraged program participants to spend time together outside of group sessions, and I went to participants' homes for meals, met for coffee, and sat outside of the treatment center talking for long stretches before and after group sessions. With their permission, I took fieldnotes on some of those interactions as well. In addition, I interviewed fifty people who had participated in diversion in the past. Because of the sensitivity of the site and the information participants shared with me, I have taken particular care to protect their anonymity. I have given pseudonyms to all of the people I write about and omitted any details that could be used to identify them. I also do not identify the location of the field site, since some participants might be identifiable if I did.

To situate these study participants and their experiences within the broader context of diversion, I collected four years of administrative data on the demographics and outcomes of diverted defendants in that jurisdiction. I also talked to treatment providers in my field site and elsewhere about their aims and motivations and the pressures they felt in their work. In all, I interviewed forty-seven mental health professionals, including diversion program directors and therapists who worked directly with diverted defendants. For additional insights into their work and concerns, I also attended two national conferences for diversion practitioners, where I observed dozens of presentations and trainings.

THE COURTROOM

To understand the role of diversion in the criminal court system, I interviewed forty-one prosecutors, judges, and defense attorneys and observed criminal courtroom proceedings over the course of two years. These interviews and observations shed light on how decision-makers understand and use diversion in their work. And because jurisdictions don't collect data on what happens in people's legal cases before they are diverted or on their ultimate outcomes, the time I spent in the courthouse also helped me to piece together the trajectories of diverted cases through the courts. To better understand case trajectories, I also collected complete court docket entries for several hundred felony diversion cases and coded them for the content and outcomes of every hearing.

The most important legal decisions are not made in the courtroom or documented in administrative data. Behind closed doors, prosecutors decide whether each arrestee will face criminal charges or walk free, and later they determine case outcomes by deciding what plea deals to offer the 95 percent of convicted defendants who eventually enter guilty pleas. To understand whether or how pretrial diversion shaped those crucial decisions, I had to take a creative approach. I designed a vignette-based experiment that described two different felony-level cases and asked seventy active prosecutors how likely they would be to file charges in each and what plea deals they would likely offer. Each prosecutor was randomly assigned to one of two versions of the survey, which differed only in that one specified that the cases would be eligible for pretrial diversion, and the other did not. Random assignment ensured that the only difference between the groups was the diversion option, so that I could measure the influence of that option on their decision-making processes.[57]

THE NATIONAL LANDSCAPE

To situate my qualitative and local research within the national landscape of diversion, I took a random sample of 20 percent of all US cities with populations over 100,000 and, with the help of research assistants, spent two years collecting comprehensive information about the diversion programs that they and the counties in which they were situated operated as alternatives to arrest, prosecution, or formal punishment, outside of carceral or hospital settings. After collecting all of the available public information, we reached out with hundreds of phone calls and emails to the programs in the sample to gather additional information about their eligibility criteria, program requirements, and other operations.

Institutional Entrenchment

Together, these varied sources of data show how—despite everyone's best intentions—diversion has become a new engine for punishment. In doing so, they also bring into focus a broader process of *institutional entrenchment*, by which reforms can shore up embattled institutions—or "symbolic systems" that order reality, such as the criminal legal system.[58] When institutions come under fire, institutional actors can shore up their positions by embracing new tools or practices that reassure the public that they can be trusted with the power they have. Once enacted within those institutions, these reforms are incorporated into powerful, long-established patterns of action, and they can help to perpetuate those patterns in new and less visible ways. That process unfolds in three parts, outlined and illustrated below with findings from my site.

LEGITIMATION

The first move in the process of institutional entrenchment is the implementation of a reform that reassures the public that an institution should retain—and even expand—its power in the social world. That is, rather than imposing external limits on the organizations that carry out the work of an institution, the reform promises that they will do their work differently and to better effect. By shoring up legitimacy not just in the eyes of the public but also internally, helping workers to feel better about what they do, this move encourages organizational expansion.

Reforms tend to emerge out of contestation, and few domains of social life have been more contested than mental health. Responsibility for the care and treatment of mental illness has shifted among the religious, medical, therapeutic, and legal professions,[59] reflecting dramatic changes in prevailing definitions of mental illnesses and ideas about their treatment.[60] The blurred, unstable boundaries around these forms of illness have lingered in part because of incomplete scientific knowledge about them,[61] which has also allowed inaccurate associations between mental illness and dangerousness, moral weakness, and poor discipline to flourish and contributed to the criminalization of many of their symptoms.[62] Now, emerging from the battles over mental illness is a growing movement to shift its management away from the criminal legal system.[63]

In response to public concern about the criminalization of illness, elected officials are expanding programs that divert people from the criminal courts into mental health treatment. Those programs assure the public that the legal system is providing people with the help they need and that, in fact, it is the most appropriate entity to administer that help. By leveraging the threat of punishment, the argument goes, courts can push people to make changes that they would not have made on their own. They also move low-level cases out of view, shifting them from the public courtroom to the hidden sites where mental healthcare is administered.[64] The invisibility of diversion allows politically diverse groups of advocates to project their own hopes onto programs that promise almost magical effects.

The expansion of diversion programs is also lending new legitimacy to criminal legal control on the front lines of legal practice, giving courtroom decision-makers additional reasons to keep people under supervision. Convinced that people who are ill benefit from the court's control, prosecutors bring criminal charges in cases they would otherwise have refused, and judges monitor people more closely and over longer periods of time. By legitimizing coercive state intervention in the minds of the people who administer it, in other words, diversion helps to expand the legal system's reach.

ASSIMILATION

The second element in the process of entrenchment is the assimilation by reformist practices of dominant institutional logics, or sets of conventions that have achieved "rulelike status in social thought and action."[65] The actors tasked with implementing reform may aim to make fundamental changes in their organizations, but they are operating under long-established pressures and constraints. As new practices are incorporated, their contours adapt to established organizational forms.

Diversion programs may be implemented with the intent of making substantive and even radical change. The practitioners in this book, without exception, emphasized their strong commitments to replacing punishment with high-quality treatment. But court-mandated mental healthcare operates in an environment concerned with maintaining visible control over people who are widely viewed as dangerous, and programs are also under immense pressure to adopt requirements that have become standard in the criminal courts, including appearing for appointments, meeting legal financial obligations, and passing regular drug tests. Treatment providers are expected to strictly enforce conformity with those requirements, despite the fact that they are often at odds with effective mental healthcare.[66]

Because court-mandated treatment operates under the shadow of punishment, criminal legal logics also seep into the day-to-day interactions between therapists and their clients. Providers try to provide the kind of care that they would offer outside of a mandated setting, but they are responsible for enforcing rules and ultimately determining the punishments their clients will face. Keenly aware that their treatment providers are also their judges, clients engage in a set of defensive and performative strategies that are informed by the logics of the courtroom. Those strategies consistently obstruct treatment providers' efforts to establish trust and provide high-quality care.

OBFUSCATION

Molded by their institutional environments, reforms become new tools for carrying out established practices. Over time, they obfuscate the continuation of those practices, making them harder to recognize even when they come into view by giving them new and more appealing forms.

In diversion programs, the traditional processes of criminal adjudication and punishment continue to operate under cover of treatment. As treatment providers enforce compliance with strict rules, they systematically move many of their clients back into the court system to be punished. But the therapeutic site sorts people largely along lines of inequality. People experiencing chronic pain, symptoms of trauma, or mental illness often struggle to avoid use of cannabis or other medications that trigger drug test failures; those who are ill, unhoused, or responsible for vulnerable family members often struggle to arrive at treatment sessions and to pay program fees; and people from groups frequently targeted by police violence and anti-Black racism in the legal system are often fearful of reporting to the program to ask for help when they fall out of compliance, and go on the run instead. People marked "noncompliant" with diversion not only lose the chance to exit the legal system but are often punished more harshly than they would have been if they had never been diverted at all.

Diversion obfuscates the allocation of punishment both by moving it out of view and by reframing it. People who enter diversion disappear from the public courtroom, and often the decisions that assign them criminal convictions are made behind closed doors. But even when their cases return to court to be adjudicated publicly, the punishment of sick people for minor offenses is colored by a new narrative: even if these vulnerable individuals did not deserve to be punished on their initial charges, they do now. By refusing the proffered help, that narrative goes, they have demonstrated to the court that they require coercive control because they are unwilling or unable to make positive changes in their own lives.

Plan of the Book

The book proceeds in three main parts. Part I documents institutional *legitimation*, or the process by which reforms help to shore up the legitimacy and maintain the reach of an institution. Chapter 1 examines the expansion of treatment-based alternatives in the criminal courts in a moment of widespread advocacy for reform, analyzing the competing pressures on public officials that make those alternatives so appealing. On one hand, those officials face fiscal and popular pressure to reduce the use of incarceration and other sanctions; on the other, they fear that simply releasing people from criminal legal supervision could be construed as neglect of public safety. Court-supervised treatment programs allow them to advertise more compassionate and effective responses to mental illness and substance use without relinquishing control.

Chapter 2 shows how reforms can help to legitimize an institution not just in the political sphere but also on the ground. In the criminal court system, treatment-based interventions lead judges and prosecutors to expand their sphere of influence by reframing and reorganizing the work they do. The chapter outlines three social processes that contribute to this expansion: Organizational norms shift, as judges and prosecutors increasingly view court-mandated programs as social services that reshape people's lives for the better. Organizational membership shifts, as treatment providers increasingly work closely with courtroom decision-makers and urge them to send more defendants to their therapeutic programs. And organizational constraints are lifted, since diverting defendants allows decision-makers to avoid the professional penalties that have traditionally discouraged them from intervening too widely. Together, these shifts encourage prosecutors to draw more people into the court system by bringing criminal charges against people who would otherwise have walked free. By legitimizing coercive state intervention in the minds of the people who administer it, in other words, diversion helps to expand the legal system's reach.

Part II documents institutional *assimilation*, showing how reformist practices are reshaped by the logics of the institution that adopts them. Chapter 3 shows that treatment programs that enroll court-mandated participants do more than provide mental healthcare: they are also tasked with supervising their clients and enforcing strict rules of behavior. Around the country, diversion programs employ remarkably similar rules and enforcement strategies. Nearly all of them hold criminal cases in suspension until participants complete their assigned programs, and they return to the court system anyone who falls out of compliance with program rules. Programs require abstinence from substances (enforced by regular drug testing), fee payment, and regular mandatory appointments. This program structure is neither legally mandated nor supported by research. Rather, it reflects powerful institutional logics of containment and control: treatment programs aim to demonstrate that they can be trusted to manage the "dangerous" people in their care.

Chapter 4 shows that the court-mandated treatment program structure, modeled on other forms of criminal legal supervision, profoundly shapes the day-to-day provision of care. Although mental healthcare providers try to insulate treatment from enforcement, they are responsible for making a range of daily decisions that determine their clients' lengths of stay under court supervision and exposure to criminal punishment. Deeply concerned about their legal case outcomes, participants engage in several strategies that are central to the traditional criminal legal process: *negotiating responsibility*, or arguing that they do not deserve to be in the legal system at all; *negotiating risk*, or trying to convince providers that they can safely be released from treatment, often by hiding any symptoms of mental illness; and *serving out time*, or simply checking out mentally to wait for the end of their allotted time in mandated programs. Those strategies often collide with treatment providers' efforts to establish productive therapeutic relationships with their clients.

Part III documents *obfuscation*, showing how reforms can perpetuate the traditional work of their adopting institutions even as they obscure it. Chapter 5 outlines the ways diversion programs, like the criminal courts, sort and mark people for sanctions. The programs adjudicate on the basis of compliance with program requirements, sending the "noncompliant" back to court to be punished. This form of adjudication systematically sorts people along lines of social inequality: because successful compliance requires health, financial resources, and legal-institutional trust, the people who are returned to court are overwhelmingly poor, Black, and sick.

Chapter 6 examines what happens to people who are marked for punishment in diversion. Many defendants are required to enter guilty pleas in order to enter diversion—with the promise that those pleas can be withdrawn when they complete treatment—so that programs' decisions to return their cases to court effectively constitute decisions to convict them. Whether people return to court to face adjudication or sentencing, judges and prosecutors often view treatment noncompletion as a black mark against them and assign harsher punishments as a result. And although court-mandated treatment itself is experienced as a punitive intervention, time spent in diversion is not credited toward defendants' sentences when they return to court. As a result of these dynamics, treatment-based alternatives can, paradoxically, result in harsher sanctions for the most vulnerable people.

The concluding chapter considers the ramifications of the research in this book for theory and policy. It further elaborates the framework of *institutional entrenchment* and considers its applications beyond the criminal legal system. Across domains, institutional reforms can help to maintain and extend dominant practices, ultimately re-entrenching established patterns of action. The chapter then considers how we might relieve courts of responsibility for managing mental disorder, laying out policies such as the provision of accessible public mental healthcare, including interventions aimed at harm reduction; the legalization of substance use and of other behaviors for which many people with mental illness are arrested, such as homelessness; and measures to reduce poverty and inequality more broadly.

∴

Part I
LEGITIMATION

∴

[CHAPTER ONE]

Rescuing Legitimacy

Treatment-Based Reforms in the Criminal Legal System

In February of 2021, drug possession was briefly legalized in Washington State. The state's supreme court, in a divided ruling, struck down its felony drug possession law because it had not required prosecutors to prove that defendants had possessed drugs *knowingly*.[1] The decision upended Washington's criminal court system. Across the state, prosecutors dropped all pending drug possession cases and recalled arrest warrants issued in those cases. Orders to vacate convictions were filed for people incarcerated or on probation for simple drug possession. People in court-ordered drug treatment were released.[2]

Responding to pressure from reformers, in a state ranked among the most liberal in the country,[3] the state legislature agreed on a temporary solution. They passed a new law that required police officers to refer people to voluntary treatment the first two times they were found in possession of drugs and made the third offense a simple misdemeanor, which carried a maximum penalty of only ninety days in jail. The legislation contained a sunset clause for those provisions specifying that they would remain in effect for just two years.[4]

When the legislature returned to the issue in early 2023, lawmakers argued that the state needed tougher penalties for drug possession so that they could court-mandate people into treatment. Simple misdemeanors, they pointed out, were not dealt with in the kinds of courts that had drug diversion programs, so people were not being sent to treatment under court supervision. The incentives to comply with treatment were also not strong enough, they maintained. As one state senator put it, "The threat of a longer sentence is a needed motivation for drug offenders to undergo treatment."[5] Steeper penalties, together with expanded pretrial diversion programs, policymakers argued, would ensure that people entered and completed treatment.[6]

The Washington legislature ultimately passed a bill that substantially increased sanctions for drug possession and expanded court-mandated treatment options. It eliminated the requirement that police refer people to drug treatment rather than arrest them and changed drug possession from just a simple misdemeanor to a gross misdemeanor, meaning that it could carry a sentence of up to a year behind bars. At the same time, it created a pretrial diversion program that offers people charged with simple drug possession anywhere in the state a chance to have their charges dismissed if they complete substance use disorder treatment.[7]

What is happening in Washington is not unique. Around the country, court-mandated therapeutic programs have become a central pillar of arguments in favor of criminalizing minor offenses. Cities are expanding diversion programs designed for people who are unhoused, even as they draw more of those people into the legal system by passing new ordinances criminalizing homelessness.[8] In Oregon, where drug possession was decriminalized by a 2020 ballot measure, mandated treatment quickly became a focal point of arguments to recriminalize. Lawmakers pushed to change the policy on the grounds that criminal penalties were a necessary incentive to get people into treatment.[9] Even the liberal executive director of the state's Alcohol and Drug Policy Commission declared that drug decriminalization "created a problem, because there are some people—the stick of jail allowed them to get into recovery. And now we don't have that anymore."[10] Oregon recriminalized drug possession in 2024, simultaneously creating new forms of diversion for people arrested for the offense.[11]

This chapter shows how treatment-based reforms lend new legitimacy to the criminal legal governance of mental illness. Public sentiment is increasingly turning against the criminal punishment of nonviolent acts often associated with mental illness, including substance use.[12] In response, many public officials are expanding programs designed to divert people out of the traditional court system and into supervised treatment.[13] Drawing on interviews with court-mandated treatment providers and program directors, a national analysis of prosecutors' campaign platforms, government reports and news articles, websites and reports published by a national sample of urban pretrial diversion programs, and a survey of the same sample,[14] the chapter outlines the ways diversion programs have helped state officials to respond to reformers' concerns while strengthening the case for the courts' jurisdiction over substance use and other symptoms of mental disorder. In doing so, it illustrates a process of institutional *legitimation*, by which reforms help to justify and thus maintain the reach of an institution.

Punishment and Mental Illness in the United States

Criminal punishment has become a central response to mental illness in the United States. Mental health services are severely underfunded, and most people with mental disorders—including substance use disorders—are not receiving any treatment.[15] Instead, many are swept into the criminal legal system. Estimates suggest that people who meet diagnostic criteria for mental illness now constitute the majority of people held in US prisons and jails.[16] A recent national survey found that people with both a substance use disorder and at least one other mental illness are *eleven times* more likely to be arrested than those without. Many in that group are arrested on minor charges multiple times every year.[17]

The criminalization of mental illness is rooted in the social construction of the category itself. Mental illness has been defined over time in opposition to societal norms.[18] The US Surgeon General famously defined it as a health condition "characterized by alterations in thinking, mood, or behavior (or some combination thereof) associated with distress and/or impaired functioning."[19] The experiences that produce distress, and the forms of functioning required to manage daily life, reflect social structures and cultural understandings that can shift over time.[20] The construct of alcoholism crystallized during the Industrial Revolution, for instance, when customary levels of alcohol consumption came to be seen as interfering with factory work.[21] Contemporary definitions of schizophrenia coalesced as part of a backlash against Black freedom movements in the 1960s as psychiatrists began to explain Black men's political protest as symptoms of mental instability.[22] Although mental illnesses produce measurable mental alterations and distress, the lines we draw between madness and sanity necessarily reflect misalignments between people's behaviors and the social structures and expectations around them.[23]

Particularly contested among common mental disorders are substance use disorders, often referred to colloquially as addictions. Over time, the patterns of substance use that we now classify as disordered have been understood variously as benign routines, as religious or moral failings, as crimes, and as diseases, and debates over their classification are ongoing.[24] But the most recent research indicates that they fall within the broad category of mental illness. A substance use disorder is characterized by sustained changes in an individual's cognition, mood, and behavior,[25] and it is defined diagnostically by distress and impaired functioning. Nearly all of the criteria for substance use disorder in the *Diagnostic and Statistical Manual of Mental Disorders*, 5th edition (*DSM-5*)—the manual used by mental health professionals to arrive at diagnoses—relate to the negative impacts of substance use on individuals' daily lives.[26] Like other mental illnesses, this disorder cannot be understood in isolation from its broader social context. The levels of distress or functional impairment that each person experiences as a result of regular drug use depend on their surroundings: whether they can get the doses they need and have a safe place to administer them, for instance; whether they know the content and the potency of the substances they have access to; what kinds of work they are required to do; and how their substance use is viewed by the people around them.[27]

People with mental illness face myriad forms of social exclusion, which often leaves them vulnerable to criminalization. Discrimination against them in hiring, housing, and other social domains is rampant.[28] Those with severe illness can also have difficulty managing the tasks required to access public services.[29] And although treatment can stabilize and even eliminate symptoms for some people and some disorders, it is not a panacea. The side effects of psychiatric medications can be terrible, and they can worsen over time. Success rates for some of those medications are low—they hover around 30 percent for schizophrenia, for instance.[30] Many of the most common treatment approaches for substance use disorder have no basis in science at all.[31] Often excluded from workplaces and even from shelters, people with symptomatic mental illnesses are substantially overrepresented among the unhoused.[32]

Millions of people with mental illness—and especially those who are poor and Black, Latine, or Native—have been caught in the teeth of a massive social shift.[33] Social services were rolled back dramatically in the 1980s and 1990s even as the punishment of low-level offenses intensified.[34] Fueled by a powerful political backlash against mass movements for racial justice and by racialized anxieties about drug use, several changes in the legal system took place in tandem.[35] Police stops and arrests of people engaged in victimless behaviors related to drug use or poverty—such as drug possession, public alcohol consumption, panhandling, windshield cleaning, or sex work—surged, mostly in neighborhoods where residents were largely poor and Black.[36] Prosecutors began to bring charges in scores of minor cases that they would previously have ignored.[37] New laws increased the likelihood and length of prison sentences even for low-level crimes such as drug possession.[38] Over the course of the 1980s and 1990s alone, the number of people in state prisons on drug convictions increased by a factor of *twelve*.[39] At every stage of the legal process, economic and racial disparities were stark.[40]

Despite growing calls for reform, policing and punishment of people who are ill continues largely unabated. Drug possession remained the most common reason for arrest in the United States in 2019.[41] Simple drug possession can still result in a felony conviction in the vast majority of US states.[42] Not only people with substance use disorders, but also those with other mental illnesses, are often vulnerable to arrest and punishment on drug charges: People with psychiatric disorders often use nonprescribed substances to self-medicate, and about half of them also develop substance use disorders.[43] And enforcement against other behaviors associated with illness and poverty may be on the rise. A recent study of 187 US cities found that the vast majority had passed municipal bans on at least some behaviors associated with homelessness—including sleeping in parks, sitting down on sidewalks, camping, living in vehicles, "panhandling," "loitering," and "loafing"—and that the number of bans had risen substantially between 2006 and 2016.[44] A movement to criminalize the unhoused is also gaining some traction at the state level: anticamping legislation was recently passed statewide in Texas and Missouri, and similar laws are currently under consideration in seven other states.[45]

The negative impacts of punishing people who are sick are hard to overstate. The most severe end of the punishment spectrum involves incarceration, which is inherently dangerous and at times torturous in itself. Solitary confinement, which is still widely used in prisons in the United States, tends to exacerbate mental illness and can even induce it in previously healthy people.[46] Incarceration also produces a range of long-term negative consequences in the lives of incarcerated people following release: reduced household wealth, damage to both short- and long-term employment outcomes, reduced mental and physical health, fear of engaging with state institutions such as schools and healthcare providers, housing and residential instability, and damage to the material security and health of family members.[47] Social and economic precarity is itself a risk factor for mental illness.[48]

Criminal convictions, whether they are accompanied by incarceration or not, carry their own long-term burdens. A felony conviction is a major barrier to employment and is associated with lower incomes over the course of the convicted person's life.[49] It can also lock people out of key forms of public assistance, including public housing, educational grants, and food stamps.[50] Even misdemeanor convictions can exclude people from some social services and workplaces or professional licensures in areas ranging from nursing to dry cleaning to beautician work.[51] By triggering widespread daily discrimination, convictions may also have negative impacts on overall mental and physical health, putting people at greater risk for psychological distress and depression.[52]

Even when it does not result in a criminal conviction, police contact itself can have serious consequences. Arrest records can trigger employment discrimination and penalties such as eviction from public housing.⁵³ Police interventions can also have devastating impacts on the material and mental well-being of people who are unhoused, as sociologist Chris Herring documents in an ethnographic study of unhoused people in San Francisco: when police force people to move away from the places where they have been staying, clear their camps entirely, or confiscate their belongings, they leave them even more vulnerable than they were before.⁵⁴ Interactions with police can also end in violence, and a recent report by the Treatment Advocacy Center finds that at least one in four—and as many as half—of all police killings are of people with untreated psychiatric disorders.⁵⁵

Contestation

After years of unbridled expansion, the US criminal legal system—and particularly the punishment of illness—is increasingly coming under fire. On the left, the Movement for Black Lives has brought national attention to the impacts of policing and punishment on Black people in the United States. The movement's mass actions in 2020, which became some of the largest protests in US history, amplified calls to "defund the police" and reallocate funding to mental health services.⁵⁶ Their ongoing political demands include the decriminalization of drug use and reinvestment in healthcare, housing, and job services.⁵⁷ One outgrowth of this social movement has been an electoral push that has swept left-leaning district attorneys (DAs) into office in at least fifty of the largest criminal jurisdictions in the United States.⁵⁸ Around the country, progressive voters are enthusiastically endorsing campaign platforms focused on reducing punishment for low-level, nonviolent offenses.⁵⁹

A simultaneous push for criminal legal reform has come from the political right, as conservatives have taken aim at the financial costs of incarceration. The fiscal crisis of 2008, which coincided with low crime rates, gave birth to what legal scholar Hadar Aviram terms "humonetarianism"—a discourse advocating frugality as a reason for reducing the size of the carceral system.⁶⁰ Conservative reformers under the banner of Right on Crime began to advocate policy changes that could "produce the best possible results at the lowest possible cost" by using lower-cost interventions and reducing recidivism rates. Around the country, other groups on the right have joined the call for strategic reforms. They aim specifically to reduce spending without sacrificing "public safety," engaging in what sociologist Christopher Seeds calls a politics of "bifurcation":⁶¹ advocacy for reduced punishment for nonviolent crimes coupled with continued or increased punitiveness against violence. In other words, they focus on new responses, particularly to low-level offenses.[62]

Attitudes toward the punishment of mental illness, in particular, are changing across the political spectrum. Although the stigma surrounding people with mental illness is still pervasive,[63] recent research suggests that it is on the decline. Advances in neuroscience and years of advocacy by individuals and organizations have pushed a growing share of the US public to view mental disorders as biological and genetic conditions, rather than as personal weaknesses or character flaws.[64] Although public attitudes toward substance use disorders are decidedly more negative than those toward other mental illnesses,[65] they are also changing. A shattering two-decade rise in opioid overdose deaths, which has disproportionately affected White people,[66] has increased support especially among White voters for treating drug use as a public health concern rather than as a crime.[67] Increasingly, substance use disorders are understood—and portrayed in mainstream media accounts—not as moral failings, but as illnesses requiring treatment from trained professionals.[68]

Along with ideas about the nature of mental illness, attitudes toward treatment are shifting. Increasingly, people in the United States express the belief that individuals with mental health conditions can recover and lead successful lives.[69] About one in six currently takes a psychotropic medication themselves.[70] And belief in the efficacy of therapy is at an all-time high. Dozens of studies find strong and increasing support for professional mental health treatment in general, and psychotherapy is the most popular method.[71] Mental healthcare is also inching closer to the mainstream medical system. The Affordable Care Act, enacted in 2010, finally required insurance companies to cover mental healthcare as part of standard health insurance plans, and Medicaid similarly expanded its coverage. That change has been particularly significant for drug treatment, which historically has operated separately—physically, financially, and culturally—from the rest of healthcare.[72] Belief in, and support for, treatment is strong across the population. A national survey by the Pew Research Center found that more than two-thirds of Americans believed the government should focus more on providing treatment for people who use drugs like heroin and cocaine, rather than on prosecuting them.[73]

Reducing the punishment of mental illness has thus become a key point of convergence for diverse groups of reformers. Those on the left are concerned about the racial disparities in enforcement against minor offenses and about using police to address social problems such as drug use and illness.[74] Those on the right are concerned about the costs of the criminal legal system and incarceration. Rather than advocate leniency for violent crimes, they focus on reducing expenditures on the low-level, nonviolent crimes for which people with mental illness are usually arrested. And people across the political spectrum increasingly believe that mental illness should be treated rather than punished.[75]

Treatment-Based Reform

In response to public contestation, institutions frequently promise reform as a means to shore up their legitimacy.[76] Systems of state punishment, in particular, rely on alignment with widely shared values and patterns of thought to justify their power to the public.[77] When the terrain of public sentiment shifts, the criminal legal institution has to reestablish its footing. Often, that reestablishment takes the form of new practices that address reformers' concerns, at least on their face. Michel Foucault famously detailed the transition away from medieval forms of punishment in the face of public outcry and sympathy with the accused, for instance. Public displays of retributive violence, writes Foucault—including hanging, torture, branding, whipping, and drawing and quartering—reached a crisis of legitimacy. He understood the shift away from those displays and toward a disciplinary approach that aimed to change people internally, exemplified by the birth of the prison, as a reform designed to appease the public and consolidate sovereign power.[78]

In the contemporary criminal legal system, the professionals who carry out the daily work of administering punishment face growing demands for reform directly, as advocates turn their attention to local elections as key pressure points. Judges and district attorneys, who together determine the fate of nearly every arrestee, are typically elected to office.[79] Their elections have historically been largely uncontested, low-turnout affairs.[80] Now, progressive groups are running new candidates and drawing public attention to the work that these officials do in courtrooms.[81] particular, the "progressive prosecutor" movement has focused on electing new district attorneys—the most powerful decision-makers in the criminal court system[82]—with tremendous success.[83]

As a result of organizers' efforts, district attorneys around the country are facing heightened scrutiny and pressure to do *something* to demonstrate their commitments to reform—whether they are newly elected or incumbents trying to hold onto their seats—but they also face some powerful political constraints. The most obvious thing a prosecutor can do to reduce the reach of the legal system is simply not prosecute: prosecuting attorneys have almost total discretion to choose not to pursue charges in any case the police bring in.[84] But that decision carries some risks. Although state prosecutors in the 1960s charged only about half of all the cases that came to them,[85] prosecution rates surged over the decades that followed until charging became the norm. Now, to deviate from that norm by letting people walk free can be damaging for DAs politically. Perceived leniency is often unpopular with voters, and political scientists consistently find that courtroom actors make more punitive decisions when they are concerned about reelection.[86]

Public commitments never to prosecute entire classes of cases have proven risky for district attorneys. Some DAs have made such commitments to "deprosecution," but only in progressive cities,[87] and even there they have often triggered serious political blowback. The governor of Florida removed Tampa's progressive DA, Andrew Warren, after he vowed not to prosecute abortion,[88] for instance; the Pennsylvania state legislature impeached Philadelphia's Larry Krasner for "dereliction of duty," responding in part to his decisions not to prosecute people arrested on low-level charges;[89] and in San Francisco, Chesa Boudin, a DA committed to nonprosecution of "quality-of-life crimes" and other reform policies, was recalled and voted out of office halfway through his first term.[90]

Backlash against deprosecution can come not just from voters and other elected officials but also from the police. Prosecutors have to work closely with police officers on a daily basis to build their cases against defendants: they rely on police officers to conduct investigations and bring in evidence, and they often rely on them to serve as witnesses in court.[91] Nonprosecution has been met with vehement resistance from police forces around the country.[92] In one interview, the policy director of a progressive advocacy group put it this way:

> I've talked to the prosecutors' office a lot about this idea of de-felonization. What they *could* do is just stop prosecuting low-level drug offenses. They could do that and it would be the biggest thing they could do to reduce the size of the jailed population. But if she did that there would be *huge* blowback from the police. They would see it as, "we saw a problem and made this arrest, and now you're not respecting that work we did!"

Unhappy police officers can make it hard or impossible for prosecutors to do their jobs. As one former prosecutor writes, "You need [police] to help you make your cases (every prosecutor has experienced having a police officer catch an attitude, sometimes in the middle of a trial, and purposely ruin your case because they don't like you)."[93] In other words, prosecutors can ill afford to adopt policies that will alienate the police.

In the context of these constraints, district attorneys around the country have turned to diversion as a palatable way to demonstrate their commitments to reform. Because they can decide when and how to move ahead with charges, individual DAs' offices can run pretrial diversion programs that send people into court-supervised therapeutic programs prior to conviction or sentencing. If they complete the programs, prosecutors drop the charges against them and let them exit the system without convictions on their records. If they don't, the cases continue through the courts. By sending people to these programs, prosecutors can demonstrate a commitment to meaningful change in the legal system and to treatment for mental illness without leaving voters with the impression that they have failed to do their jobs. Or, as one former diversion program director observed in an interview, "If they divert a case, it helps them avoid political blowback. . . . It's resolving the situation in some way. Diversion is seen as 'doing something,' whereas dismissal can be seen as 'not doing your job.'" Pretrial diversion programs have become pillars of DAs' political platforms around the country, have garnered hundreds of millions of dollars in grant money, and have been taken up as a gold standard for reform by groups across the political spectrum.[94] The rest of this chapter outlines the emergence of diversion as a popular response to reformers' diverse concerns and source of legitimacy for the criminal legal management of illness.

DIVERSION

Diversion programs emerged in prosecutors' offices in the late 1960s in response to a federal reprimand. In 1967 the US federal government released a major report on the state of crime and criminal justice in the United States titled *The Challenge of Crime in a Free Society*. The report raised concerns that prosecutors were using their broad discretion to dismiss too many cases: "Approximately one-half of those arrested are dismissed. . . . First offenders are often dealt with in this way. So are persons whose offenses arise from drinking or mental problems, if the offenses are minor."[95] Rather than releasing these people, the report instructed, prosecutors were to ensure that they prosecuted anyone who "merit[ed] criminal sanctions" and diverted the rest into treatment or other community services.[96] In other words, the report advocated for diversion programs as a means to avoid not too much punishment but too much leniency, asking prosecutors to maintain supervision over people whose cases would otherwise have been dismissed. A brief expansion of pretrial diversion programs followed release of the report.[97] By 1977, sociologist Malcolm Feeley counted at least 200 pretrial diversion programs nationwide,[98] accounting for a large majority of the 298 programs estimated to be in operation forty years later.[99]

Prosecutor-led diversion built on a longer history of therapeutic interventions managed by the criminal courts. Beginning in the Progressive Era, in the first decades of the twentieth century, reformers had articulated an enhanced role for the court as an institution that could use its punitive powers to transform individuals. Calling on the state to take a more active role in preventing and addressing social problems such as crime, they pushed for an expansion of welfarist services within the legal system as well as outside of it. Urban court systems swelled with new personnel, including probation officers, social workers, doctors, and psychologists, who advised judges on the best treatments to assign to the people who passed through their courtrooms. State legislatures also expanded judicial discretion by extending the range of possible penalties beyond incarceration and fines to include probation, parole, indeterminate sentences, and mandatory treatment. Judges around the country began to move beyond the administration of the law to incorporate techniques borrowed from social work and medicine in efforts to address crime through therapeutic treatment of individual behavior.[100]

The Progressive Era courtroom tradition also gave birth to another key intervention, decades after the emergence of pretrial diversion: the drug court.[101] The first such court was established in 1989, as the war on drugs gathered momentum and court systems contended with surging numbers of drug cases and diminishing judicial discretion. Promising reductions in punishment to people who complete outpatient treatment programs and consistently turn in negative drug tests, drug courts involve frequent, in-depth interactions between judges and program participants in the courtroom setting and typically punish violations of program rules with jail time.[102] Most (72 percent in my national sample) require people to plead guilty as a condition of entry. Drug courts played an important legitimizing function for a court system thrown into turmoil by surging numbers of drug cases, finds sociologist James Nolan,[103] and they continue to draw overwhelming support from government agencies and the general public.[104] Now numbering about four thousand across the United States, they have given birth to a range of "specialty courts"—including mental health courts and veterans' treatment courts—which use the same structure to treat different groups of people.[105]

As reformers become increasingly aware of the costs of criminal conviction and of prolonged involvement with the criminal court system, pretrial diversion run by prosecutors has reemerged as a favorite treatment-based reform among advocates aiming to reduce the reach of the legal system.[106] Operating with far more separation from courtrooms and jails than the drug court, it allows people to avoid conviction altogether and typically spares them from regular contact with the courts. Advocacy groups from across the political spectrum have hailed pretrial diversion as an ideal reform: conservative political leaders champion diversion as a cost-cutting proposal that is "smart" on crime,[107] grassroots groups on the left recommend it in the same breath as social services such as housing and healthcare,[108] and researchers and liberal advocacy groups praise it for reducing the number of people under criminal legal control while addressing the "root causes" of social problems.[109] President Joe Biden declared that diversion into treatment should be the default response to drug possession.[110] Ninety-eight percent of the progressive prosecutors currently in office campaigned on promises to expand pretrial diversion,[111] and candidates for district attorney around the country advertise their commitments to those programs, regardless of their political affiliations and those of their constituencies. In an analysis of thousands of news articles, I turned up not a single instance of criticism of an elected official for using or expanding a typical pretrial diversion program.[112]

The structure of the pretrial diversion program directly addresses liberal and leftist reformers' calls for less punishment and more treatment for low-level offenses. The programs promise to let people leave the court system without criminal convictions or formal sanctions, and they move people directly into treatment for mental health conditions. (Although only about 16 percent of the pretrial diversion programs in my national sample limit participation to people with diagnosed mental disorders, nearly two-thirds of those from whom I was able to collect more detailed information about program content reported that they require all participants to receive mental health treatment, and 94 percent said that they mandate drug testing for everyone.[113] Even programs that do not mandate treatment across the board reported that they assign it individually to many or most of their participants.) Some of the programs also promise to connect participants with other kinds of social services. And across the board, they contend that their practices are "evidence-based" and highly effective, citing a long list of diversion program evaluations that have found better outcomes among people who finish diversion programs than among those who remain in the traditional system.[114]

Pretrial diversion programs also promise to improve public safety even as they cut costs, speaking to two of the central concerns of more moderate or conservative reformers. To demonstrate their commitment to safety and avoid any appearance of leniency toward dangerous crime, they typically limit eligibility to low-level, nonviolent charges.[115] Many limit eligibility even further: nationally, I estimate that nearly one in five limit it to drug- or alcohol-related charges, and another 23 percent limit it to other specific low-level offenses, such as loitering or disorderly conduct.[116] As one program director I interviewed explained that standard practice: "Diversion is a gift given to people we believe are not a public safety risk.... We don't take any weapons, any violent crimes, or any heavy distribution like distribution of methamphetamine or heroin. The public would definitely shut us down." Her concern that expanding the program to include a wider range of charges could trigger backlash is not unfounded. When San Francisco DA Chesa Boudin started a diversion program that did not explicitly exclude people facing charges of sexual abuse and domestic violence, for instance, the harsh criticism that followed—including from the California District Attorneys' Association and from staff in his own office— contributed to his recall and removal from office.[117]

Advocates of diversion programs also emphasize that they save taxpayer dollars. Some contend that they reduce immediate case processing costs by reducing attorneys' caseloads and shortening court dockets. Staff in one large DA's office, for instance, convinced the local council to fund a large new pretrial diversion program by showing them that it would ultimately save money by reducing per-client fees paid to the public defenders' office. Most programs also refer participants out to nonprofit or private centers for treatment rather than providing services directly, meaning that they can operate on very small budgets. This practice of engaging voluntary organizations, which has become a key strategy for the penal sector in other sites, is often an effective way to facilitate and justify the expansion of new forms of criminal legal intervention in the context of economic retrenchment.[118] In addition, many practitioners argue that diversion programs save money on policing, prosecution, court costs, and probation or incarceration by reducing recidivism rates, declaring that they enhance "public safety through addressing the *root cause* of the arrest-provoking behaviors of the defendant,"[119] "reduce the risk they pose to the safety of the community,"[120] or "prevent future criminal conduct."[121] Across public websites and reports nationally, programs advertise the public monies they can save by preventing people from committing further crime.[122]

Diversion programs are a nearly ideal reform: they address the concerns of reformers with a wide range of perspectives and commitments, reconciling competing visions of criminal punishment and of state investments in service provision. The secret to their striking success lies in part in their invisibility.

INVISIBILITY AND LEGITIMACY

Part of the magic of diversion is that it can be anything to anyone. In a kind of sleight of hand, it moves people and their legal cases out of the public courtroom and into a hidden site that is left almost entirely to the imagination. Researchers and journalists cannot get behind the curtain to observe without official permission, which is rarely forthcoming. Meaningful data on what happens to diverted defendants is nearly impossible to access, because in many cases it is not collected in the first place. Even basic information about what goes on in the places we cannot see—what services are provided, exactly, and what it takes for people to make it through the programs—is often elusive. Diversion programs' public-facing materials typically promise mental health treatment, and some mention other services such as job training, but details are scarce. Further complicating matters, every program is different. Each is part of the fiefdom of the district attorney, whose office determines its aims, funding and staffing structures, and eligibility and participation requirements. What information and records programs *do* maintain have to be collected directly from each jurisdiction individually, and I found that very few are willing to provide them to researchers.

The ambiguity of the term *treatment* adds another layer of obscurity. Pretrial diversion programs typically don't specify the approaches they take but say only that they tailor treatment to the needs of each individual, which leaves a wide-open field of possibilities. Mental health treatment can take the form of medication or individual or group psychotherapy; it can be outpatient or residential; it can involve appointments at any frequency or duration; and it can be provided by psychiatrists, psychologists, licensed counselors and social workers, or people without formal credentials. Even within these categories, the variations can be enormous. Psychotherapy can mean cognitive behavioral therapy, which focuses on identifying and changing negative thoughts and behaviors; psychodynamic therapy, which aims to help individuals understand and resolve unconscious conflicts that contribute to their mental health conditions; or group therapy, which focuses on bringing together people who share similar issues and offering a supportive place to discuss their feelings and experiences, to name only a few approaches. Peer-led mutual support groups like Narcotics Anonymous are also often referred to as treatment for substance use disorders.[123] Interviews with diversion practitioners point to some standard practices: programs usually rely on outpatient group sessions, for instance, and refer only participants in acute crisis into residential programs or psychiatric treatment. But even this limited information is not included in public-facing materials.

These various barriers to inquiry make it hard to evaluate the claims made by advocates of pretrial diversion. Close analysis of the published research on pretrial diversion reveals that we actually know very little about its impacts on participants, how it affects recidivism rates, or what its financial implications are for jurisdictions. The available program evaluations draw on limited observational data rather than assign people randomly into different conditions to isolate the impacts of the programs, and they do not compare different therapeutic interventions or disaggregate the effects of those interventions themselves from the reductions in punishment that often accompany them.[124] As a result, they tell us very little about whether or how diversion changes people's outcomes. This paucity of research likely reflects more than the difficulty of getting access to the data we would need to rigorously assess program outcomes. The hiddenness of diversion means that we don't even know what kinds of data to look for or what questions to ask. Because the programs operate largely in the dark, we don't know what we don't know.

Diversion programs' invisibility allows advocates to project their own visions onto them. Progressive advocates tend to picture them as providers of much-needed social services that free people from the criminal legal system, while conservatives celebrate the money they save and the firm hand with which they reshape behavior and lower recidivism rates. In the absence of evidence to support or refute either vision, reformers can imagine diversion as both a generous source of government services and a measure to cut public spending; an escape from coercive state control and a necessary mandate into treatment for those who would not have entered voluntarily; a rollback of the carceral state and a forceful intervention to improve "public safety." By satisfying a wide range of concerns, diversion reassures advocates that the legal institution can manage mental health concerns effectively.

Conclusion

Opposition to the criminal punishment of mental disorder has surged across the United States,[125] and a growing number of public officials are responding by expanding treatment-based alternatives to legal sanctions. These interventions, which focus almost exclusively on the low-level offenses on which most people with mental illness enter the court system, promise dismissal of criminal charges when people complete assigned therapeutic programs. They have been met by enthusiastic support from groups across the political spectrum and taken up by elected officials and political candidates around the country. The alternatives are able to satisfy diverse sets of interests in reform—promising to provide treatment and other social services while also cutting costs, for instance—in part by moving the courts' contested work out of view. Whereas courts are open to the public, and government datasets compile detailed information on interventions like imprisonment, probation, and parole,[126] diversion programs only rarely allow observation or make data on their work available. In the absence of clear information about the programs' operations and impacts, each advocate can imagine the programs as the particular panacea that they hope for. Court-mandated treatment has thus become a powerful tool to legitimize the continued criminalization of minor behaviors often associated with mental illness.

The legitimation of criminal legal control over those behaviors has important implications for people's lives. Even if everyone arrested for low-level offenses were successfully diverted, the arrests and criminal charges would have their own negative long-term impacts on them. And the criminalization of those offenses, in itself, can harm people's health and well-being. Fear of arrest drives people to use drugs less safely, for instance, leading them to share or stash supplies in unsanitary places to avoid carrying anything incriminating with them and to use drugs in hidden places where they are less likely to be found if they overdose and need medical care.[127] Criminalization also drives drug markets underground and prevents regulation of their products, meaning that people cannot know what is in them. People who use drugs experience a wide range of health problems, up to and including fatal overdoses, because of the unpredictable and often dangerous substances in the available supply.[128]

The findings laid out in this chapter illustrate a process by which reforms can help to shore up the legitimacy and reach of an institution. Such processes have been of broad interest to researchers, who have found that the stability of institutions is due in large part to organizations' tendency to adopt new practices that align with those institutions' dominant logics and practices. The pursuit of legitimacy leads organizations to adopt those practices even when they are at odds with interests in efficiency and output.[129] The professional groups associated with particular institutions are also motivated to push for responses to social problems that will strengthen, rather than weaken, their own power and influence over those problems.[130] One key body of research examines an approach to reform that allows organizations and their workers to shore up legitimacy by adopting practices that publicly signal commitments to desirable values without producing any substantive changes to their daily work—a process that legal scholar Lauren Edelman refers to as "symbolic compliance."[131] This chapter draws out another approach to reform, in which organizations may make real changes to their daily work while maintaining control and discretion in the hands of the same workers. Those reforms can lend legitimacy in large part by operating out of public view. Established systems of accountability and transparency may be sidestepped when organizations adopt new and apparently benign practices, enabling reforms to appeal to groups with different and even conflicting interests. As those reforms become widespread within organizations affiliated with an institution, they can help to shore up the position of that institution in the social world.

Ultimately, this chapter has shown how diversion allows courtroom actors to advertise more compassionate and effective responses to mental illness within the bounds of the criminal legal institution, helping to shore up the legitimacy of that institution in the face of mounting critiques. The argument for court-mandated treatment is being taken up well beyond the courts—in places like the Washington State legislature—and used to advocate for the continued criminalization of mental illness. The next chapter zooms in on the daily operations of the criminal courts themselves to outline the ways that diversion legitimates criminal legal control over illness not just at the level of policy, but also in the everyday practices of legal decision-makers. In doing so, it encourages often invisible forms of system expansion on the ground.

[CHAPTER TWO]

Extending Control

Diversion and the Interventionist Courtroom

On one sunny morning in court, Judge Hamilton was calling people up one by one for diversion status hearings. Changing the subject halfway through one hearing, she addressed the men silently waiting on the benches a few rows ahead of me: "How many of you spend time thinking about when am I gonna get off paper [court supervision]?" All of the men raised their hands. One raised both hands for emphasis. "But you're still going to be living the same lives, just without our support!" she retorted. "What's really going to be different when you're off paper?" In the silence that followed, Darrell, the Black man standing for the hearing, answered, "Drug tests are a waste of time. I haven't failed one since 2011." The judge turned to look hard at him, and he continued uncomfortably, "I'm just saying, I think my time could be better spent." The judge, sounding irritated, responded: "Better spent on what? What else would you be doing?" The judge shook her head as a formerly incarcerated diversion counselor came gently to the man's defense, noting that he had been applying for jobs and listing other requirements, such as fee payments, that would be lifted when they finished. She cut him off mid-sentence. "Nothing really changes when you're off paper," she admonished the group. "This program isn't about trying to trip you up! It's about what are you doing this month that's different from last month?"

Around the country, advocacy groups seeking to reduce the reach of the criminal legal system are championing diversion programs that promise therapeutic alternatives to punishment.[1] People who have been arrested—and, in most cases, charged with crimes[2]—are given the option to enter therapeutic programs that typically require participation in mental health treatment programs and drug testing. If they complete program requirements, they can exit the legal system, often without criminal convictions. Those programs are widely understood as tools to reduce the size and social costs of the criminal system by channeling people out of that system before they have been exposed to the negative consequences of legal involvement.

As national reform organization the Vera Institute for Justice declares on its website in large red type: "Instead of expanding the criminal legal system's reach, diversion programs minimize contact."[3]

But this chapter shows that, in practice, inserting mental healthcare into the criminal courts can encourage the *expansion* of criminal legal control by lending it new legitimacy in the eyes of frontline workers with the power to pull more people into the court system. Drawing on interviews, ethnographic fieldwork in courtrooms, and an experimental survey, it outlines three key social processes that together drive that expansion: First, organizational norms shift as courtroom decision-makers begin to view their roles differently and more expansively. Taking hold of therapeutic tools that they believe can reshape people's lives for the better, officials like Judge Hamilton come to see themselves as service providers with a duty to keep people under court supervision for their own good. Second, organizational membership shifts as diversion staff and other treatment program workers join the courtroom workgroup. Those new workers encourage legal decision-makers to draw more people into the legal system to take advantage of the services they offer. Third, organizational constraints are lifted as the professional penalties that have traditionally discouraged decision-makers from intervening too widely are removed. One key result of these changes is a shift in the way prosecutors make decisions: they are more likely to bring charges when they know they can divert people into therapeutic programs. Taken together, the dynamics outlined in this chapter illustrate the ways reforms can strengthen dominant institutional practices by lending them new legitimacy in the minds of decision-makers on the ground.

Criminal Courts as Service Providers

As the criminal courts have come to play an increasingly important part in the state's management of illness, courtroom decision-makers are taking on new roles. Prosecutors divert people into treatment and track their progress, promising to drop charges against them if they complete their assigned programs.[4] Judges run diversionary programs like drug courts or mental health courts, supervising treatment for defendants or people on probation.[5] Even standard courtroom interactions often focus on mental healthcare: among the hearings I observed, nearly one in four involved assignment to an intervention related to behavioral health. Judges discussed defendants' medications, substance use, treatment attendance, and possible treatment options at length, often spending far more time talking about these aspects of defendants' lives than about the legal merits of their cases.

Down the hall from Judge Hamilton's courtroom, I watched another typical interaction between judge and defendant play out. In a chilly, windowless room, Judge Sayers was working through her docket for the day. The prosecutor called a name, and a young Black man named Julian walked to the front to face the judge. The judge read through his charges and noted that he was out on bond. "What's your drug screen gonna show?" she asked. "Marijuana," Julian answered. "Just marijuana?" the judge replied suspiciously. "Nothing else? Can you stop smoking on your own? Can I give you a reason to?" He assented. "All right, I want you to take a screen today and quit smoking weed." Julian's public defender conferred briefly with the prosecutor and the clerk, and they set a February date for the next court hearing.

The young man made a move as though to walk away, but Judge Sayers was not done. "Are you depressed?" she demanded. "Is that why you smoke weed? You want to go to counseling?" He mumbled something inaudible from the benches, and the judge loudly recapped: "So you lost both your mom and your—well, is marijuana helping?" She answered her own question without pausing: "Not really." Turning again to the young man's public defender, she said, "Have him come back in November so I can prove him wrong." Addressing Julian again, she concluded: "You're going to find out you can't stop. I'll see you on November 16. If it's positive you're going to go into counseling." The public defender looked confused and asked if they were disregarding the February date. "No," the judge told him, "he still has February. This is just for a marijuana check."

The judges I observed and talked with saw themselves as more than legal arbiters; they viewed referring people to services as a central aspect of their work.[6] As another judge described the role of the court, "There just isn't funding for [crisis centers or hospitals]. So unfortunately, the court becomes a social service agency. I guess I feel like if the court doesn't become that, then who does?" Keenly aware that the poor people who pass through their courtrooms on a daily basis have desperate needs that are going unmet,[7] she and her colleagues took their responsibility as service providers seriously. Judges, probation officers, and prosecutorial diversion programs frequently required defendants to participate in drug treatment or other services as a condition of pretrial release or an alternative to other sanctions. Some judges sent defendants to be drug tested every time they came to court and mandated treatment after any positive test result, including for cannabis. Over and over, they expressed certainty that *something* had to be done to help defendants and that, if they did not use the power of the court to intervene, nothing would be.

Although courtroom decision-makers lamented at times that social services were not more accessible outside of the court system, they also saw a clear role for the courts in administering therapeutic programs. For one thing, they often viewed those programs as important tools for crime prevention. Prosecutors talked regularly about the effectiveness of court-mandated treatment in changing people's behavior, for instance: as one of them put it, diversion "turns defendants around and keeps them out of the criminal justice system, more effectively than anything else." Nearly all of them pointed to the single-digit recidivism rates among people who completed diversion as the primary evidence of the programs' value. These effects, they emphasized, reflected the fact that the programs addressed the underlying causes of behavior. As another prosecutor described it, diversion was a key approach to discovering "what the person actually needs. Why is it that they're committing the crime? Let's get to the root of this." One judge in my field site put an even finer point on the connection between mental healthcare and crime prevention, declaring, "I'd bet that any guy sitting in jail or in my court—50 percent of them have mental illness as the issue that's probably underlying. But that's what makes them scary. You don't just wake up one morning and rape or murder somebody. And you can look at them and see it!" Drawing on a common narrative about the association between mental disorder and dangerousness,[8] decision-makers described treatment as a key approach to reducing future crime.

Officials also saw the courts as uniquely equipped to ensure the effectiveness of therapeutic interventions in people's lives. When those interventions are administered by the courts, they are accompanied by criminal legal supervision and backed by the threat of punishment. In fact, that threat is often the courts' *only* contribution, since they typically refer people out to community-based organizations rather than funding treatment programs themselves. Judges and prosecutors frequently described legal coercion as necessary to ensure that people made real efforts to improve their lives—just as Judge Hamilton presumed that keeping defendants like Darrell in diversion as long as possible could only benefit them, and Judge Sayers saw adding drug tests and court dates to monitor Julian's cannabis use as a way to help him. In drug and mental health courts, punishment is a particularly prominent aspect of treatment: the judges who oversee those specialty courts can send people to jail at any point as a therapeutic tool.[9] As one judge who runs a mental health court reflected: "If we feel like we need to get someone—not scared straight, but more in line with—if we know they have the mental capacity to do something but aren't willing, putting them in jail tends to jump-start that." But even for mandated treatment programs that do not have the capacity to jail their participants—including pretrial diversion programs run by prosecutors—the same ideas apply.

Another judge described the legal supervision of treatment as something that "people benefit from even if they don't know it. A lot of people are only complying with treatment because of the court." Or as one of her colleagues put it, more bluntly: "The penal element is *very* important to the treatment. The threat of really screwing up your life. Your life is pretty screwed up now, but it could be *really* screwed up." In other words, decision-makers saw the threat of punishment as a crucial tool for motivating people to change their behavior.

The notion that their capacity for coercion makes courts ideal service providers for the largely poor, Black people they manage aligns with long-standing narratives about poverty and racial inequality.[10] Political scientists such as Joe Soss and Barbara Cruikshank have shown, for instance, how public policy is shaped by the idea that people who are poor are too irresponsible to act in their own interests. Because they are unable to handle their own lives, the narrative goes, the state has a responsibility to step in to supervise and guide them.[11] Those deep-rooted ideologies about poverty have been found to shape other practices of punishment: viewing poor people as unable or unwilling to take care of themselves, criminal legal actors often conclude that state control is needed to transform poor people and thus pull them out of their social stations.[12] Dominant constructions of Blackness as dangerous—which have become so ingrained in the public imagination over time that they shape even such basic neurological functions as visual perception—also affirm the idea that people who come into the contact with the legal system should be tightly controlled and surveilled for the protection of the public, irrespective of their legal guilt.[13]

By reframing coercive control as service provision, therapeutic reforms help to legitimize the maintenance and expansion of that control among workers on the ground. As judges and prosecutors come to see themselves as caregivers providing crucial aid to the people who pass through the court system, they are encouraged to intervene even more intensively in the lives of those people. That encouragement also comes from the treatment providers who increasingly work closely alongside them.

Expanding the Courtroom Workgroup

Research on criminal courts documents the importance of the *courtroom workgroup*, or the group of prosecutors, judges, and defense attorneys who spend their days in sustained interactions inside and outside of the courtroom itself. Even though each of the three professional groups within the larger workgroup has its own agenda and interests that can be at odds with the others', they constantly collaborate to move cases through the legal process and dispose of them. They have to agree on plea deals, date changes for hearings, and other small daily decisions. More fundamentally, they spend most of the day together in the same spaces, week after week and year after year. Over time, these groups develop shared norms and standard approaches designed to minimize friction among them, and members are incentivized to align their decisions with the norms and values shared by the people working around them.[14]

As courts become more involved in the provision of mental healthcare, new members join the workgroup, adding capacity and pushing their own priorities. Diversion program staff and other treatment providers are often present in court and in judges' and prosecutors' offices, where many physically work full-time. Trained as counselors and social workers, these providers bring to the workgroup a commitment to therapeutic intervention cultivated by many years of professional education. Most are passionate believers in the power of mental health treatment to help people and address the "root causes" of their involvement in the legal system. As Sue, a diversion program director, reflected, "Unless we find out what the problem is, and if we're not referring you to appropriate services like heroin treatment, then we're not solving the root of the problem. Now we can't fix everything, but while you're in our program we're going to do our damnedest to try." Sue was passionate about extending their services to as many people as she could, and administrative data from her jurisdiction confirmed that the number of people entering diversion every year had skyrocketed since she had taken over the program. As she recalled,

> When I first came in, we saw three to four hundred adults a year. Now we're doing two to three thousand at all times. When I took over juvenile, about a hundred and twenty cases a year. Now we have four to five hundred at all times. Because before, the mindset was that government mindset: just do what I can do between 8:30 and 4:30.... But I get here at 8 in the morning, sometimes earlier, and I'm here till 8:30, 9, 10, 11 at night because I'm so obsessed with opening the program to everyone who wants this opportunity.

Sue's vision of diversion as an invaluable opportunity that should be made available to as many people as possible was widely shared by treatment providers, who were highly motivated to recruit more people into their programs.

Treatment providers tended to advocate for more referrals to diversion even when that meant drawing more people into the legal system. Staff in my field site, for instance, openly lamented a policy that eliminated arrests and charges for marijuana possession, replacing them with citations. As Marie, the diversion program director, reflected: "My concern with that is, I don't believe that the interventions are in place to actually help that person look at their behavior and see if there is something that needs to be changed." She argued that if anyone were arrested with cannabis more than once, "we should still get them here." In other words, they should be criminally charged in state court so that they could be diverted. Marie did not acknowledge that bringing people into court would expose them to other forms of punishment. Not only would they have charges on their records, but they would likely fail to complete diversion and end up in the traditional court system: prior to the policy change, 42 percent of all defendants who had entered her program on marijuana charges had been unable to finish the program and were returned to the court system for punishment.[15]

In some cases, diversion staff took direct measures to encourage prosecutors to bring more cases into the court system so that they could be diverted. One program coordinator recalled a conversation with a screening prosecutor about a young man who had been arrested for shooting paintballs in his neighborhood in which she pushed the prosecutor to accept the case so that it could be diverted:

> They didn't want to give me him at first. They were going to refuse the case. But I was like, "We are *not* refusing this case. I want to talk to this kid. I want to have a conversation with him about what's going on through his head, and let's find a more productive use of his time than shooting at things." Because that's just—I know it's a paintball gun, and I had to listen to [*in a high-pitched voice*] "it's just a paintball gun, nah nah nah"—I understand that! There's still a process that's happening here, and we need to work through it.

The prosecutor did agree to bring charges against the young man and sent him to diversion. To this diversion coordinator, that decision was a clear positive for the defendant and for society, since it allowed her to intervene and work to prevent more serious behavior in the future.

Courtroom decision-makers interacted not only with diversion program directors, but also with a range of outside treatment providers who stressed the tremendous value of referring defendants to them. One strange day in court highlighted the involvement of this latter group with particular clarity. When I walked into an afternoon session usually reserved for status updates on diversion participants, the courtroom was packed with nearly two dozen unfamiliar people in suits and ties, many of them White men. The first to speak was a researcher who had been contracted to evaluate the judge's diversion program and who announced, to enthusiastic applause, that he was finding that recidivism rates among people who had completed the program were substantially lower than the jurisdiction's average. Next was a tall White man who introduced himself as director of Turning Point Treatment Center and emphasized the "very high success rates" of their therapeutic services, adding that they had recently hired an addictionologist who was available for one-on-one appointments. "Does the addictionologist do group sessions as well?" the judge demanded, and the man stammered that she didn't currently but probably could. He was followed by a long list of representatives of similar programs—nearly all offering outpatient treatment for substance use disorders—who each stood when called on and breathlessly delivered sales pitches for their services, emphasizing their proven effectiveness. The judge fixed each with an eagle eye, often cut them off to ask questions, and took careful notes.

Finished with their pitches, most of the people in suits stayed as the judge began to call up program participants, one by one, to check in on their progress in treatment. When he mentioned that one man's alcohol ankle monitor had given some positive results, the man from Turning Point stood back up. "I believe he needs to see our addictionologist," he announced. "He should come to a one-on-one. We'd do an exam on him to confirm if he's drinking or not. But we can only do that if we can get him in the office." The judge nodded and gestured to a back corner of the courtroom. "Y'all go talk over there," he instructed.

This unusual courtroom scene illustrates a dynamic that continually shapes the landscape of service provision in the criminal courts. External treatment providers often interacted with courtroom decision-makers, accompanying their clients to hearings or coming in to meet with judges and advertising the value of their services. The legal system has become a central source of referrals into therapeutic services, nationally; for drug treatment, it is now the largest source.[16] Although the inpatient treatment centers in the city had long waiting lists, the outpatient programs into which most people are court-mandated were often actively seeking more court referrals.[17] These programs rely on reimbursement from Medicaid or on grants for which client numbers are crucial, and the external organization directors I interviewed estimated that court referrals constituted around 90 percent of their clientele.[18] They knew that their survival depended on a steady stream of referrals from judges and others in the legal system, and a central aspect of their work was to assure those decision-makers that coerced treatment made huge positive impacts on people's lives.

New members to the courtroom workgroup consistently reassure legal decision-makers that more intervention into the lives of people under the court's control will have positive benefits for them. By making the argument for their services day after day, they help to legitimize criminal legal governance of mental disorder in the minds of frontline workers. At the same time, the diversionary options that they offer provide convenient solutions to some of the dilemmas those workers face.

New Pathways for Prosecution

The most important point in the criminal court process is at its start, when prosecutors decide whether or not to bring criminal charges against a given individual.[19] If they do not bring charges, even after an arrest, then the person walks free.[20] If they do, those charges set in motion a chain of crucial events. People facing criminal charges can be kept in jail until their cases are resolved, or required to pay large sums of money in order to be released pretrial; they have to engage defense attorneys to represent them; and they will be made to appear regularly in court for months or even years.[21] The majority of individuals charged with felonies in the United States are ultimately convicted, about 95 percent of them through guilty pleas,[22] so that by some calculations, increases in charging rates have been the primary driver of the explosive growth in US prison populations over the past few decades.[23] And even if a defendant ultimately avoids conviction—by completing pretrial diversion, for instance—the criminal charges can trigger deportation proceedings and harm employment prospects by reemerging perpetually on background checks and in Google searches.[24]

Diversion creates a new pathway for prosecution that can make it more appealing to bring charges in low-level cases. Although legally prosecutors have full discretion to decide when to bring charges and when not to,[25] past research indicates that prosecutors are more inclined to charge higher-level cases and those in which they think they can ultimately secure convictions:[26] their charging decisions have tended to track factors such as the quality of the evidence against the suspect, the severity of the alleged offense, and the suspect's prior legal record.[27] Prosecution is resource-intensive, and members of the courtroom workgroup typically aim to conserve their own (and others') time and financial resources by disposing of cases as quickly and efficiently as they can,[28] including by choosing not to pursue cases in which judges or juries are less likely to convict. But when prosecutors can divert defendants out of the traditional court system immediately after charging them, they no longer have to worry about burdening their caseloads with minor or unwinnable cases. In the absence of that concern, diversion is an appealing path forward for prosecutors, since it lets them avoid the small risks associated with refusing cases and align their work with a courtroom culture that values therapeutic intervention.

The cases that prosecutors charge and then refer to pretrial diversion are very rarely rejected by diversion programs. Because programs can refer participants to external organizations if they do not have staff capacity to provide services to them, none of the program directors I interviewed were concerned about getting too many referrals. As one screener in a prosecutors' office described the decision to divert, "Sending cases to diversion is up to them [prosecutors]. It's not like they're going to get in trouble if they send a case that doesn't apply. That's never going to happen. That [diversion] unit does really try to get as many cases as they can get." A lot of program directors actively encouraged prosecutors to send them more cases irrespective of their legal merits, as Marie did in the case of the paintball gun. But even when staff had doubts about the quality of the evidence in cases they received, they didn't challenge prosecutors' charging decisions. One former diversion program director, for instance, recalled encountering a number of diverted defendants with extremely minor charges or cases in which the evidence looked weak to her: "There were cases where I would get it on my desk and I'd be like, 'This is such bullshit! Why was this not refused?' You know? But . . . 'Should it be prosecuted?' is a question that's like, unfortunately not my—I'm not allowed to answer." Diversion staff were all clear that if a prosecutor chose to charge a case, they had no room to criticize. Aware that they relied on the district attorneys to continue funding their offices and the line prosecutors (the attorneys who carry out the day-to-day work of prosecuting defendants) to keep sending them cases, they were careful to cultivate goodwill in all of their interactions with prosecutors. As one diversion director, Lillian, reflected, "I'd rather have them every now and then divert one case that maybe they couldn't—maybe they'd have this difficulty prosecuting than create, like, some sort of situation where they feel like we don't trust them and they stop diverting as many cases."

Defendants who are charged and then offered diversion nearly always accept. In theory, entering a diversion program is a voluntary decision, and defendants can opt instead to fight their cases in court. In practice, prosecutors and defense attorneys agreed that the latter choice is extremely rare.[29] Many program participants told me that they had mistakenly believed that entering diversion was obligatory. Even those who knew they had a choice, on paper, almost never considered refusing the diversion offer. If they were being detained in jail pretrial, then accepting that offer allowed them to go home right away, whereas refusing meant staying behind bars indefinitely. And because most cases that are prosecuted end in conviction, and no one could know what plea deal they might be offered if they did turn down the diversion offer, refusal presented a very serious risk.[30]

Even when diverted defendants returned to court without completing treatment, those cases don't necessarily generate additional work for prosecutors. Many diversion programs require defendants to admit guilt as a condition of entry, for instance. Those who complete the programs can withdraw their guilty pleas and have their charges dismissed, while the rest proceed directly to sentencing on their convictions. So the prosecutor does not have to do any more work to prove the case when people come back to court from diversion.[31] Some programs also require participants to waive other legal protections when they enter pretrial diversion. One large jurisdiction requires defendants to waive preliminary hearings at entry, for instance, meaning that the cases are easier to prosecute if they do return to court. And prosecutors always maintain the option to drop cases after they return from diversion rather than prosecuting them in the traditional court system.

Assured that people who are charged with crimes and then offered diversion will almost certainly be removed from their caseloads, prosecutors are also affirmatively motivated to bring charges and divert rather than to refuse cases. Not only do they work in a courtroom environment in which therapeutic interventions are valued—as one diversion program director observed about prosecutors, "They want them [arrestees] to like get services, so it might be a case where it's like, they feel like they're really like at risk and the prosecutability of it might be kind of on the fence but they know that they need something, so they might send it our way"—but they also face some organizational pressure not to refuse or dismiss cases. As one former case screener in a district attorney's office, Lisa, observed about the prosecutors she worked with:

> They would just drop the case otherwise [without a diversion option] because it's such a small amount of drugs, or they're going to have a difficult time proving that they were—you know, it's like evidence problems. But if they have that kind of thing [diversion], they can use it as a negotiating kind of chip, right? Instead of dropping the charge, you can say, "Well, I'll send you to this program." . . . A lot of prosecutors don't want to drop a case, especially if they're sort of like a line prosecutor and they have a manager above them, someone watching what they're doing. A lot of times they have to chat with the manager before they drop a case.

By diverting people rather than just letting them go free, line prosecutors can avoid the scrutiny that can come with deciding not to prosecute a case at all. In other words, specific organizational incentives align with pervasive courtroom logics to encourage prosecutors to charge more divertible cases.

Prosecutors Widen the Net

Almost since the inception of the therapeutic alternative, scholars have been raising concerns that it may expand the reach of the criminal legal system. Criminologist Stanley Cohen coined the term *net widening* to describe that expansion in 1979 and later outlined his now classic metaphor:

> Imagine that the entrance to the deviancy control system is something like a gigantic fishing net. Strange and complex in its appearance and movements, the net is cast by an army of different fishermen and fisherwomen working all day and even into the night according to more or less known rules and routines, subject to more or less authority and control from above, knowing more or less what the other is doing. Society is the ocean—vast, troubled and full of uncharted currents, rocks and other hazards.... The alternatives had merely left us with "wider, stronger and different nets."[32]

In an effort to prevent such net-widening effects, the primary professional organization for diversion practitioners (the National Association for Pretrial Services Agencies) has warned prosecutors against bringing charges in weak cases simply in order to divert them. "As a matter of fairness," its standards read, "no case should be diverted which can not be prosecuted. Without merit, such a case warrants neither diversionary resources nor those of the courts and should be dismissed."[33]

In practice, it is hard to know whether prosecutors are in fact widening the penal net, since they make their decisions behind closed doors. As political scientist Marie Gottschalk observes, prosecutors have largely been "exempted from the modern regime of restraints and reviews on administrative discretion that applies to other government actors."[34] Because prosecutors do not need to account for their charging decisions to the public or to the judiciary, data on their decision-making processes is hard to come by.[35] Information on the influence of alternative tools like diversion on those processes is even scarcer. Study of the impacts of those tools would require comparison between offices that do and do not make them available to their

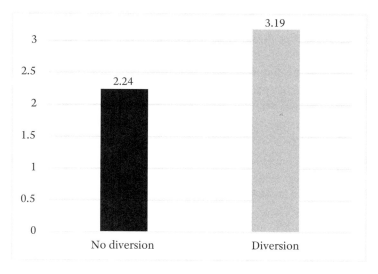

FIGURE 1

staff. But offices that offer pretrial diversion likely differ in other important ways from those that do not: factors such as prosecutorial culture and jurisdiction demographics may be associated with *both* use of diversion and particular approaches to charging and other decisions,[36] making it difficult to isolate the impacts of diversion itself.

For additional insights into the ways that prosecutors charging processes might be shaped by the availability of therapeutic alternatives—and the social processes described above—I designed an experiment that could hold constant everything except the availability of pretrial diversion. I asked seventy state prosecutors from two different urban offices to review descriptions of two different low-level felony cases (a drug case and a check fraud case) and to draw on their experiences to rate the likelihood that they would file charges in each case. The software I used randomly assigned each respondent to one of two versions of the survey. The case vignettes and questions were identical in both versions, but half of the respondents were told that the cases would be eligible for pretrial diversion, and half were not. Because prosecutors were distributed randomly between the two versions, there were no systematic differences between the people in each group.[37] This study design effectively isolates the influence of the diversion option. (More details about experimental survey studies in general and about the design of this study in particular can be found in methodological appendices A and B.) The results of the study are shown in figure 1.

The average likelihood of case acceptance reported among prosecutors in the diversion condition was 3.19 out of six, compared with 2.24 among respondents in the other group. In other words, prosecutors with access to diversion reported a much higher likelihood that they would file felony charges—about 42 percent higher, a very large effect. In other words, prosecuting attorneys were far more likely to make the weighty decision to bring criminal charges against people whom they knew they could divert into treatment.

Conclusion

Diversion programs promise to reduce the reach of the criminal legal system by providing services as in place of detention, conviction, and other forms of punishment.[38] But in practice, treatment-based alternatives to traditional punishment lend new legitimacy to coercive control among courtroom decision-makers, encouraging them to expanding the reach of that control. Judges and prosecutors increasingly embrace more expansive roles for themselves, shifting focus toward the use of therapeutic tools that they believe can reshape people's lives for the better. As they do so, they are often motivated to intensify or lengthen the time individuals are required to spend under criminal legal supervision. As one diversion coordinator summarized the reigning logic about defendants in the courtroom: "It's not going to hurt them to go through this program! . . . Everyone would do better if they were forced to comply with rules that make them stay on the straight and narrow." At the same time, treatment providers are becoming regular members of the courtroom workgroup, touting the effectiveness of their services and encouraging legal decision-makers to draw more people into the legal system in order to divert them into treatment. And because prosecutors can divert cases irrespective of the strength of the evidence in those cases, constraints that have traditionally discouraged them from expanding their reach are being lifted. Together, these shifts encourage prosecutors to bring charges in a wider range of cases, widening the entrance to the criminal court system.

The widening reach of the criminal courts has immediate implications for people's lives. Each person charged by prosecutors is another person subjected to a costly legal process likely to drag on for months or years. Regardless of the severity of the charges or the strength of the evidence, they will often face lengthy periods of incarceration and, in most cases, criminal conviction.[39] Even if defendants are not ultimately found guilty or if the cases against them are dismissed following successful completion of a diversion program, charges can harm their employment prospects and online reputations for the rest of their lives.⁴⁰ Additional interventions at later stages of the legal process, including mandated treatment or drug testing, increase not only the court's demands on people's time and financial resources, but also the odds that they will face even harsher punishment. Previous research indicates that court-mandated behavioral requirements like these have very few positive effects but do make people more likely to fail to meet the terms of probation or parole and to be sent to prison, as a result.⁴¹

In illustrating how reforms can shore up the legitimacy of an institution not just in the public eye but also in the minds of the professionals who carry out its daily work, this chapter sheds light on the forces that can drive penal net widening. Warnings by scholars such as Stanley Cohen that the introduction of "alternatives" to traditional punishment can extend the reach of the legal system are taking on new significance as those supposed alternatives expand,⁴² but our understanding of how and where that extension happens in practice has been limited. Most research on net widening simply shows that the overall numbers of people under criminal legal control tend to increase after implementation of programs such as electronic monitoring, community service, or drug courts.⁴³ A few key studies by sociolegal scholars have explored factors that can contribute to these outcomes: Forrest Stuart has examined police officers' motivations for giving out more citations in order to refer people to therapeutic programs, for instance, and Michelle Phelps has identified state-level policies associated with net widening in the context of probation.⁴⁴ This chapter advances our understanding of the social and relational dynamics that can drive the expansion of coercive control in the criminal courts, where therapeutic alternatives are proliferating.

Taken together, the findings laid out in this chapter show how reformist tools give frontline workers new reasons to double down. By recasting their work in a more positive light, bringing in new workers who are motivated to apply those tools more widely, and removing established constraints on decision-making, they can expand workers' spheres of influence. In lending new legitimacy to the exercise of institutional power on the ground, in other words, reforms can strengthen and broaden its reach. Part II considers how, once situated within an institution, reformist interventions themselves can be invaded and powerfully reshaped by their environment.

∴

Part II
ASSIMILATION

∴

[CHAPTER THREE]

Managing Risk

The Design of Mandated Care

Makayla woke up to the sound of an officer tapping on her windshield. As he pulled her out of the car where she and a friend had fallen asleep after using heroin, she tried to explain that she had just started treatment and was trying to turn things around. It didn't make a difference. He arrested her on charges of heroin and drug paraphernalia possession and took her in to the county jail. Makayla managed to post bond, and for the next four months she went to a clinic every day for doses of methadone, which reduces the symptoms of opioid withdrawal and attenuates the effects of the opioids themselves.[1] By the time she appeared at her first court hearing, she had avoided heroin use for three months straight.

When the prosecutor offered her the option to enter a pretrial diversion program, Makayla took it enthusiastically. The program would let her avoid a felony conviction if she did some additional drug treatment, her lawyer explained. And the treatment program she would enter used national best practices, employed only therapists with graduate degrees, and boasted a recidivism rate of under 4 percent—a success rate unheard of in the worlds of both drug treatment and the criminal courts. She left court walking on air.

Three months later, Makayla found herself $4,500 dollars in debt, pushed off of methadone treatment and using heroin daily, and so alienated from her therapist that she didn't even call her to say that she wouldn't be coming back to the program. She went back to court to enter a guilty plea and be sentenced on a criminal conviction, packed up and moved back in with her parents, and started over at the methadone clinic.

What happened here? Makayla had entered a diversion program run by a dedicated team of staff, had been assigned to an experienced, well-trained counselor who cared about her, and had come in determined to get better. Diversion programs rely on low recidivism rates to make the case for their efficacy, so they are incentivized to do everything they can to help people improve their longer-term outcomes. And they are given near-total autonomy to operate as they see fit, without legislative constraints on their content or operations.[2] This chapter analyzes the program structure that produced Makayla's outcome and examines the institutional forces that have put that same structure in place in jurisdictions around the country, even though that structure is neither legally mandated nor supported by research.

Once treatment is situated within the criminal legal system, providers face new pressures from the courtroom and the public that are often at odds with the administration of quality mental healthcare. Drawing on ethnographic data from my field site, a national survey of diversion programs, previous studies, and interviews with prosecutors and program directors, I show how diversion programs have come to be structured by practices designed not to promote behavioral health but to signal that they are managing perceived risk by exercising standard forms of control. In doing so, I draw out a process of institutional assimilation whereby a reformist practice is profoundly reshaped by dominant institutional logics.

The Structure of Mandated Treatment

Diversion programs nearly all share a common structure: they keep participants under criminal legal supervision while they are in treatment, and they require regular appointments, abstinence from most substances, and some financial investment. The results of my national survey of pretrial diversion programs suggest that all of them keep their participants' legal cases pending for the duration of the program; and among those for which information about program requirements was available, 88 percent require all participants to attend regular treatment sessions or classes designed to alter their daily behavior in some way (and the rest mandate attendance on a case-by-case basis); 94 percent regularly drug test participants to enforce abstinence from intoxicating substances; and 94 percent require participants to pay program fees. The high degree of similarity among these programs is striking, particularly since these standard practices are not mandated by any national legislation and are largely unsupported by research.

THE LEGAL STAKES

At Makayla's first hearing in district court, prosecutors announced that they would be bringing felony charges against her and then conveyed an offer to her attorney: if Makayla completed drug treatment through a pretrial diversion program, all of the charges against her would be dropped. The offer was pre-plea, meaning that she didn't have to admit guilt in order to take it. If she came back to court without completing the program, she would still be able to negotiate a plea deal or take her case to trial. Makayla took the offer.

A defining feature of court-mandated treatment is that it happens under the shadow of a legal case. Treatment can begin at any of several stages in the case, and it can have several different implications for its outcomes. Traditionally, pretrial diversion programs accept people after they have been criminally charged but before they have made any admission of guilt, as in Makayla's case.[3] But some jurisdictions have begun to divert people even before charges have been filed, and many more require people to admit guilt before entering a program.[4] If the individual completes all of the program requirements in the latter case, the plea is withdrawn and charges are dismissed. If they don't, they return to court with a criminal conviction and proceed straight to sentencing, without the possibility of a trial or plea deal. More than half of the jurisdictions in my national sample operate at least one post-plea program, and interviews indicate that they are growing in popularity among prosecutors, since they ensure that once cases are diverted they can never return to their caseloads. In my field site, the percentage of diverted felony defendants who were required to enter guilty pleas nearly tripled over the three years for which I have data.[5]

Once in a diversion program, participants are closely monitored by their treatment providers, in the understanding that they will be returned to court to face punishment if they fall out of compliance with program requirements. As a result, people are under significant pressure to meet the demands placed on them, even when those demands increase midstream. Treatment providers typically do not send people back to court the first time they miss a requirement. They begin by intensifying supervision—adding more drug tests or appointments, for instance—or extending participants' time in the program. This means, in part, that the time and resources people have to put into diversion to make it through successfully can be very unpredictable—even for the participants who enter with a clear understanding of what will be required of them, which many do not. The legal stakes mean that they have to do what they can to meet every requirement as it comes.

APPOINTMENTS

At intake, Makayla was assigned to a diversion counselor and told that she would need to attend a combination of individual meetings and group therapy sessions for at least two years. Her individual sessions with the counselor were on different days from her group therapy sessions, so she had to arrange her work schedule to let her make her way to the treatment center every Monday and Tuesday and to travel periodically to the courthouse for drug tests. Roslyn, her assigned therapist, had a graduate degree in counseling and had been in the job for nearly a decade. Unlike some of the other therapists, who spent only a few minutes checking in with each client outside of group sessions unless there was a serious issue with program compliance, Roslyn tried to take at least fifteen minutes with each client every week. At minimum, she monitored Makayla's attendance in group sessions and drug test results and warned her about any issues that might endanger her status in the program.

By six weeks into the program, Makayla had reduced her methadone treatments and stopped smoking weed so that she could demonstrate progress on her drug tests, and she was struggling. At seven weeks, she tested positive for heroin again. Roslyn increased her requirements to include an external "intensive outpatient program" (IOP) that required daily attendance. Luckily, Makayla had insurance. She found a program down the street from the diversion office that could take her for evening sessions after work. That program almost immediately sent her on to inpatient treatment.

Inpatient treatment can take a variety of forms. In some cases, people spend thirty days at a time in facilities that offer therapeutic sessions and support for abstinence. In others, they go into hospitals or facilities with medical support for about a week to go through detox. Ending regular use of some substances—including opioids and alcohol—is not just miserable but also dangerous. Missing a dose will trigger withdrawal symptoms, often including fever, vomiting, and dysphoria, and the symptoms can be life-threatening if left untreated.[6] Medical professionals can monitor people during the withdrawal period and give them medications to ease the process.

Makayla spent a week in a nearby hospital going through detox. The facility discharged her after seven days—despite her concern that seven days had not been enough time for her to detox fully in the past—because her insurance would not cover more time. She left with a prescription for buprenorphine (Suboxone), which was intended to manage any subsequent symptoms. But in the middle of her first night at home, she woke up vomiting over and over. Another dose of the medication did not help. Finally she called a friend for some heroin and, as she told me later, "Within three minutes, suddenly I'm fine."

The effectiveness of the mental health treatment that people receive in diversion is hard to study. For one thing, concerns about client confidentiality make that treatment something of a black box. The official program records that can be obtained via public-records requests don't include anything about the intensity or forms of care that diversion participants received. The fact that Makayla went to an IOP and to a hospital in addition to the usual outpatient therapy sessions, for instance, is not recorded. For another, most diversion participants are receiving drug treatment, which varies widely in quality in the United States.[7] Treatment programs for substance use disorders are severely underfunded around the country. Work in those programs is difficult and poorly paid, and many programs employ inexperienced counselors because they cannot attract or retain experienced, well-trained providers.[8] The programs vary widely in terms of quality, and there are almost no centralized standards, external checks, or avenues for other organizations or potential clients to learn about the kind of care they offer. As one prominent researcher recently observed about substance abuse treatment in the United States: "Anybody can make any claim they want and get away with it. . . . It's essentially an unregulated industry."[9]

The studies of court-mandated treatment that we do have tend to focus on drug treatment alone, and most find minimal or no effects on people's health or legal outcomes. A recent meta-analysis found that of nine studies of the impacts of compulsory drug treatment, only two documented reductions in rearrest rates and self-reported substance use, and those reductions were small and measured shortly after treatment had ended. Five studies found no changes, and two found that outcomes were worse for people who received mandated treatment.[10] One consistent research finding is that the risk of overdose is substantially higher among people who go through court-mandated treatment—between 2 and 3.67 times higher—than among people who do not. Because tolerance for substances drops after a period of abstinence, people returning to drug use after such a period can experience overdose when they use what would previously have been a normal dose for them.[11]

DRUG TESTING

Once in the diversion program, the first thing Makayla was asked to do was to return to the criminal courthouse to take a drug test—the first of many. She made the walk back in the hot June sun, passed through the metal detector and security check, gave her name at the drug testing area, and waited to be called. Twenty minutes later, in a bathroom in the back, a staff member watched Makayla collect her urine sample, eyes on the toilet where she sat. Makayla finally stood and walked out as quickly as her legs would carry her, submitting her sample on the way out. Drug test results were emailed to her counselor, Roslyn, who would interpret the colors on the document and decide how to respond to any positive results.

Use of any illegal drugs, alcohol, and cannabis (even in states where the latter is legal) was prohibited by every program I spoke with. Programs also often disallow use of prescription painkillers, even for people with valid prescriptions. They can also require them to test negative for methadone or buprenorphine—both common and highly effective treatments for opioid use disorder[12]—before they can be released from supervision.[13] Although the National Academy of Sciences recommends long-term use of either medication as the safest option for treating the disorder,[14] providers often described that use as "substituting one addiction for another," because both medications occupy the same receptors in the brain that are activated by opioids.[15] Makayla's first test was positive for methadone, as were the ones that followed. Roslyn reminded her in every session that she needed to be tapering off of that treatment.

The standard court-mandated drug test screens urine using the quick and inexpensive "immunoassay" method,[16] which uses antibodies to detect the presence of particular substances. Immunoassay tests can be tricky to interpret and can return false positives, so they are meant to be confirmed by lab tests, but most programs don't have the funding for that or even know that it's recommended.[17] The tests are often "10-panel," which means they are designed to detect THC (tetrahydrocannabinol, the psychoactive compound in marijuana), cocaine, amphetamines, opiates, and methadone, among other substances.[18] Some programs add panels to detect additional substances such as alcohol or buprenorphine. Depending on the substance and the quantity consumed, the tests might detect it for only a day after use or for well over a month.[19]

There is little evidence that using drug testing to enforce abstinence over the course of a court-mandated program can reduce drug use over the long term. The treatment providers I talked to were firm believers in such testing as a way to help people recover from substance use disorders, and the National Association of Drug Court Professionals' Best Practice Standards confidently declares that the more frequently programs "perform urine drug testing, the better their outcomes in terms of higher graduation rates and lower drug use and criminal recidivism."[20] But in fact, several randomized controlled trials (high-quality studies that test the impacts of an intervention by randomly assigning some people to receive that intervention and others not to and then comparing their outcomes[21]) have now measured the effects of subjecting people to frequent random drug testing as a condition of probation or parole and immediately punishing any positive results with jail time. Two of those studies found that people assigned to the intensive drug testing condition had lower rates of drug use and rearrest while they were still being tested, but the effects did not last. When the authors of one of the studies followed up with study participants five years later, they found that the drug-tested group had been charged with new crimes at the same rate as the comparison group. The authors of the other study found that the differences between their two groups had disappeared just a year after the drug-tested group had been returned to standard parole.[22] Two other studies using very similar methods found that the testing had minimal or no effects even in the short-term.[23]

Research findings on the effects of drug testing for abstinence are consistent with what we know about the nature of substance use. Drugs can be used to self-medicate for long-term illnesses such as depression, post-traumatic stress disorder (PTSD), or anxiety, which are still present when drug testing ends and the person can return to medicating without the threat of a positive test result.[24] Once people develop substance use disorders, the situation becomes even more complex. Those disorders are characterized by long-term and possibly permanent changes to the brain's motivational systems and to the control of the prefrontal cortex over decision-making.[25] Common neuroadaptations involve reduced self-control over consumption of the substance, reduced enjoyment of other experiences, and sensitivity to environmental cues that trigger desire for the substance.[26] Abstaining from a particular substance for a period of time does not undo those neurological changes. In fact, belief that abstinence is a requirement for positive change is associated with higher rates of relapse.[27]

FEES

A few weeks after she had been discharged from the hospital where she had gone to detox, Makayla got a bill for $4,500. When I last talked to her, three years later, she still had not paid it off.

The third nearly universal requirement among diversion programs is payment. The financial costs of participation can vary widely, but they are hard to avoid completely. Even when programs themselves don't charge for enrollment, participants often have to pay external organizations for drug testing, treatment, or breathalyzers. Most also have to pay for drug testing. Those arrested for theft or similar property crimes are often required to pay restitution. Each of these costs becomes a legal financial obligation, in that failing to pay it means being sent back to court for sanctions. As in Makayla's case, the largest fees often come when clients are mandated to get outside treatment as a condition of staying in the program. Some programs help their clients apply for Medicaid to cover the costs, but millions of people are both uninsured and ineligible for Medicaid,[28] and even those with insurance can face substantial out-of-pocket costs.

Fees could also add up quickly when people were required to rent or buy external equipment. Breathalyzers or other alcohol monitors were usually required for people charged with driving under the influence, for instance, and they were usually provided by private companies at exorbitant rates. A young man named Leonard described his experiences with the breathalyzer payments in an interview: "It's a little preposterous, you know, to go there, wait an hour and a half, pay eighty dollars, and it's the same thing [every month]. They hand you a new little piece of plastic." If he missed a payment, his car would shut down entirely. The system could also shut down the car for unrelated reasons. Leonard recalled driving through some water on the way home from work in a rainstorm late one night, for instance. The breathalyzer system shorted, and the car wouldn't turn back on. He had to call someone for a ride and pay the company another eighty dollars for a reset code before he could rescue his car. Although these were not direct fees charged by his diversion program, failure to pay them would have had the same effect: if Leonard missed a payment, he would risk removal from the program and the punishment that awaited him on the other side.

Many diversion programs also charge fees directly. In my field site, all participants were required to pay $200 before the end of the program, in addition to paying for their own drug testing and any additional treatment. It is hard to know how that fee compares to those of other programs nationally, because most don't make their fee structures public. But the information I was able to gather indicates that the fees can be hefty. Several of the programs in my national sample charge fees of over $1000, and one charges each participant between $10,000 and $15,000 for treatment and ignition locks.[29] A recent *New York Times* examination of 225 prosecutor-run pretrial diversion programs around the country concluded that an average cost was impossible to calculate because fee structures are so complex and nontransparent, but they did note that two-thirds of the defense attorneys they surveyed reported that diversion fees were a barrier to participation for their clients.[30]

In some cases, diversion fees generate income for prosecutors' offices. In 2018, for instance, a group of plaintiffs in Arizona filed a lawsuit against the Maricopa County Attorney's Office and a treatment center (the Treatment Assessment Screening Center, or TASC) in Phoenix. They alleged, in part, that the office had used a pretrial diversion program to collect nearly $15 million in revenue from mostly indigent defendants. Over the previous decade, the office had run a felony diversion program that charged each participant about $1000 in program fees and had required them to stay in the program until they could pay off those fees. One result, the plaintiffs argued, was discrimination against poor people in violation of the Due

Process and Equal Protection Clause of the Fourteenth Amendment.[31] Settlement negotiations are ongoing as of 2023, but Maricopa County has already overhauled its pretrial diversion programs in response to the lawsuit. As a staff member in the County Attorney's Office put it in an interview, "Ultimately, the drug diversion program and felony pretrial diversion program were eliminated and we started from scratch." The program dramatically reduced participation costs. TASC has permanently closed its doors.[32]

To distinguish themselves from programs like these, most of the program directors I interviewed were careful to emphasize that they do not profit from the fees they charge. "I don't make enough to pay for my own pencils and paper," one told me. Another director, Sue, explained at length that her program operates in the red and purposely so:

> There are programs who never even see a client and they charge them a fee. But we earn our fee, and I can tell you that every DA's office goes through a legislative audit, and all of the financials for diversion are probably posted on the Secretary of State's website. . . . We have always lost money on our program, and the DA wants to always lose money on our program, because he doesn't want anyone to say that this is all about money.

Sue's program employs in-house therapists who provide much of the treatment, so she likely does lose money. Still, the program charges felony participants $1500 to enroll in the program, and close to half of their participants are referred out to other programs (like Makayla's intensive outpatient and inpatient treatment), for which they may also have to pay.

Some program directors described their fees in therapeutic terms. Emily, the associate director of an organization that provides much of the court-mandated treatment in my field site, explained that asking participants to come up with the payments for sessions was an important way to teach them responsibility and accountability. "They'll push it, and be like, 'Well, I can't pay for the session today. Can I still come?' No! Because it's part of that therapeutic model, you know? Of taking responsibility in multiple ways." Others emphasized the importance of charging fees for treatment as a means of ensuring that people would value and feel invested in that treatment. "People don't value things that they don't pay for," the leader of one training session told her audience.

But research on legal financial obligations finds that those obligations have unequivocally negative effects on people's lives. They increase housing instability and both acute and chronic health stress, and they can result in driver's license suspensions, damaged credit, incarceration, and prolonged involvement in the criminal legal system as people work to pay off their debt. They can also harm the families of people with legal debt, increasing financial strain, emotional distress, and interpersonal conflict among relatives.[33]

Taken together, the available evidence does not suggest that standard diversion program practices promote improvements in mental health or even reduced contact with the criminal legal system. So why—given programs' near-total autonomy in choosing their own practices—do they use this standard structure so consistently?

Assimilation of Institutional Logics

In the fall of 2022, a heated debate raged in King County, home to the city of Seattle. The district attorney, Dan Satterberg, had founded two pretrial diversion programs with an almost unprecedented design: staff referred people to services and then permanently threw out their cases, without further surveillance or requirements. One of the programs was for adults facing felony charges. Satterberg described the approach to me in an interview: "[Our staff] try to figure out which of these community groups they should be connected to and connect them. Once we do that, they're done. They're not on any kind of probation with us—we consider justice to have been done once they're with that community group." Now Satterberg was set to retire, and his chief of staff, Leesa Manion, was running to replace him. Running against Manion, Jim Ferrell broadcast his critiques of the current diversion programs in the very first paragraph of his campaign website, under the heading "KEEP YOUR FAMILY SAFE": "I believe in second chances, but not revolving doors where the same criminals are repeatedly committing the same crimes. Let me be clear: I will hold offenders accountable. *I know how to use our county diversion programs effectively so we can keep the public safe while changing lives.*"[34] A unique approach to diversion triggered a unique turn of events: for perhaps the first time, pretrial diversion became the central issue in a major political race.[35]

In interview after interview, debate after debate, Ferrell made his argument. The current DA's office had adopted an approach that deviated markedly from established practices, he maintained, and in doing so was abdicating its responsibility to protect public safety. Calling the program an "outrageous breach of public trust" that was "not a diversion program" but a "look-the-other-way program,"[36] he declared, "It's astounding to me. I've got 19 years of experience as a prosecutor. I've never heard of a diversion program in which there was never a checkback to say, 'Did you show up?' 'Did you complete what they asked you to do?'"[37] His criticisms resonated widely. Prominent supporters—including the local Democratic Party, several Democratic representatives, the mayors of nearly every town in King County, and Seattle's major newspaper—took up Ferrell's banner. "Public safety must be the main concern," announced *The Seattle Times* in its endorsement of his candidacy.[38]

The debate at the center of this political race is a striking illustration of the powerful norms surrounding diversion and the pressures DAs face to demonstrate that they are maintaining control even as they provide treatment. Ferrell, a hardline prosecutor who had changed his party affiliation from Republican to Democrat only when he began running for public office in King County, ultimately lost his race in a county consistently ranked among the most progressive in the country. But his platform, and the broad support it garnered, highlight not only the homogeneity of diversion programs in the United States but also a powerful assumption undergirding the contemporary criminal legal institution: that the people who tend to come into contact with that institution pose a risk to society and thus must be kept under particular forms of surveillance and control.

INSTITUTIONAL LOGICS OF CONTROL

Organizational theorists understand institutions as shared "symbolic systems" that order reality:[39] the capitalist market, for instance, or the bureaucratic state, democracy, the nuclear family, or the criminal legal system. Each embodies a distinct set of conventions that have achieved "rulelike status in social thought and action."[40] In other words, the conventions at the heart of each institution are generally taken for granted, informing assumptions and expectations across a wide range of groups and individuals. Those conventions, often referred to as *institutional logics*, operate not only through individual cognition, but also through continual social enforcement and reinforcement. In particular, they are expressed in and reproduced by organizations, the coordinated systems of activities that have become central carriers of institutions.[41]

Organizations thus come into being within powerful institutional fields. Their legitimacy depends in large part on their alignment with the dominant logics in those fields, and they need that legitimacy to survive. Researchers have repeatedly found that organizations' decisions to adopt particular practices are driven *not* primarily by the pursuit of efficacy, but by external pressures from other organizations, the state, and the professions. In other words, it is less important that they do their work in a way that efficiently advances their purported goals than that they appear legitimate to others in their institutional fields.[42]

Scholars widely agree that the US criminal legal system is dominated by a logic of control that envisions the people who enter that system—who are disproportionately poor and Black[43]—as dangerous or uncontrolled and in need of state oversight.[44] That logic has deep roots. The construction of Blackness as criminal began as a rhetorical move to justify enslavement and has been perpetuated ever since,[45] and poor people have long been understood as too irresponsible to act in their own interests and therefore in need of state control.[46] But beginning in the 1970s and 1980s, the focus of criminal legal praxis shifted toward containing those groups in perpetuity and away from reintegrating individuals back into society. At the center of that shift was the prison: rehabilitative aims gave way to approaches centered on controlling risk by warehousing the marginalized groups that society marked as "dangerous populations."[47] In thrall to these logics of containment and control, the United States has become home to the largest prison population in the world.[48]

Although the prison stands as the ultimate manifestation of control, only a small percentage of people who come into contact with the legal system ever find themselves behind its walls. The vast majority are supervised by the courts and by probation and parole agencies while they live in their own homes.[49] Each of these agencies has had to find ways to exercise control over people society sees as dangerous while they move freely outside of carceral institutions. As decades of scholarship tells us, risk—and thus risk management—is politically constructed, reflecting shared values and frameworks.[50] As legal scholar David Garland has observed, "Risk begins where certain knowledge ends."[51] Ideas about appropriate modes of control can thus become inscribed into policies and practices irrespective of the value of those practices in actually controlling behavior or changing outcomes.[52] In the contemporary US legal system, those ideas have been inscribed into a set of practices that are employed almost universally by the agencies tasked with supervising people outside of carceral facilities.

Several key practices have come to represent appropriate levels of control across the criminal legal system. Primary among them is the mandated physical appearance. People on pretrial release, probation, or parole are usually required to appear for regular appointments in court or with supervising officers—in addition to attending any other programs that might be mandated for them—and these appearances are taken so seriously that they can be sent to prison or jail for missing even once.[53] These appointments function as a powerful form of social control and metric by which legal decision-makers gauge people's "governability," according to sociologist Issa Kohler-Hausmann.[54] A second central practice of control is the drug test. Beginning in the 1970s, the use of frequent testing to enforce abstinence from substance use spread rapidly throughout the criminal legal system as a highly visible, measurable form of control. People under legal supervision now find themselves tested regularly, usually via urinalysis, irrespective of their histories of substance use. For many of them, a positive test result can mean the difference between incarceration and freedom.[55] Finally, nearly every form of criminal legal supervision places legal financial obligations on supervisees. These obligations have expanded particularly since the early 1990s and, like required appearances and drug testing, they have become a key form of social control: not only do they place demands on people's finances on pain of punishment, but they also often require people to continue to appear in legal settings for months or years just to make payments on their debts.[56]

CONTROL LOGICS AND THE STRUCTURE OF DIVERSION

Although diversion programs are usually run by licensed social workers and therapists, they are situated squarely within the criminal legal setting. The programs operate as extensions of district attorneys' offices, which fund and house them and which have the power to alter, expand, or eliminate the programs at any time. They also rely entirely on case referrals from line prosecutors, who have discretion to decide whether and how often to send them cases. Program directors are thus highly motivated to adopt practices that align with prosecutors' aims and expectations—and prosecutors, in turn, are sensitive to public perception. Institutional logics operate as a kind of common sense that defines goals and expectations across a society,[57] meaning that dominant ideas about appropriate control inform not only what people *within* the legal system do, but also what the wider population expects from them. Public support is critical for prosecutors, who are elected directly in forty-six of the fifty states,[58] and attempts to cater to the electorate have tended to push elected legal decision-makers toward more punitive decisions.[59] Those logics are shared by police, on whom prosecutors rely to bring in evidence for their cases.[60] One deputy district attorney, Randy, described the importance of enforcing participant compliance with standard program requirements: "There's a fair amount of public pressure. Law enforcement also comes with a certain level of expectations. Perhaps even from victims . . . I think there is a fair amount of expectation. It's all based on a distrust that somebody's going to follow through. And if they don't, we're going to catch them."

Diversion program directors thus did their best to demonstrate to DAs that they could be trusted to use the appropriate measures to supervise and control the people who were referred to them. Program director Lillian reflected on her reasons for using a set of practices that is common in the criminal courts, noting that she had done so in large part to reassure prosecutors that her program could be trusted to manage people the public saw as dangerous:

> I think it's really hard to be a political entity tasked with public safety and to choose to not prosecute somebody. . . . In the back of their mind they have this, like there's that pressure, you know? Like your boss is an elected official, people want defendants punished, they think that they're causing crimes. You're choosing not to punish somebody every time you send them to diversion. . . . And that's one of the reasons like we're switching some of our screening processes. . . . Then we can tell the DA that we're using a validated risk assessment and it's not just like our personal judgment. Which I think might make them feel a little bit better.

Although the program did not change after implementation of the risk assessment at intake—defendants were still subjected to the same standard requirements—the risk assessments were an important gesture. As a standard part of the criminal courts' management of "subjects who must be dangerous,"[61] the assessment broadcast that the program was attentive to the dangers their participants could pose and the importance of calibrating control accordingly.

The rare diversion programs that did try to deviate from standard practices of monitoring and control invariably encountered pushback. Often it came from other decision-makers within the legal system. Allison, a founder and former leader of a diversion program that used restorative justice processes—which convene community meetings, or "circles," to decide on consequences for wrongdoing rather than imposing standard requirements on participants—recalled the way her program changed over time under pressure from courts and funders. Initially, most of the plans the circles produced did not include drug treatment because, as Allison put it, "the community providers and community people know that mandatory treatment is not particularly helpful." But the grant that was funding the program required that a certain percentage of participants be in drug treatment, and all of the treatment programs they could find required drug testing. Even for participants who weren't in treatment, she recalled, "We started to hear from the judges and the state's attorneys like, 'Why aren't more of these people doing drug testing?'" The courts began introducing more control mechanisms, adding drug treatment requirements to community circle plans that did not include them and extending the time that people had to spend under their supervision. By the time she resigned, Allison said she felt about the diversion program "like it's this demon baby that I birthed."

In other cases, members of the public intervened directly to push for higher levels of control over diversion program participants. Another former diversion program director, Miranda, recalled phone calls from a couple of alleged victims that, as she put it, "made the prosecutors shake in their boots": "They [the prosecutors] didn't want angry victims. . . . No matter how many good cases you have, if you have two people making a fuss that this is a slap on the wrist, then the DAs are like, 'Of course, it *is* just a slap on the wrist! Oh God, like you're not even punishing them?'" In the wake of two complaints that the diversion program was too lenient—one lodged by a woman from a powerful political family—the district attorney in Miranda's jurisdiction pressured her to make her program more regimented and increase standard requirements for diversion participants. She left the job as a result, and the changes the DA had asked for were made after her departure.

But for the most part, directors did not try to deviate from the standard program structure. Most seemed caught off guard when I asked how they had decided to put each program requirement in place. Nearly all of them told me that the requirements were "best practices" in the field, that the structure had just been in place since long before their time, or both. Although many had made minor changes to their programs—adjusting eligibility requirements or partnering with new treatment providers, for instance—none had altered the fundamental tenets of oversight and enforcement of standard performance requirements. The widespread adoption and maintenance of practices that are common within an organizational field, irrespective of those practices' effectiveness, has been well documented in the literature on organizations. The pursuit of legitimacy leads organizations to model themselves on other organizations perceived as appropriate or successful in their fields, in a process scholars refer to as *mimetic isomorphism*. By adopting standard practices, organizations protect and shore up their own legitimacy, reproducing and further validating those practices in the process.[62]

Conclusion

Diversion programs around the country employ very similar structures. They keep participants under court supervision until they have completed their assigned programs and return them to the traditional legal system if they fail to meet program requirements. Those requirements include regular drug testing to ensure abstinence from all substances, financial payments, and regular therapeutic appointments. This standard structure is neither legally required nor supported by research. But because it so powerfully signals a commitment to managing perceived risk to protect public safety, it has become almost universal. Facing pressure from courts and the public, treatment providers adopt many of the techniques and practices that dominate in criminal courtroom settings. Once situated in the legal system, in other words, treatment assimilates institutional logics of control.

As a result of this assimilation, diversion programs employ a range of practices that have not been found to promote improvements in behavioral health and may even harm it in the long run. One large randomized controlled trial found that adding drug testing and more appointments to probation or parole did not reduce rates of rearrest but did lead to higher rates of technical violations and, as a result, to higher rates of incarceration.[63] A similar study recently reproduced that finding and additionally discovered that people assigned to the more intensive supervision condition absconded at higher rates. It also found that positive drug tests were listed as the reason for probation revocation at *ten times* the rate observed in the control group, indicating that more frequent drug testing contributed directly to higher rates of incarceration.[64] These studies align with a larger body of literature indicating that increasing supervision requirements can have devastating impacts on people's lives.[65]

On their face, research findings about the ineffectiveness of the specific practices employed by pretrial diversion programs look out of keeping with the dramatic reductions in recidivism often seen as the main indicators of those programs' effectiveness. But in fact, the impressive success numbers cited by proponents of diversion could *depend* on the high rates of failure caused by intensive supervision and technical violations. Program evaluations typically examine recidivism rates among people who complete the programs and exclude noncompleters from their analyses.[66] By excluding from analysis the participants who are unable to complete the rigorous program requirements—as many as half of all those who enter diversion[67]—they likely bias their results. As I will show in chapter 5, the people who are able to complete all requirements are also those less likely to be rearrested. In addition, practitioners and researchers are unable to separate the effects of the program components themselves from the effects of avoiding criminal punishment.[68] Because formal sanctions produce a host of negative long-term consequences,[69] people who avoid those consequences as a result of completing diversion might have better outcomes even if the impacts of program participation itself are neutral or even harmful.

More broadly, this chapter has illustrated a process of institutional assimilation, showing how reformist practices absorb and integrate the logics of the institution that adopts them. In doing so, it builds on a broader literature on the encroachment of criminal legal logics into the social service sector. In his classic book *Punishing the Poor*, sociologist Loïc Wacquant wrote that the penal arm of the state had inserted its punitive logic into social programs.[70] Recent ethnographies have documented that insertion in granular detail. Scholars Susan Dewey and Tonia St. Germain, for instance, explore how initiatives to offer therapeutic treatment to people who do sex work in Denver have come to adopt the mandates of policing. Those initiatives have ultimately drawn social-services professionals into the project of regulating women through arrest, incarceration, and court-mandated treatment.[71] Similarly, gender studies scholar Jennifer Musto has written about the ways that interventions purportedly designed to protect and care for people deemed at risk for sex trafficking—who can include adults who freely choose to engage in sex work—increasingly involve punitive state control over their lives, drawing them into what she calls the "carceral-assistential net."[72] This chapter builds on their work by documenting a process that takes place specifically in the context of reform: an organization adopts a new practice that promises transformative change, but once implemented, powerful institutional pressures and constraints drive it to assimilate the logics already dominant within the organization.

Diversion, in this case, purports to operate as an exit ramp off of the highway of the criminal legal system and into supportive community treatment.[73] But in practice, program directors operate within and under immense pressure from that system, and as they work under those pressures over time, the contours of new programs come to resemble established institutional forms. The next chapter explores how programs' assimilation of criminal legal logics shape daily interactions between therapists and their clients.

[CHAPTER FOUR]

Coercing Care

Therapist-Enforcers and Client-Defendants
in the Therapeutic Space

The group of a dozen people filtered into the waiting room out of the warm sun of a spring evening. For the last half hour or so, I had been sitting on the front steps of a squat gray building with a small crowd of people who had all been promised that the criminal charges against them would be dismissed if they completed an outpatient treatment program. The program required frequent group therapy sessions, which often focused on drug use but embraced a general aim of treating the root causes of each person's involvement in the criminal court system. The sessions met here most evenings, and I joined them as a researcher. Most people arrived too early, subject to the timetables of city buses or of the friends or family members who dropped them off. On nice days like these, nearly everybody stayed out on the front steps of the treatment center as long as they could, talking and smoking and glancing down a little nervously to check the time. Just before 5:30 that evening, the spirited conversations died out as everyone stood up, groaning a little, and began to file inside through a metal detector, past a sign-in station where an unsmiling man checked IDs. We joined the couple of people already settled into chairs in the silent waiting room, one fast asleep. Some of us stared at our phones while others closed their eyes and leaned their heads back against the wall.

That evening, the group therapist was a little late opening the locked door to let us into the back room. After a few minutes of silence, a tall, bald White man I had never seen before came through the front door and greeted a middle-aged Black man named Andrew. Their voices echoed in the quiet room as they reminisced about the last time they had seen each other, some years back. "How long you got in here?" Andrew asked the newcomer. "Two years," he answered with a long sigh. "How long did you get?" Andrew said he got just twelve months. The bald man nodded, frowning. They both fell silent again, contemplating the floor.

Finally Eric, the therapist in charge of the group that night, opened the door, looking uncharacteristically harried. A couple of people moved to get up to walk back for group, but Eric was just holding the door for one more person to come out. It was a young Black welder named Bryan, coming out of the one-on-one check-in that everybody had to do with one of the counselors every week. Bryan lived almost two hours away, so he had been given the coveted check-in slot with Eric right before the group session to save him an extra trip every week. Bryan also looked more stressed than usual, and he dropped into a chair as Eric strode outside to smoke a cigarette. The group waited in silence for Eric to come back in and open the door to the back for us. When he did, his greetings were perfunctory as we trailed past him, single file, down to the windowless room where we would spend the evening.

Eric was well liked. He remembered details about everyone's lives and could make even the grouchiest group member smile. He was a huge Black man in his fifties who had used and dealt crack around the city for twenty years before becoming a therapist, and there was no story anybody could tell that he could not top with an even more harrowing version. Outside of sessions, group members talked about him with affection and in slightly awed tones. Most days he offered hugs to everybody as we filed past him to the room at the back, but on that evening he could hardly look at us. When we had all settled into our chairs, Eric asked us to "check in," which meant going around to say how we were doing. But before most of us had answered, he interjected:

> I want y'all to get *out* this shit. Because I know it's like a straitjacket. I want y'all to get through this shit and keep pushing. I don't want to hold y'all up. But y'all don't hold me up! Let me help you! Be clean [test negative on drug screens], make the one-on-ones, so it won't be a problem when I turn the paperwork in to my director and she say "you out." Then when you done, if you wanna blow [use], blow! You won't be under no pretense or guidelines of the program. But you say "work with me"—I do! But if you don't come, don't call, I'm supposed to risk my job?

Assuming that this outburst was directed at him, Bryan started telling Eric that he wasn't trying to say Eric should risk his job, that he had just had a hard couple of weeks and slipped up but was turning it around. Eric shook his head. "This for everybody! Everybody wanna go to heaven but nobody wanna die! The way you get out is by going through this! Because I ain't gonna lose my job. I got a high-ass rent."

Eric was unusually troubled that evening, but the themes in his speech came up regularly in sessions. They point to a tension at the center of court-mandated treatment: therapists are not just treatment providers but also enforcers, and their clients are also defendants. Therapists badly want their clients to stay clear of the harsher forms of criminal punishment that would follow removal from the diversion program, but they are nonetheless required to enforce the program rules. This chapter draws on ethnographic fieldwork inside of a mandated treatment program to examine the ways this central tension shapes the interactions between providers and their clients. Aware of therapists' enforcement obligations and anxious to extricate themselves from their legal entanglements, mandated treatment participants engage in a set of defensive and performative strategies that are common to the courtroom environment. They attempt to demonstrate that they are not culpable for the actions for which they have been criminally charged; to convince providers that they present a low risk of recidivism, typically by hiding symptoms of ill health; or just to quietly serve out their allotted time in the program. These strategies often collide with and thwart therapists' training and goals. In the process, the logics of the criminal legal institution permeate and profoundly shape the day-to-day provision of care.

Therapist-Enforcers

"My job as I understand it, and as I want to follow it, is to be an agent of healing in any capacity," a young White diversion therapist named Mira reflected from her seat on my couch. Like all of the diversion therapists I spent time with, Mira had been through many years of professional education that trained her to place her clients' mental health needs at the center of her work and professional identity. She now sits daily in an office where she sees clients, performs mental health assessments, and facilitates group therapy sessions. No one surveils her work with clients, dictates which therapeutic approaches she can use, or asks her to report in detail on what occurs in her sessions. So far as her treatment work is concerned, she has full professional discretion, with no clear institutional pressures from the criminal legal system. The courts will never ask her for notes on her sessions, and she keeps them brief and vague just to be safe. She works hard, she told me repeatedly, to assure clients that therapy is a confidential and nonjudgmental space in which they are safe to share their experiences and emotions openly.

Therapists in my field site were committed to a variety of approaches and techniques, including cognitive behavioral therapy, acceptance and commitment therapy, and existential therapy (Mira's preferred approach). In group sessions, the younger providers seldom talked about drug use or substance use disorders directly. Instead, they brought in exercises designed to teach general "coping skills" for navigating mental health challenges and trauma, to elicit open conversations about challenges participants were facing, or to encourage reflections on close relationships and how they might be improved. Eric—like most drug treatment providers around the country[1]—combined his formal training with frameworks and language taken from Narcotics Anonymous, a twelve-step group in which he was active: he encouraged storytelling, and he constantly reminded his clients that addiction was a disease that required total abstinence and lifelong vigilance to keep in remission.

Regardless of their therapeutic approaches, all of the providers emphasized that trusting relationships with their clients were fundamental to their work. Their project, as they had been trained to view it, was the alteration of patterns of thinking, feeling, and behavior through the establishment of those relationships.[2] As one classic text defines it, psychotherapy is a "psychological form of treatment in which a trained professional *establishes a relationship with a patient* to achieve particular goals by psychological means."[3] Study after study has found that the effectiveness of therapy rests on the quality of the connection between the therapist and client.[4] The providers in my field site were firmly committed to building those connections.

But therapists like Eric and Mira are also tasked with a set of duties that stand in stark contrast to their therapeutic work.[5] They have to monitor their mandated clients' compliance with program rules, including their attendance at treatment sessions, drug test results, and fee payments. Those reports are subject to review by supervisors. If a client misses any sessions, tests, or payments, or has a positive drug test result, the therapist is usually supposed to increase requirements like treatment sessions or drug tests. If those steps don't bring the client back into compliance, they have to return the case to court.[6] That return was more likely than not. Therapists in my field site returned about 55 percent of their felony cases to the courts, a rate similar to those recorded in court-mandated treatment programs around the country.[7]

Just as Eric did that night, the therapists tried to distance themselves from their roles as enforcers by emphasizing repeatedly that decisions about their case outcomes were out of their control. They often told their clients that they were advocating for them with their superiors and that they were holding off on enforcement as much as they could without endangering their own jobs. Although they did have some degree of discretion in determining how to respond to their clients' noncompliance, they downplayed it in group sessions. As Eric often explained the process to the group: "I don't make the decision to release you from the diversion program. I just give a summary. My director makes the decision, and if your notes and groups and meetings aren't in line like she want them, she'll send them back—send the case back to the courts. . . . My director won't allow me to allow you to move forward if you got dirty urines. Simple." By presenting themselves as advocates whose hands were tied when it came to case closures or other punitive consequences, therapists tried to protect the therapeutic interaction from the institutional pressures of the court system. But their success was limited.

Client-Defendants

Therapists administer treatment in their offices and almost never have any reason to enter a courtroom; their clients, however, enter treatment after months of intensive interaction with the legal system as criminal defendants. By the time an individual enters pretrial diversion, they have been arrested and often spent time in jail. One in ten people in my field site is incarcerated on an unaffordable cash bond up until they enter diversion, and the rest pay substantial sums for their pretrial freedom. The median time spent in the system prior to entering diversion is four months, and court dates during that period are frequent.[8]

In court, defendants stayed laser-focused on freedom and on the performances that would get them there. For the most part, they came to court on time. They pled not guilty and admitted to nothing. They followed the dress code. They showed deference to judges. They brought their grandmothers along. They reassured the court that they had committed to personal change, given up drug use, and dedicated themselves to finding or keeping employment. Courtrooms have a tight script, and defendants knew what it was: They had to show the judge not just that they were innocent, but also that they were low-risk subjects.[9] Over the course of weeks or months, defendants worked to demonstrate that they were economically and mentally stable and willing to comply with any demands the court made on them. The stakes of these performances could hardly be higher; the cost of failure could be the loss of freedom, financial stability, housing, and family.

For defendants, diversion was another step in the high-stakes criminal court process. Although program directors and prosecutors emphasized that entering treatment was entirely voluntary, defendants rarely experienced it that way. Nearly half of the people I interviewed expressed confusion when I asked them how they had decided to participate in diversion and replied that they had had no choice. Seven were so taken aback by the question that they misunderstood it entirely and started telling me how they had decided to participate in my study. And even those who did see diversion entry as a decision invariably described it as a coerced choice. As one participant explained when I asked how he had decided to enter diversion: "Oh, it was a easy process. It's called you're sitting in jail, then they give you an opportunity to get out of jail called the diversion program. If you don't take that opportunity, you're sitting in jail and you're waiting for trial. So I decided to do what many broke people do: take the diversion program." For incarcerated defendants, accepting the diversion offer meant almost immediate release to return to their families, jobs, and other responsibilities, while refusal meant remaining in jail indefinitely. Even for people who were out of jail pretrial, diversion could put an end to the endless string of court dates, each of which took a psychological and financial toll. More importantly, it offered a way to avoid the terrifying fate that likely waited at the end of the pretrial process. Although I couldn't find a jurisdiction that kept data on pretrial diversion offer refusal rates, the prosecutors and diversion coordinators I interviewed all agreed that refusal was very rare. For most defendants, diversion was another unavoidable step in the long progression through the criminal court system.

Once in treatment, defendants' case outcomes still hung in the balance as they worked to meet the state's demands on them. Failure to meet any of the programs' requirements—which included drug testing and fee payments as well as attendance in group therapy sessions—could send them back to court and to jail. And the face of enforcement was the therapist, who was tasked with tracking each client's conformity with program requirements and returning cases to the courts as needed. The knowledge that their therapists could put them behind bars at any moment could be acutely stressful for program participants. As Steve, one participant, described the experience of being in diversion, "It's like they're holding a gun to your head and if you step out of line, they're going to pull the trigger."

Relational Dynamics of Coerced Care

Although treatment providers did their best to protect the therapeutic environment from the pressures of the criminal court system, those pressures had profound effects. Program participants entered treatment far less concerned about its impacts on their mental health than about its implications for their legal cases. Cognizant that therapists were now their judges, they brought familiar strategies from the criminal courts to their ongoing efforts to win their freedom. They worked to convince therapists that they should be released from court supervision and to serve out their time in the program as efficiently as they could, but their efforts were at odds with therapists' own commitments and tended to produce tense and mistrustful relational dynamics without moving them toward their goals.

NEGOTIATING RESPONSIBILITY

On her first evening in group therapy, a young Black woman named Shanice recounted the circumstances of her arrest, directing her story to the lead therapist, Eric, in a pleading tone: "I had some furniture from the Rent-A-Center. I missed a payment because I had lost my card, and they came to my job, called the DA and all that!" The volume of the group rose as other members expressed indignation that she had to go through the program just because of a missed payment, and others began to recount the stories of their own unjust arrests. After a couple of unsuccessful attempts to redirect the conversation, Eric raised his voice, gesturing at Shanice: "Yeah, but that's how they do though! That's how they get theirs! That's how they cover the insurance or whatever. You know something about life, though? Life like this. It ain't about what happened to me, or the circumstances that caused me to be here. It's about how I respond to it! I know you won't do Rent-A-Center no more." Shanice looked down, and the group fell silent. Eric redirected with a conversation prompt about gratitude.

Therapists and their clients entered the treatment environment with very different institutional investments. Participants often came from months in courtrooms where the denial of guilt and discussion of mitigating factors were the norm, and they were eager to convince therapists—the new decision-makers in their cases—that they did not need to be in the system. Therapists, by contrast, entered with their focus trained on the therapeutic aims of altering individual psychology and behavior. Psychotherapy is grounded in the idea that people have to recognize their own behaviors in order to change them. Therapists were also steeped in the language of drug treatment—a central focus of their work with many court-mandated clients—which tends to frame an individual's *admission* that their substance use is problematic as an indispensable first step toward recovery.[10] As one therapist described his work with mandated clients, "The first struggle is, they have to admit it. If they don't admit it we're going to start using terms like denial and resistance." Wary of any attempts to avoid taking full responsibility, therapists countered participants' defenses by encouraging them to own their mistakes and consider directions for personal growth and change.

Because people were often mandated into therapy for reasons that did not boil down to individual responsibility, therapists' redirection could heighten tensions between themselves and their clients, at times along lines of race and class. In one exchange, for instance, several young Black men took turns putting forward their case defenses as their two White therapists, Marly and Libby, tried repeatedly to refocus the conversation onto the men's own behavior. A Black high schooler, Dalton, told about the search at the front doors to his school during which police had found marijuana on him and put him under arrest. He reflected on how minor the offense was and how counterproductive it had been to take him out of school and put him in jail, concluding, "I feel like if I was in my old school or any school where there wasn't all them cops, like if I wasn't in that type of environment I probably wouldn't have even went to jail." Marly interjected: "Do y'all feel like change needs to happen?" and Dalton asked, "Within the system?" Frowning, Marly replied, "I feel like we can't really talk about the system, because if y'all ask me questions about the legal system I'll just be like 'I don't know.' But looking at yourself, and the way things are going now, *your* choices, *your* actions, do y'all feel like a change needs to happen? . . . if you value your freedom—being free and not being in jail—how do you live your life around that value, where you don't want to go to jail?" Libby nodded, adding, "That's more of our role. Looking at what you do have control over." Dalton frowned and replied, "Ain't much that you got control over." A White participant, Brad, jumped in: "In life, you can be a victim and choose to be like 'this ain't fair and why me?' or you can look at it like 'this is happening for a reason, I'm supposed to be learning from it.'" Libby nodded in agreement, reminding Dalton that he had made the choice to stop smoking marijuana and to come to group to confront his drug use. Sounding frustrated, Dalton replied, "But as far as the system and how stuff's set up, like, when you get arrested and all that, you don't have no control over all that. . . . I mean, you can try to do better, but you're going to be in the same category from the outside. Like I said, I got partners in jail. And being a Black young male anyway, right?" Here Libby changed the subject, and the group moved on as Dalton continued to frown at the table.

Outside of the group, participants said that they read therapists' persistent focus on individual decision-making as moral judgment that elided the social realities of participants' lives. Keenan, a Black man in his thirties, described the group treatment sessions: "I just kind of thought they were just total bullshit, which is what they were. Because everybody had a different thing that they were there for, and they were just like, 'You're all the same. You're, like, bad, immoral people.' . . . Adam clearly has a problem, he's clearly super poor. I don't have the same problems as Adam—I'm not super poor. He's stealing because he has two kids to worry about, which makes me feel sad." I never heard a therapist describe any of their clients as bad or immoral, but participants often said they heard the accusation implied in therapists' insistence that they were responsible for their circumstances. In this context, the therapeutic goal—to elicit reflection on and alter individual behavior—clashed with clients' legal goals. Focused on freedom, defendants returned again and again to the reasons they did not deserve to be held hostage by the state.

As therapists and their clients negotiated responsibility, their conflicting frameworks often collided in tense interactions that eroded trust. Program participants, preoccupied with their legal cases, sometimes tried to convince their therapists that they were not "bad" or even guilty of the offenses they had been charged with—in other words, that they did not require court supervision. But the therapeutic structure did not allow for evaluation of legal evidence of guilt, nor could it redress systemic wrongs. Therapists tried instead to engage their clients in self-examination by redirecting attention to individual behavior. This countermove often alienated clients further, as attempts to attenuate their guilt in therapists' eyes were met with what they often perceived as vehement rehearsals of their individual culpability.

NEGOTIATING RISK

It was a late summer evening in group therapy, and Libby and Marly were struggling to fill the silence. After two of her prepared discussion prompts fell flat, Libby paused and observed that it can be hard to share with people one doesn't know well. She asked the group to go around and tell the others what it took for us to trust other people. When everyone had answered and the room had fallen silent again, she asked if it had helped to hear each other's answers. There was a long pause. Finally Anton, a Black high school senior who was one of the group's most active participants, asked, "Helps you what?" Marly clarified: "Feel like you can trust us! Feel like you can share." Anton paused for a second and then said, "It's like, I'm not gonna trust y'all to tell you everything that I do or been through. Like y'all said, y'all job come first. Y'all hear something, y'all gonna go and tell 'em. So it's a different level." Tay, another Black high schooler, agreed: "We trust y'all to a business point." When Marly asked what he meant, Anton clarified: "We might mess up your head with something where you wasn't even there. And y'all gonna go back and tell your supervisor. And your supervisor mess with the courts. All that go back, and I'm bit in the ass because of something I told you. . . . I just can't tell y'all all the shit that be on my mind and that I be doing, shit that has really traumatized me." The other participants were nodding and making sounds of agreement. Libby's and Marly's frowns deepened, and Marly assured the group that, apart from the few things she was mandated to report, what was said in the session stayed there. Anton shook his head, not satisfied. "Everybody in this program is trying to get out. That man [*nodding at another participant*] could tell you something like that and y'all could feel like, 'He crazy. He need more time in here.' He told y'all something and it came back and bit him in the ass. So you gotta stay in your lane." He ended with a note of finality, and an older Black woman in the group repeated his words in a murmur: "Gotta stay in your lane." The therapists, looking uncomfortable, thanked everyone for sharing and noted that it was time to check out and wrap up group.

Therapists tried in every session to elicit sharing from their clients about their struggles with substance use, relationships, or exposure to violence; but nearly all of the treatment participants I spent time with said that they made efforts to give therapists the impression that they were healthy and at low risk of reinvolvement in the legal system. They were acutely aware that the information they shared could have serious implications for their legal outcomes and that the best outcome for them would be to convince their treatment providers that they could be safely released from the program. Current participants often asked me and others to confirm, before they shared sensitive details about their lives, that we would never mention the information in front of treatment providers. Those reflecting on past participation in mandated treatment consistently recalled similar concerns. One young White man summarized their shared sentiment: "I would have been very hesitant to reveal any deeper, any difficult struggles that I may have been having, for fear of being in the program longer or, you know, or getting kicked out."

Concerned about their clients' reticence, therapists pushed them to share more about themselves. Some participants responded by moving beyond just withholding sensitive information to actively performing the personae they thought their therapists wanted to see. Shawn, a Black man in his mid-thirties, recalled his realization that he might ease his progress through the program if he shared more during group therapy: "I finally realized, 'Oh, they need to see that Shawn has changed.' So after like five classes, I got much more participatory, started answering the questions in a way that I thought they would like to hear them." This was a common story among participants. As Kyla, a young White woman, put it, "I kind of took on a whole new person when I was in there. Just kind of like, 'Oh yeah, it's totally bad. You know, I'm addicted because of my parents.' Stuff like that, that's basically what I shared. . . . They have to see an improvement in you, that's what I felt like. I feel like if they don't see an improvement in you, they're going to keep you there longer, and I do not want that." Aware that their legal outcomes would be determined by treatment providers' assessments of their mental health and progress, participants were highly motivated to perform the low-risk subjects that they thought therapists would be willing to release. Their efforts consistently thwarted therapists' attempts to build the trusting and authentic relationships that form the basis of therapeutic interactions.

SERVING OUT TIME

On one particularly well-attended evening, seventeen of us filed silently into our chairs for a group session. Eric, still pulling in extra chairs from surrounding offices as he did every week, stuck his head in and instructed, "You know this is so repetitive that y'all could just start checking in when you get in here. Instead of just everybody sitting here grabbing on their fucking chins like 'I don't wanna fucking be here.' And I understand that! But y'all know how it go. One person start, then we go around." We all gave our names and said how we were doing that week, moving clockwise around the circle as we did in every session. Most common among the check-in reports were brief variations on the phrase "just trying to get through this." Half of the attendees did not speak again for the rest of the session. Three asked questions about their cases, such as whether charges show up on background checks and what happens when cases go back to court. Four relatively new arrivals carried the conversation with Eric all evening, describing how completely they had turned their lives around since their arrests—the commitments to abstinence, the new jobs. As soon as Eric announced that the session had ended, everyone leapt up and was out of the room before I had even gathered up my papers and pencil, even those who would spend the next hour waiting outside for a ride.

The group's silence constitutes a third technique, borrowed from a legal system that asks people to wait out long periods of time in prison, on supervised release, or even just repeatedly sitting in court: many of the participants just withdrew into their own minds to wait for the day when their time in the program would be done. Victor, another young Black participant, described that technique: "When I was in [treatment], I was in there and I wasn't in there. I would just be sitting in there. Just my presence was there but my mind wasn't in that shit. I just went 'cause I had to. . . . it's like, it's jail but it ain't jail." Victor was among the many who thought of the treatment sessions primarily in terms of serving out time. They sat largely in silence, sometimes texting or putting in earbuds when the group was large enough that they could go mostly unnoticed. This dynamic aligned with many participants' efforts to avoid any self-revelation that could increase their riskiness in therapists' eyes. But as Victor signals, here the logic shifted away from that of the criminal court, in which punishment might still be negotiated with the right arguments or behavior, to the carceral, in which time just had to be served.

Some participants came into the program already determined just to wait for release. Others began by trying to negotiate responsibility or risk and later gave up, joining the ranks of the absent-while-present. A young Black man named Ty, for instance, had come into the program with high hopes for an early release. From the start, he had not only carefully curated the information he shared about himself but had also been the most active participant in his group, joking with therapists and stepping up to answer questions. But one evening Ty walked into group with an uncharacteristically tight face and eyes locked on the floor. When we checked in, he said curtly that he was "drove" (angry), and he was less patient than usual when the group therapist didn't understand the word. After check-in he put an earbud in and closed his eyes, even though there were just seven of us around the table that night, and stayed quiet for the rest of the session. Afterward, Ty told me that the counselor in charge of his case had given him permission to miss some appointments when he had no transportation from his family's house in a distant suburb. But she had told him today that the program director had looked over the notes and said his time in the program should be extended because of those missed sessions. Ty's voice rose with emotion as he recalled the conversation: "I was mad today! Like, 'I'm doing *everything* y'all asked me! You hearing me? And I'm still in here!' . . . That's why I'm really drove. I feel like I'm really trapped in that stuff now! I was supposed to get out a month ago. . . . And my counselor, she ain't messing with me. She like my progress. But it's really up to her supervisor, and I don't know how the supervisor—the supervisor don't know me, she just know the notes." The notes that Ty mentions reflected only tallies of his attendance in treatment, drug tests taken and passed, and fee payments. In other words, it became clear to Ty that no matter how hard he tried in treatment sessions themselves, these metrics—which he often experienced as beyond his control, in the case of a lack of transportation—would determine his fate. Ty said he was "done trying," and he rarely spoke during the remainder of his group sessions.

Therapists were patient with clients who made clear that they would prefer to be anywhere else. All had been trained in graduate school not to reprimand clients or pressure them into participating against their will. As one therapist reflected, "There's an enormous amount of resistance and resentment, which makes a lot of sense . . . that's pretty common when you have a mandated client: being like, 'I'm not going to fucking talk to you!' Like, 'Okay, you don't have to!'" Eric assured his clients in nearly every session that he understood that they were suffering and anxious to be done. Even Libby, the most enthusiastic believer in the program I met during my fieldwork, told me without hesitation: "Nobody wants to go to treatment. I shouldn't say nobody, but like a lot of them, they don't want to go to treatment. They want to just get this off their record." Therapists very rarely called participants out for using their phones during sessions—one of the few times that Eric drew the line was when someone answered a phone call in the middle of the group.

Painfully aware that their clients felt trapped, many of the treatment providers shifted their focus away from the daily reality of treatment and toward the days their clients would finish the program and be free. When I asked them about the best and worst parts of the job, for instance, their answers were usually related to clients' legal outcomes. They dreaded sending people back to court, and seeing them make it through the program, on almost any terms, was what kept them going. As one therapist immediately exclaimed, in answer to my question about her favorite part of the job: "Completing people! . . . For so many people they're like, 'I did it, I'm done, I can't even'—there's so much disbelief about like, 'I can't believe this is over.' It's like the happiest day, and I can't even describe to you how many people have come in crying that day." Therapists' focus, like their clients', often moved ahead to the day of completion.

The frustration that could follow participants' attempts to negotiate responsibility or perform health was attenuated when they resigned themselves to waiting out the time together. But the idea that one can serve out time in treatment and then walk free is often an illusion: over half of the program participants were eventually sent back to the court system, where they received no credit for "time served" in diversion.

Conclusion

Reformist practices assimilate the dominant logics of the institutions that adopt them, and their daily operations are reshaped accordingly. Even mental health treatment, which is shielded from outside pressures by professional practice and by privacy laws, is permeated by the logics of the criminal courts when they mandate it. Keenly aware that their treatment providers could give them freedom or send them to jail, mandated clients engage in a set of defensive and performative strategies in efforts to make it through the assigned treatment. Each translates into the therapeutic space a tactic that is central to the criminal legal system. First, clients *negotiate responsibility*, attempting to convince treatment providers that their past actions do not warrant placing or keeping them under criminal legal supervision, even as therapists push them to take responsibility as a first step toward personal transformation. Second, they *negotiate risk*, trying to perform health in order to convince therapists that they can be safely released from treatment while therapists try to elicit honest sharing about their mental health challenges. Finally, they *serve out time*, putting their bodies in the seats and keeping their minds far away while they wait for their assigned time in treatment to run out. Each of these techniques shapes interactions between clients and their therapists in distinct ways, and they often overlap. But each disrupts and transforms the therapeutic space, thwarting treatment providers' efforts to build trust and provide meaningful care.

The complexities of therapeutic engagement with court-mandated clients raise questions about the costs of coercing care. When treatment providers are positioned to mete out punishment to their clients, even indirectly, they may find it more difficult to engage and establish trust with them. This matters especially because, in many cases, court-mandated treatment is not a *supplement* to voluntary treatment but a *substitute* for it. Diversion programs rarely contribute more public mental health resources to an environment in which those resources are scarce. Typically, court-mandated clients enter treatment in community organizations, where they often enter ahead of voluntary clients who are waiting for spots to open. Even in a national sample limited to urban district attorneys' offices—typically the most well-resourced—91 percent of the responding pretrial diversion programs reported that they do not provide any treatment services themselves but refer all clients out to community organizations.[11] They often have established relationships with organizations that allow them to move mandated clients into programs even ahead of long waiting lists. In some places, journalists report, this process has produced an environment in which the only way to get into treatment may be to be arrested and mandated by the criminal legal system.[12]

The findings laid out in this chapter also have implications for scholarship on institutional trust and mistrust. Researchers have found that people's confidence in the criminal legal system has important impacts on their lives, shaping their relationships with their own attorneys, their interactions with judges in the courtroom, and their feelings about the law and its validity broadly.[13] Numerous studies have examined factors that contribute to low trust in the system, including racism among police and other criminal legal decision-makers and procedural injustice in the legal system more broadly.[14] This chapter extends that work by showing how mistrust can emerge in the criminal legal context *even when* state workers adhere to official procedures and do their best to help and build trusting relationships with the people in their care. Although other factors exacerbate it, some degree of mistrust may be structural: the legal system asks most of its workers to mete out punishment, and most people do not want to be punished. This fundamental collision of interests impedes openness, as people try to avoid punitive consequences by hiding anything about themselves that might expose them to blame or reveal their vulnerabilities.

More broadly, this chapter has shown how the assimilation of dominant institutional logics can reshape the daily operations of reformist practices, even when workers do their best to resist the intrusion of those logics. Other studies have examined the ways that social services can be fundamentally altered by placement within the criminal legal system when service providers are pressured to do their work differently. Therapists providing mandatory services to people who report experiences of domestic violence to the legal system, for instance, push people to rewrite their experiences into particular accounts of survivorship. To demonstrate that they are worthy of state support, finds sociologist Paige Sweet, participants are asked to build their own narratives around psychological recovery and minimize the structural elements of violence.[15] Similarly, nurses providing healthcare to people who report sexual violence have altered their work to accommodate criminal legal logics, focusing on collecting evidence for potential court cases, even at the expense of caring for their patients. Although their efforts to gather evidence typically make little difference to case outcomes, writes anthropologist Sameena Mulla, they fundamentally reshape patients' experiences of healthcare.[16] The findings laid out here expand on these accounts by showing how reforms can be powerfully molded by their institutional context even when workers attempt to keep that context at bay, in part because it shapes the expectations and concerns of clients themselves.

In part III, I show how mandated treatment programs, powerfully reshaped by the logics of the criminal system, become hidden sites of adjudication. Carrying out the traditional work of the criminal courts even as they obscure it, mandated treatment programs sort and mark people for punishment.

∴

Part III
OBFUSCATION

∵

[CHAPTER FIVE]

Sorting People

Adjudication by Social Structure

Isiah was arrested on a humid summer day and found himself held in the county jail without money for bail. It was his first time there, but as a young Black man from a heavily policed neighborhood, he had plenty of friends with stories. People inside had died of dehydration or been beaten to death by deputies. Stabbing deaths were not uncommon. So when his public defender visited him with an offer from the district attorney that would allow him to go home that same day, he took it without hesitation. He would enter a guilty plea, and as soon as he completed a substance use treatment program, the plea would be withdrawn and the charges against him dismissed. For a few weeks he went to treatment sessions and went in for drug testing. But he could not pay the program fees on the limited income he made mowing lawns, and a drug test came back positive for cocaine. He was afraid to talk to diversion counselors about his situation. When I mentioned them, he just shook his head. "They look at you *different* from everybody, know what I'm saying? Like, diversion for fuck-ups. . . . Like you less than them. Like you ain't shit. Know what I'm saying? Like you ain't got control over your own life." Just two months after entering the treatment program, he was marked noncompliant and sent back to court. He returned with a felony conviction and with no opportunity to go to trial or negotiate a plea deal.

People who are diverted into treatment by the courts will stay under legal supervision until they have completed their assigned programs, and as many as half of them never do.[1] Instead, they are marked as noncompliant with treatment and returned to court, where they may face automatic convictions, like Isiah, or a range of other sanctions.[2] This group of people is disproportionately poor, Black, and contending with substance use disorders, like Isiah. In my field site, 70 percent of people assessed as "highest risk and need"—a determination made on the basis of poverty, illness, and prior criminal legal contact (itself a proxy for race and poverty[3])—are returned to court, twice the rate recorded among people in the lowest risk/

need category.[4] Over 60 percent of diverted Black felony defendants in my field site are returned to court from diversion, versus just 45 percent of White defendants. Similar racial, economic, and health-related disparities in completion characterize other court-mandated treatment programs around the country.[5]

This chapter outlines the ways that people are sorted for punishment along lines of inequality in the hidden sites where treatment is delivered. Drawing on ethnographic fieldwork and interviews with participants in mandated treatment programs, it shows that successful compliance with treatment requires health, financial resources, and confident self-advocacy before the state. Programs typically require regular appointments, drug tests, and payments over months or years. People who are ill or living in precarious situations are frequently unable to get to all of the required treatment sessions and to pay program fees. Those dealing with chronic pain, symptoms of trauma, or mental illness are often unable to avoid substance use and pass drug tests. Exacerbating those difficulties, people who have learned to distrust the legal system tend to be fearful of reporting to the program to ask for leniency when they miss appointments or have positive drug test results. As a result, the most vulnerable participants are systematically labeled noncompliant and marked for punishment. Adjudication is thus carried out in a new guise, under cover of social services and using unacknowledged criteria for judging people and allocating punishment. This chapter illustrates how reform can obfuscate the work of an institution by giving it a less recognizable form.

Compliance as Resource Exchange

For many people, compliance with diversion requirements is a straightforward exchange. They give time, money, and abstinence, and in return they get clean criminal records. Mindy described one such simple trajectory in an interview a couple of years after her charges had been thrown out. A White woman in her thirties with perfect teeth and a white-collar job, Mindy pulled up to our meeting spot in a shiny car and insisted on buying her own coffee. She had been arrested on cannabis charges a couple of years ago, she told me, and the diversion offer was presented to her as "your easy way out." "Easy way out," she mused, "but it was so long. . . . It was a lot of traveling to meet with the little diversion counselor and do the drug tests. It was very invasive and just seemed a long time. I often wondered what the sentence would have been, not that I ever want to go inside jail, but [*laughs*] weighing the options, but they don't present that to you." Although she hated the program, Mindy recalled, she fell into a routine pretty quickly. She dreaded the long drives out to her group therapy sessions, but she found that she could combine them with workouts at a gym nearby. She was frustrated that the program only gave twenty-four hours' notice before each random drug test, but she was able to pay for testing at a private site, so she didn't have to make it to the courthouse before it closed. She could leave after work, drive to the site, and usually be done with the whole errand in just over an hour. She missed smoking cannabis at night, but she never worried about slipping up and failing a test. And she had no trouble paying the $600 in fees associated with the program.

Mindy had time, abstinence, and money to spare to the program's demands for compliance. It was not easy, she emphasized repeatedly. But she could choose to leverage her resources to get from start to finish: put some miles on her car, give up the pleasure of cannabis, reduce her free time after work, let her bank account take a hit. For people whose lives had narrower margins, compliance was not so straightforward.

Health

Among the most important obstacles to successful compliance with mandated treatment was, paradoxically, ill health. Although treatment programs are putatively intended for people with mental health conditions, the eligibility criteria for diversion means that many defendants enter without behaviors or conditions typically diagnosed as mental illness or disordered substance use, and that degrees of severity vary widely. The stigmatized marks of illness then crucially shape individuals' capacities to meet program requirements. Participants with substance use disorders, those dealing with symptoms of trauma, and those with other forms of mental illness often struggled to get to the required in-person treatment sessions and to pass drug tests. As a result, they were often marked noncompliant and removed from the program.

SUBSTANCE USE DISORDER

Michael, a slight young man in square black glasses, walked into his first group treatment session escorted by a counselor and leaning on a cane. He sat down in silence and stared down fixedly at the table. Tanya, the counselor in charge of the group, passed out worksheets and started a group discussion about coping techniques for maintaining abstinence from substances. Michael scribbled a straight line on his worksheet, back and forth, in a movement that grew increasingly agitated until the pen bore through the paper and it tore. At a mention of heroin, he finally broke in, nearly crying: "You're always going to want that feeling again. Thirty years from now—I could not use for thirty years, and I will never forget what it feels like." He choked out the story of his drug use, beginning with his discovery of heroin as a painkiller following his diagnosis with multiple sclerosis. Then he fell silent again as Tanya returned to a discussion prompt about recovery, and when the session ended he nearly ran out the door.

Michael's case was returned to the courts soon after. He missed his first court date, but after the judge issued a warrant for his arrest without bond, he appeared the next day with a private defense attorney. The prosecutor noted that Michael had been "put out" of the diversion program and still faced felony charges for possession of heroin and paraphernalia. Because he had not been required to enter a guilty plea prior to diversion entry, his case was set for motions. Six weeks later, he pled guilty and took probation. When his probation was revoked six months later because of positive drug tests, he served out the rest of the time behind bars.

Anyone who enters a mandated treatment program with a substance use disorder immediately faces an enormous obstacle: to consistently return the negative drug tests required to make it through the program, they have to beat the odds. Nearly everyone with a substance use disorder will return to substance use repeatedly. Medical research has shown that that disorder is a chronic condition characterized by long-term—possibly permanent— changes to the brain's motivational systems and to the control of the prefrontal cortex over decision-making.[6] Not a single person among those I interviewed years after treatment had stopped using long-term, and several said they went back to using immediately after the last required drug test. And many people with substance use disorders are not able to finish treatment at all. Although arrest on drug possession charges is not a clear proxy for substance use disorder, it is worth noting that nearly two-thirds (62 percent) of treatment participants in my field site who had been charged with possession of drugs other than marijuana were returned to court, compared with just under half (48 percent) of those on all other charges. These patterns align with research in the drug court context, which shows that participants with more severe substance use disorders complete treatment at substantially lower rates than others.[7]

Although programs aim to facilitate recovery from substance use disorders, their requirements can become obstacles to successful recovery. Brooke, for instance, was a young tech worker who had been arrested on heroin charges. She was able to bond out of jail and get into treatment at a methadone clinic, where she went daily for doses of medication that reduces heroin cravings. By the time she was offered diversion and entered the mandated treatment program, she had been on methadone for six months. In her first two group sessions, she reflected cheerfully on the six months of abstinence from heroin and her hopes for a full recovery. But over time, she stopped talking in group and often looked close to tears. She told me that her counselor, Mia, had told her that she would also not be allowed to complete the program as long as she was still testing positive for methadone. As she reduced her daily dosage, she felt sick all the time—methadone withdrawal symptoms are typically protracted—and she was finding it increasingly difficult to stay off heroin.

Brooke eventually began using heroin again and was mandated into a more intensive outpatient program after a drug test came back positive. That program immediately referred her on to an inpatient program, where she checked in right away. Brooke was leaving the hospital a week later when she got a call from Mia. As she described the conversation to me, "She's calling me acting like I absconded or something! Because I didn't meet her. And I was like, 'You told me to go to treatment, so I went to treatment. And here you are yelling at me!'" Certain that Mia was going to kick her out regardless, Brooke stopped calling or going in for appointments. Her case was returned to the courts soon after, and she entered a guilty plea in exchange for six months' probation.

Diversion programs' abstinence requirements can extend to methadone and buprenorphine, medications that are highly effective treatments for opioid use disorder. Both medications are synthetic opioid agonists, meaning that they occupy the receptors in the brain that are activated by opioids (called mu-opioid receptors). By occupying those receptors, they reduce the symptoms of opioid withdrawal and attenuate the effects of shorter-acting opioids such as heroin, codeine, or oxycodone.[8] A number of high-quality randomized controlled trials have found that the medications substantially reduce mortality and improve health among people with opioid use disorders (OUD).[9] As a 2019 research review by the National Academy of Sciences, Engineering, and Medicine concludes, "The verdict is clear: effective agonist medication used for an indefinite period of time is the safest option for treating OUD."[10] But these medications can fall outside of diversion programs' substance use parameters. The US federal government classifies methadone and buprenorphine as Schedule II and III drugs, respectively, putting the former in the same category as morphine and fentanyl.[11] Providers often referred to prescribing agonists as "giving you opioids," since they occupy the same brain receptors and can cause a high if taken in very large doses. Judges often strongly discourage use of agonist medication among defendants in their courtrooms for the same reason. As one judge put it succinctly, "People end up addicted to it." Although the medications are legally prescribed in every state, prohibitions on noncriminalized substances are not uncommon in mandated treatment contexts: all of the surveyed programs ban alcohol and cannabis, for instance, even in jurisdictions where both are legal.

The obstacles to program completion faced by participants with substance use disorders affect a substantial share of people. Nearly two-thirds of diverted felony defendants in my field site were facing drug possession charges, and studies suggest that most of the people arrested on typical diversion-eligible charges—usually low-level, nonviolent offenses such as drug possession, theft, or "public disorder"—meet the clinical criteria for substance use disorders.[12] Those disorders also overlap with symptoms of trauma and other mental illnesses, which frequently co-occur.[13]

TRAUMA

Andrietta was a Black grandmother and home health worker in her sixties who had used cannabis for years to manage stress and symptoms of PTSD. She had never used other drugs and did not identify as having a substance use disorder, and she was able to stop smoking and pass all of her drug tests for twenty-two of the twenty-four months she was required to spend in the treatment program. Two months before the end of her treatment, her younger brother fell out of contact, and she went to his house to check on him. As she told me afterward, "I found my brother in his house dead. And I really didn't even know how to come downstairs to tell my mother. But I had to tell her because when my son got killed, they didn't come tell me. The news told me. So how you think I felt? So I came downstairs and I went in my mom's house and got my mom. I carried her hand, I held her hand all the way till we got to his house. I said, 'Your son up there dead.'" Following her brother's death, she experienced intense anxiety and frequent flashbacks to the death of her son. She returned to smoking marijuana to manage the stress. Concerned about facing penalties for positive drug tests, she stopped going in for drug tests. Her case was returned to the court system, and she was sentenced on a felony conviction.

Severe trauma is common among participants in mandated treatment programs. A growing body of research has shown that exposure to past and ongoing trauma is ubiquitous among people involved in the criminal legal system in general.[14] And over the year that I spent in treatment, nearly every Black group participant mentioned at least one recent unexpected death of a family member or close friend. In a single treatment session in July, three of the four young Black men present had lost loved ones in the previous week. More often than not, people in the treatment program were navigating extremely difficult life events and their psychological impacts as they struggled to complete program requirements.

For many of the participants I spent time with, marijuana was the primary source of relief from flashbacks, anxiety, and other symptoms.[15] Most of them had no access to quality healthcare or any formal treatment for trauma. As one diversion counselor reflected about her clients, "They smoke a lot—they smoke *so* much—but they're smoking for PTSD maintenance." Giving up marijuana as a medication for symptoms of PTSD could take a heavy toll. One young Black man in his last year of high school, Eason, told me that before entering the program he had smoked marijuana every day, usually when memories came up of his cousin's death in a shooting or of violence he had witnessed against his sister. Determined to get through the program, he started spending most of his time alone in his room to ensure that there would be no marijuana around when the flashbacks came and he was tempted to smoke for relief. When his brother was killed three months into the program, Eason stopped coming out of his room altogether for weeks and lost a frightening amount of weight. Over and over, participants struggled to make appointments and to pass drug tests in the aftermath of trauma as they dealt with flashbacks and the physical and psychological stresses of grief.

OTHER MENTAL DISORDERS

Beyond substance use disorders and trauma, other mental health concerns could also present obstacles to program completion. Severe psychiatric disorders such as mania and psychosis could make compliance nearly impossible, but even depression and anxiety—which affect about a third of the adult population to some degree[16]—played an important part. Lester, a Black veteran in his seventies who lived at a homeless shelter several miles from the courthouse and did not have a phone, came close to having his case returned to court after falling out of contact with his therapist for nearly a month. He suffered from PTSD and severe depression, and when he lost the expensive breathalyzer that he was required to carry with him and blow into three times a day to prove that he had no alcohol on his breath, he became so depressed that he wasn't able to leave the shelter for weeks. When he eventually managed to come back to group, his therapist told him that he had already begun the paperwork to return his case to the courts. In tears, Lester explained:

LESTER: I lost my breathalyzer, and I had struggled with it for a whole month and passed, and it wasn't easy. Now I lost it and I don't know if I'm gonna be able to get it back. I lost it on the bus! . . . This got me completely depressed with myself, you know? To me, it was like the devil was just on my shoulder—

ERIC (THERAPIST): I don't believe it be the devil! I believe it be me, fucked up! I don't believe in something outside of me that motivate things, I believe it be me with my negative shit. You still could've came and caught the bus at, or you could've gone to the office where you live at and called over here, my man!

LESTER: I'm not saying I didn't call you. I called you a couple times but I didn't get through. I'm not using anything as an excuse. I'm just telling you how I felt! . . . I knew what to do but I couldn't make my feet go in the direction that my brain was telling me.

Lester's inability to "make my feet go in the direction that my brain was telling me" is reflected in a large body of research showing that people suffering from depression and other mental illnesses frequently miss scheduled appointments, even those that can make the difference between life and death.[17] But when participants in mandated treatment programs failed to appear for appointments, regardless of the reasons, providers had to return their cases to court.

Difficulties for participants struggling with mental illness could also be exacerbated when they had previously relied on medications like cannabis—commonly used to reduce psychological distress, including clinical anxiety and depression[18]—that were prohibited by the program. Melana, for instance, was a young Black woman who had relied on cannabis as a treatment for anxiety and depression for a decade. When she had to stop smoking, she started having frequent panic attacks at work and spending long periods of time in the bathroom during her shift as she waited for them to pass. Some days she could not bring herself to go in to work at all; she described days spent crying in bed while her girlfriend held her. She eventually lost her job and, as a result, her apartment. "I'm surprised I didn't commit suicide—most people would," she reflected on that period later, after finally finishing the program and returning to regular cannabis use.

By setting requirements for compliance that leave little room for experiences of mental illness, mandated treatment programs not only mark for punishment the very people they are putatively designed to help, but also produce inequalities along a few intersecting axes. First and most obviously, they produce inequalities by health and ability. People with substance use disorders, symptoms of trauma, or other mental disorders experience severe forms of social disadvantage as a group. The daily challenges of earning income and performing other daily tasks necessary to survival are compounded by widespread discrimination against people with mental illness in hiring, formal education, criminalization, and personal relationships.[19] Second, marking people who are ill for punishment amplifies disparities across race and class: People suffering from mental disorders are far more likely to be poor,[20] people who are Black are much more likely to experience trauma—including gun violence and its long-lasting physical and psychological effects—than their White counterparts,[21] and access to mental healthcare outside of the legal system is lower among poor people and Black and Latine people.[22]

Financial Resources

Mandated treatment requires that participants show up at the treatment center for regular appointments and drug tests, often for months or years, and usually that they pay various fees. Compliance with those requirements cost money. Transportation was difficult: many people struggled to find the $2.50 for a roundtrip bus fare, and others lived in areas not served by buses. Some participants arrived at the center on foot, sometimes in the blistering heat and after walking hours on the shoulders of highways. Time off work for sessions or drug tests often meant lost income. Childcare could be expensive, and people who couldn't access it sometimes brought their children with them to treatment sessions, to their counselors' dismay. But for most, the fees were the most taxing financial requirement. Participants in my field site are required to pay $200 by the end of the program and $15 each week for drug tests, in addition to any restitution they owed.

The program's financial demands could also increase at any point during the program if therapists mandated participants into additional treatment. Bryant, for instance, was a young man who made a living gathering scrap metal with his girlfriend. He entered diversion on crack and heroin charges and was almost immediately assigned by his therapist to an additional mandatory outpatient treatment program. When he went to that treatment center for intake, he learned that the center charged $100 for the initial appointment and did not accept Medicaid or offer payment plans. Already unable to buy food on some days, he saw no way to proceed with the program and met with his counselor to ask whether the additional requirement could be lifted or any of the costs covered. When they told him that it could not, Bryant told his public defender that he needed to leave the diversion program. He was able to negotiate a misdemeanor plea deal with the prosecutor, but he was then assigned a sentence well over the statutory maximum by a judge who berated him for demonstrating "no interest in changing" by leaving diversion.

The difficulty of paying program fees is often compounded by the very fact of participants' ongoing involvement with the court system. Those who had lost jobs when they were arrested or were otherwise looking for work often found that the marks on their records kept them from passing background checks. People who had been required to enter guilty pleas in order to enter diversion could have felony convictions on their records for the duration of the program. Even those who had not yet pled to anything could face similar obstacles. While some judges formally dropped charges as soon as defendants entered diversion, others left the charges pending for months. Whenever the topic of job searches came up, participants googled themselves and showed me the results on public websites on their phones: an arrest record and often a conviction or a bright notice of "charges pending."

Often finding themselves locked out of the formal job market, the poorest participants often took measures that put them at greater risk of rearrest. A participant named Jasper, for instance, could not make ends meet while supporting his family and covering diversion program costs. He had a full-time job, but it didn't pay enough to cover program and drug testing fees in addition to covering rent, utilities, and groceries for the relatives who lived with him. He also felt an increasing urgency to come up with the money to move out of his neighborhood, where the temptation to return to using heroin was everywhere, so that he could keep passing drug tests to stay in the program. Later, he told me that he had finally gone back to selling heroin to cover those expenses:

> JASPER: I started getting heroin, started getting packages, because I knew everybody. I found myself selling that to people. I couldn't touch it, because I was in diversion, so I wore gloves, had a handkerchief over my head, had my glasses, like I'm a chemist now. I packaged it up to sell. I was selling hundred-dollar packs.
>
> RESEARCHER: So to make it through drug treatment you had to start selling drugs?
>
> JASPER: [*laughs*] I had to survive. Because they was so strict . . . I had kids to feed, bills to pay, and then I had to pay every time I had to go take a urine test. And I didn't like where I was living at. I had to get out of that place. I needed extra money, so I did that. I knew I couldn't touch it because it'd be in my pores, so I'd wear a long-sleeved shirt and a face mask so I wouldn't breathe it in.

Jasper was one of the lucky ones. He was never caught, and he made it through the program. But it was a formidable risk: rearrest while on diversion meant facing the penalties associated with program noncompletion in addition to any new charges.

Sorting people for punishment on the basis of financial resources tends to produce inequalities not only by class but also by race and health. Poor participants who were able to finish treatment in my field site typically did so with financial help from family members or friends, but on average, Black individuals in the United States have less wealth in their networks than Whites.[23] Involvement in the criminal legal system also tends to be a greater liability for Black people than for White people when looking for work.[24] And requiring financial resources also disadvantages people who are ill. People with mental health concerns experience poverty at disproportionately high rates and, like Bryant, are often mandated into additional treatment. The financial burdens involved in that treatment can add obstacles to the successful performance of compliance.

Institutional Trust

A third central factor shaping treatment outcomes is institutional trust. Defendants have no legal representation in the therapeutic setting, so they have to represent themselves in moments when they miss appointments or payments or test positive on drug screens. In practice, most people who continue to call or show up and reassure therapists that they are trying to get back on track are allowed to remain in the program until treatment providers have tried a range of options other than termination, including extended time in diversion, additional drug tests or treatment sessions, or referrals to more intensive treatment elsewhere. But because therapists are given discretion to respond to noncompliance in a variety of ways—including termination—their clients are given no assurances as to what will happen if they miss a program requirement, and they are not told how many rule violations are permitted before their cases are returned to court. Defendants' expectations about what is likely to happen in the event of a violation thus vary widely, and those expectations critically shape their responses in moments of uncertainty.

Brad was the White owner of a successful business who entered the treatment program with a serious substance use disorder. By the time I met him, he had already been in diversion for well over two years because his time in the program had been extended several times because of positive drug tests. Brad frequently reiterated that therapists were there to help and would always work with participants to help them finish the program, and he consistently showed up after positive drug tests and emphasized his commitment to recovery. He was often baffled by other participants' panic about missed requirements, as illustrated in an exchange with Steven, an older Black man who supported himself and his brother with his minimum-wage job. Therapists had just begun to give the group a discussion prompt when Steven interrupted:

> STEVEN: [*in a panicked voice*] My daddy just passed away. I just came from [a nearby city] to sign the papers. I'm in charge of everything. That made me suffer even more—I had to drive down there and I thought I was going to miss the group. We were rushing, trying to make it back. I had to come here. If I'd have missed it, I'd have been to jail. They'd have locked me up. They don't have no sympathy for me or what I'm going through. They were about to put me in jail!
> BRAD: [*calmly*] I feel like they would give you more chances as long as you're really trying.
> STEVEN: [*voice rising in agitation*] I do try! I been trying!
> BRAD: [*still calm*] No, like I mean, if you've been—
> STEVEN: [*voice continuing to rise*] I been coming to Eric every Wednesday and I only missed two classes here! Then my daddy passed away!
> BRAD: So you had missed twice?
> STEVEN: Yeah!
> BRAD: And you let them know you were going to miss?
> STEVEN: [*now almost crying*] No, I ain't called, I had lost the card [with the diversion office number]! I'd been looking for it! They were fixing to lock me up!

People who, like Brad, were confident that therapists would forgive violations could push past myriad hurdles to finish the program. They consistently came in after missing required meetings or failing drug tests and assured therapists that they were committed to continuing to progress. Disproportionately White and middle-class, those defendants tended to express high levels of institutional trust and more positive opinions of the US criminal legal system.[25]

In contrast, people with low levels of legal-institutional trust very rarely assumed that therapists would work with them to keep them in the program. Martin, for instance, was an unhoused Black man with a heroin use disorder who had circulated through the court system on low-level charges too many times to count. Since childhood, he said, he had also seen his family members and friends harassed by police and targeted for punishment over and over just because they were poor and Black. In a conversation about the diversion program early on, he abruptly said, "I see the true intent." Caught a little off guard, I asked, "You see what?" "The true intent," he repeated. I asked what he thought the true intent was. "The same thing the judicial system in America is," he answered without hesitation. "Lock my ass up."

Like many of the poor Black program participants, Martin had learned from a lifetime of experience to fear the criminal legal system. In his mind, diversion program staff were not his allies but representatives of an institution whose ultimate aim was just to put him behind bars. So when he later used heroin again and missed some appointments, he didn't call or go back in to meet with his counselor. Instead, he went on the run. Because his housing was unstable, he never got the notice about his next court date, and he said he wouldn't have shown up for it anyway. There is still a bench warrant out for his arrest.

Overwhelmingly, people with low levels of trust in the legal system responded with panic to moments of crisis in the program. They didn't try to advocate for themselves in those moments. Instead, they disappeared. As one woman described her decision that it would be better to run than to return to the program: "I wind up still smoking and drinking, because once you're on diversion you're not supposed to do none of that, you're supposed to just fly straight with the program. . . . So I'm like, 'They gotta catch me.'" She kept a low profile and managed to stay free in the same city for another two years. Some people went back to court when the subpoena came, and others never did. Among the diverted cases that I tracked through the system, 43 percent of defendants did not appear for court dates when their cases were returned from diversion. Roughly a third later reappeared—typically after rearrest on bench warrants—and about two-thirds have not been found.

When people are sorted for punishment along lines of institutional trust, inequalities emerge at the intersections of health, class, and race. Positive drug screens and missed appointments or payments are most common among people who are poor or sick, so these people are the ones who most often need to ask for leniency. And the defendants with lowest levels of trust in the legal system are overwhelmingly Black and usually poor, both in my field site and elsewhere. Sociolegal scholar Monica Bell describes the legal estrangement produced among Black individuals when the state offers them violence and hostility rather than protection.[26] A substantial body of research—most recently by political scientist Vesla Weaver—shows that familiarity with the biases and harms of the criminal legal system has left

Black people with substantially lower average levels of trust in that system.[27] Poor and working-class people are also more likely to mistrust the criminal legal system,[28] and that mistrust often shapes poor defendants' interactions even with their own legal counsel.[29] More broadly, those who grew up outside of the middle and upper classes are often not trained to advocate for themselves with institutions and authority figures.[30]

Conclusion

As a growing share of the people who enter the criminal courts are diverted into treatment, the courts' adjudicative work is shifting to a new and hidden location. People stay under legal supervision until they have completed their assigned programs, which usually require regular appointments, drug tests, and payments over months or years. Those who are able to meet all of the requirements win their freedom and exit the system, often without any criminal convictions. Those who are not able to meet the requirements— as many as half of the people who enter—are marked for punishment and returned to court. People who are ill, who lack financial resources, and who mistrust the criminal legal system, in particular, struggle to meet the demands of the programs and complete them. Because those social categories are tightly interwoven and associated with extreme marginalization in the United States,[31] sorting individuals on the basis of program compliance is likely to produce stark inequalities in punishment outcomes.

This finding has key implications for inequalities in punishment more broadly. For decades researchers have examined biases among prosecutors and judges, pointing to more punitive charging and sentencing decisions in cases involving Black or Latine defendants, for instance.[32] They have also pointed to the inequalities embedded in the legal characteristics of cases— such as the type and severity of arrest charges and the arrestees' criminal legal histories, which are among the strongest predictors of case outcomes in criminal court[33]—because of racial and class biases in policing.[34] Less attention has been given to the disparities that can emerge from the structure of court supervision itself. The performance requirements common to diversion programs—regular appointments, abstinence from drugs and alcohol, and fulfillment of financial obligations—are also placed on millions of people in other criminal legal contexts. As sociolegal scholar Issa Kohler-Hausmann has observed, the lower courts often make their decisions based less on legal considerations than on evaluations of defendants' behavior— such as consistent appearances in court and compliance with mandated programs—gauging their "rule abiding propensities" and adjusting levels of control accordingly.[35] In the contexts of probation and parole, too, individuals' (non)compliance with performance requirements can be the factor that determines whether they will go free or be sent to prison.[36] This chapter suggests that adjudicating cases on the basis of compliance is likely to widen inequalities along lines of race, poverty, and illness.

The finding that inequalities in program completion are built into the structure of court-mandated treatment also signals a need for new research on pretrial diversion programs specifically. Evaluations of these programs have overwhelmingly concluded that they are effective in lowering rates of recidivism—that is, subsequent arrest or conviction—among participants.[37] But the evaluations typically compare recidivism rates among people who *complete* treatment to rates among those who stay in the traditional system, dropping from analysis those who enter but do not complete treatment.[38] This chapter suggests that these evaluations may be affected by selection bias: the people who are likely to finish diversion are also likely to avoid rearrest, because they have more financial resources and less severe mental health concerns and are more likely to be White. As a result, lower recidivism rates among program completers may be attributable to their preexisting characteristics rather than to the programs' impacts on them.

More broadly, this chapter shows how reformist practices can become new tools for carrying out established patterns of action within institutions and can obfuscate those actions as they do. Systems of accountability and visibility are built over time, so they may not immediately capture the dynamics and impacts of institutional practices when those practices change. Reforms can be well situated to obscure contested acts both by moving them outside of established venues and by making them harder to recognize. Social theorists such as Michel Foucault and Loïc Wacquant have written about the powerful impacts of making social crisis, and state responses to crisis, less visible. Foucault proposed that the modern state had quelled public protest by abandoning the practice of public torture in favor of subtler forms of discipline—including the prison, which hides the prisoner behind impenetrable walls, and a wide range of approaches to social control that appear benign and even helpful on their faces.[39] Wacquant later argued that the widespread criminalization of poor Black men helped to hide social crisis in the context of welfare retrenchment, both by physically warehousing marginalized people in prisons and by obscuring the crisis ideologically behind racialized rhetoric about crime.[40] The court system has not often been conceived of as a site concerned with hiding crisis. Unlike the prison, it cannot physically remove people from urban space over time. But the courtroom is a public forum in which some seventeen million people every year are subjected to open display and discussion of painful aspects of their lives and to punishments that will exacerbate their suffering,[41] and courts have come under increasing scrutiny from reformers and the public in recent years. Therapeutic programs move defendants physically out of that public forum and away from the systems of accountability provided by defense counsel and public scrutiny. They also obscure the criteria by which case outcomes are decided—sorting people for punishment on the basis of compliance with largely unknown program requirements rather than of law and evidence—making processes of adjudication harder to recognize and therefore to contest.

The next chapter considers what happens to people who are marked for punishment in diversion. It shows how the treatment-based alternative can obfuscate the administration of sanctions not only by carrying it out behind closed doors, but also by offering new justifications for punishing people on minor charges.

[CHAPTER SIX]

Punishing Treatment

The Costs of Diversion

"So they get a letter—the lawyers call it the golden ticket—they get the golden ticket, and it says they can come here," explained the director of one large pretrial diversion program, leaning back in the desk chair in her sunny corner office. Her desk was piled high with files and cluttered with family photos, and her walls were almost entirely obscured behind framed diplomas and certificates, photographs, and posters. A large sign behind her read, "What is in the past and the present is far less important than what is *within* us." Warm, cheerful, and self-assured, the director told me with confidence that her program offered defendants a life-changing lucky break: a pathway out of the criminal courts and into a supportive mental health treatment program that would help them to build new lives.

The vision of diversion as a "golden ticket" out of the court system prevails in courtrooms, media sources, and research. National datasets treat pretrial diversion as a disposition, the final resolution to a case.[1] But many of the people who had accepted that ticket saw things differently. As one such participant, George, described his decision to leave the traditional court system for diversion: "If you're sitting in a skillet and the skillet burn you but you never stuck your hand in a fire before to know that fire's hotter than the skillet, you're just trying to get out of the burning situation. And then you get in the fire and you're like damn, I should have stayed in the skillet." For George, as for countless others, the apparent escape that diversion offered only landed them in more painful positions. Diversion programs require that people comply with requirements like drug screening, fees, and regular appointments, often for years. Those who are unable to complete the requirements are returned to the traditional courtroom, where they often find their exposure to punishment *increased* as a result of their time in diversion.

This chapter shows how punishment is allocated in the context of diversion. First, diversion programs can trigger automatic criminal convictions when they send people back to court because of the legal concessions required for program entry. Second, diversion noncompletion becomes a black mark against defendants in the courtroom, where prosecutors and judges assign harsher punishments to people they view as unwilling to change. Last, diversion extends the total time spent under punitive supervision for people who go back to court: they experience their time in mandated treatment as a punishment, but that time is not credited toward their ultimate sentences. In each case, the assignment of punishment is obscured not only physically—by the closed doors of the treatment center—but also ideologically, by a narrative about compassionate help rejected by the ungovernable individual. The dynamics outlined in this chapter illustrate how reformist practices can obfuscate the ongoing work of an institution by perpetuating it in new and less visible ways.

Formal Penalties for Noncompletion

More than half of the jurisdictions in my national sample currently run at least one diversion program that makes participants' legal outcomes entirely contingent on their performances in diversion.[2] Often referred to as *post-plea* programs, they require that each participant enter a guilty plea with the court as a condition of entry, with the promise that their plea will be withdrawn and criminal charges dropped if they complete treatment. If, instead, the program returns their cases to court, the guilty plea remains in place and the individual is sentenced. The consequences of these convictions are grave. Misdemeanor convictions can carry jail or probation time, require payment of large court fees, trigger deportation proceedings, and disqualify people from some social services and jobs.[3] Felony convictions have even more severe consequences: they carry longer carceral sentences or probation terms, shut people out of even more lines of work, exclude people from a wide range of social services and educational opportunities, and trigger serious discrimination on the job market.[4]

People who return to court from post-plea diversion are likely to end up with more serious convictions and sentences than they would have received if they had never entered diversion. In the traditional court system, defendants nearly always negotiate their charges downward when they enter guilty pleas. Prosecutors often prepare for this negotiation by "stacking" charges initially—that is, charge people with more, and more severe, offenses than they believe they could be convicted of at trial—to increase the pressure on people to accept plea deals and in the expectation that those deals will involve reducing or dropping some of the charges.[5] When people are required to plead guilty as charged to go into diversion, they plead to *all* of those charges. They also give up the chance to negotiate a sentence as part of a plea deal, so if they return to court they are entirely at the mercy of the judge at sentencing. Harsher penalties for defendants who return to court from post-plea diversion are usually not made explicit, but in some cases they have been formalized: at least one mental health court requires defendants to plead guilty to offenses *more* serious than those they had initially been charged with, for instance.[6]

Participants often understood the post-plea program as an underhanded maneuver to get them convicted and sentenced. Some had accepted diversion because they had not realized they had a meaningful alternative. Others, like George, had no idea what kind of "fire" they would be getting into if they left the "skillet" and were surprised by the demands of the diversion program once they entered it. Still others believed that the program would be the help they needed to finally stop using drugs and were excited about the resources it promised. When participants found themselves removed from the program and sent back to court—as the majority of the people who entered post-plea diversion in my field site did—they often felt deeply betrayed. As one defendant, Victor, put it: "You got me to plead and you know I'm a person and I'm on drugs, so you hold my addiction against me to get a conviction." The sense that failure in the program was inevitable for people facing obstacles such as substance use disorders (discussed in depth in chapter 5) led many to conclude that the post-plea program structure preyed on their vulnerabilities and left them worse off than they had been before.

Hidden Penalties for Noncompletion

People who return to court from diversion are supposed to pick up their cases exactly where they left off. National standards for pretrial diversion, published since 1977 by the National Association for Pretrial Services Agencies (NAPSA), dictate that people who return from diversion should resume adjudication without facing any penalties for program noncompletion.[7] Formally, pretrial diversion simply pauses the progression of a case and has no bearing on the rest of the legal process. Many defense attorneys, especially the less experienced, accepted the claim that participating in diversion could not harm their clients' legal cases. As one such attorney put it, "With pre-plea [diversion], if you screw up, you're in exactly the same place as you were."

It is true that when pre-plea diversion participants return to court, the processing of their legal cases resumes without any formal penalties for program noncompletion. Diversion coordinators and therapists also try to protect their clients' privacy by giving no details about the reasons for a case's return, so judges and prosecutors usually don't know what happened inside the treatment program.[8] But courtroom decision-makers do know which defendants have come back from diversion. Usually the case file indicates that the defendant has returned due to noncompliance with the program, but even without that indicator, the case timeline would be a clear tell. Low-level cases with no activity in the file for months or even years "stick out like sore thumbs," as one defense attorney put it, signaling returns from diversion.

It is hard to assess whether or how legal decisions are shaped by courtroom actors' knowledge that people have come back without finishing treatment.[9] Nationally, around 95 percent of felony convictions result from plea deals negotiated between prosecutors and defendants in private.[10] Because prosecutors have such broad discretion in charging decisions, they can offer to drop or reduce some of the initial charges in exchange for guilty pleas from defendants. State court prosecutors can also usually specify particular sentences, which judges will rubber-stamp at the formal sentencing hearings. These deals are negotiated in private and are not subject to regular judicial review, so we have very limited information about whether or how treatment noncompletion might shape them.[11]

We do know that the initial plea offer that the prosecutor makes is crucial. Although the language of "plea deals" and "negotiation" implies a give-and-take between prosecutor and defense attorney, in practice it is the prosecutors who decide what the deal will be. The pressures on defendants to accept what they are offered and plead guilty, whether there is evidence against them or not, are overwhelming. Tough sentencing laws and legal advantages on the prosecutors' side make taking cases to trial a formidable risk for defendants. Even when the risks might not otherwise be too steep, prosecutors can stack on additional charges to increase the pressure on defendants to take a plea deal.[12] And people who can't afford to pay bail are often stuck in jail until their cases are resolved, making them even more likely to accept any deal that is offered.[13]

To understand whether or how prosecutors were influenced by diversion noncompletion when they assigned sanctions, I asked seventy state prosecutors from two different urban offices to review descriptions of two different felony cases and to draw on their experiences to select the plea offers they would be most likely to make in each case. One group of prosecutors was told that the defendants in question had entered pretrial diversion but returned to court without completing it, and a second group was not. Each respondent was randomly placed in one of those two groups, so that the only difference between them was the mention of diversion noncompletion.[14] This design effectively isolates the effects of noncompletion on prosecutors' decisions by removing all other sources of variation.[15]

When prosecutors design plea offers, the most influential decisions they make are those that change the possible sentencing or conviction outcomes. Each charge they bring carries a particular range of sentences—in terms of fine amounts and years of supervision or incarceration—meaning that a reduction in charges automatically reduces the severity of punishment. Lower-level felony charges are also frequently reduced to misdemeanors as an inducement to defendants to take plea deals, since misdemeanor convictions carry lighter sentences, fewer civil penalties, and less social stigma than felony convictions.[16]

Figure 2 shows the differences in prosecutors' decisions about charge reductions when they were and were not told that someone had returned to court from pretrial diversion. They selected substantially more punitive plea offers for people who had previously been diverted. Each respondent had a possible score between 0 and 2: 0 would indicate that they selected misdemeanor plea deals for both cases, and 2 would indicate that they selected felony plea deals for both. When respondents were shown a regular, nondiverted criminal case, they averaged a score of 0.5, meaning that they chose to reduce charges from a felony to a misdemeanor 75 percent of the time. When they were shown a case in which the defendant had failed to complete diversion, they opted to reduce charges only 51.5 percent of the time. In other words, when presented with otherwise identical cases, prosecutors selected felony-level plea deals 94 percent more often when they were told that defendants had returned to court from pretrial diversion.[17]

Prosecutors were then asked to select the length and type of supervision they would offer in a plea deal to each defendant.[18] Here, there are no statistically significant differences between conditions, although there is some indication that sentences may be longer when prosecutors are told that a defendant has returned from diversion. Descriptive results are shown in figure 3. It is worth noting that, because comparisons were made *within* each supervision type, statistical power is reduced here compared with the analyses shown in figure 2; a larger sample size may be needed to properly test for differences in sentence lengths for people with different diversion outcomes. But these findings are also in line with those of previous studies that have found that nonlegal factors influence sentence type but not sentence length.[19]

Courtroom decision-makers work in contexts of uncertainty, and they make constant imputations about people's characters and riskiness to inform their decisions.[20] Previous studies indicate that those decisions revolve

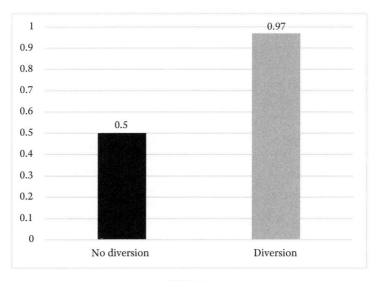

FIGURE 2

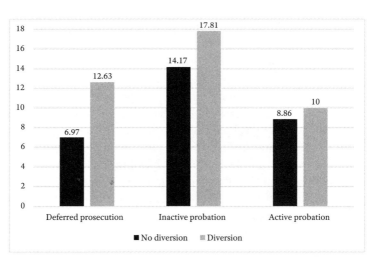

FIGURE 3

largely around their assessments of people's "blameworthiness"—or what they deserve for past behavior—and their "dangerousness"—or what they are likely to do in the future.[21] To make those assessments, researchers have found, prosecutors and judges evaluate the severity of each individual's alleged offenses, the strength of the evidence against them, and their history of contact with the criminal legal system. They also factor in, consciously or unconsciously, things like the individual's behavior in court and their apparent gender and race.[22]

Success in treatment has become a key heuristic used to assess defendants' deservingness and riskiness. In particular, decision-makers saw it as a litmus test of people's motivation to change. That motivation, they declared over and over, could independently explain the past and predict future behavior. One judge, for instance, reflected on the difference between people who complete diversion and those who do not: "The person has to want to change themselves.... Some people are motivated, and some are not. Some are not. You can have two children, and one can be—you know, the moon is, the world is theirs, and the other is like, meh. It's basically just, it's personality traits." A district attorney explicitly called diversion a means of "testing" for defendant riskiness: as he saw it, those who completed treatment were motivated to avoid further harmful behavior, and those who did not probably posed a danger to public safety. People who "failed out of diversion," he told me with a sigh, were not likely to "change their ways and stay out of the criminal justice system." Because they lacked the crucial quality of motivation to change, in the eyes of courtroom decision-makers, people who did not finish treatment were seen as requiring more punitive control.

Assignments of harsher punishment to people who do not finish treatment reflect more than these evaluations of their characters. Prosecutors and judges often expressed levels of indignation that implied personal affront when they perceived that people had failed to take advantage of the second chances they had offered. As one prosecutor reflected, frowning darkly, after telling me that he made less generous plea offers to defendants who returned to court from diversion: "I don't like it when they come back. I'm like, 'Dude, you had a chance! What are you doing?!'" He almost shouted the last sentence. A longtime public defender described the thought pattern that she observed among prosecutors like him, among judges, and among her own colleagues: "'Good people do X. Good people go to treatment. Good people do these things we ask them to do. If you don't do them, you're not good.' That flip happens *so fast*, even for defense attorneys. 'You had a way to avoid this outcome. You had a way to avoid me getting mad at you, but you didn't do it!'" The anger that the defense attorney described, and that the prosecutor expressed as he reflected on his plea negotiations with people who did not complete treatment, played out almost daily in the courtroom.

In one hearing, for instance, a White judge nearly screamed through a conversation about a Black woman she had mandated into treatment a few weeks before. The woman had not appeared for her hearing that day, and the judge's face was dark as she yelled at the woman's public defender:

JUDGE MERRILL: You *begged* me to put your client in this program and give her one more chance! Now she's not going to treatment, and she's so high she can't leave her house! She *wants* to be living under a bridge!

ATTORNEY: I don't think she wants to live under a bridge. We'll look at what's going on and try to come up with a plan.

JUDGE MERRILL: If you don't have an inpatient drug treatment program in place by Monday, I'm putting her in jail.

ATTORNEY: The difficulty is that she's on the [sex offender] registry, so those programs won't take her. I've been calling—

JUDGE MERRILL: I need an officer to go out to her house.

ATTORNEY: She's on the docket now for next Wednesday, if we could wait—

The conversation continued for a few more minutes, punctuated by two more directives from Judge Merrill to her clerk to put out a capias (an arrest warrant commonly issued for failure to appear in court) and send an officer to the woman's house immediately. Finally, the judge grudgingly agreed to wait until the following Wednesday. But she ended the conversation sounding as angry as she had when the conversation began: "If she doesn't come in, then I'll issue a warrant. And if she gets here and y'all don't have a plan for her, I'm putting her in jail."

Decision-makers' often angry judgments reflected a deep confusion about *why* people were refusing to comply with programs that aimed to help them. In effect, the subject they tended to imagine was one who was able to appear for appointments and court dates on time, pass drug tests, and pay program fees at will. Like themselves, that subject would be a healthy, well-organized person with a car, a calendar, and a wristwatch. As one defense attorney observed:

> Where I was growing up in the burbs, if I had a 10 a.m. appointment I could make it. I had a car and a house. If I left at the right time, I'd arrive at the right time. Things like public transportation, the idea that buses are late, people with power in the courts don't take that seriously. Or the idea that if a bus is late, you don't have another option. If my bus were late, I would jump into an Uber! But a lot of people don't have that option. Or even the idea that somebody doesn't have bus fare—I regularly hear that scoffed at in the courtroom. And when I started this job, I didn't believe it either. I thought everybody had $2.75 in their pocket to get to a court date or an appointment. But that's not the case. There's lots of people who are dead broke! They don't have the fare. But there are *lots* of judges who

don't believe that. They just don't. They believe that everybody's lives are approximately as chaotic as theirs are. Which is not very chaotic.

As outlined in the previous chapter, noncompliance with court-mandated treatment was an inevitability for scores of people at the bottom of the social hierarchy. But over and over, the people who held the power in criminal court talked about mandated treatment requirements as reasonable, even minimal, and about noncompliance with those requirements as a free choice that signaled a need for more coercive intervention.

Extended Exposure to Punishment

Participation in mandated treatment can also increase exposure to punishment by substantially extending the time that people spend under criminal legal supervision. When they go back to the traditional system, none of the time or money they have spent is credited toward their ultimate sentences. One elderly Black woman, Andrietta, recalled the pain of finding herself removed from diversion and sent back to court for sentencing, after nearly two years in a post-plea pretrial diversion program: "I was just *that* close to finishing [diversion] and then I had to go like start all over again [on probation]. But now I'm a convicted felon. That really hurt me.... They had done turned my life from a diversion program to a whole convicted felon. That really hurt me. I was really depressed. Sometimes I felt suicidal, that's how depressed I was getting with that." Andrietta had already pled guilty to cocaine possession as a condition of diversion, so she was sentenced on a felony conviction. The conditions of her probation were very similar to those of the diversion program, but now she was "starting all over again" after struggling through twenty-three months under court supervision. Like everyone else who returns to court from diversion, Andrietta not only lost the crucial opportunity to exit the legal system without a criminal conviction but also saw her punishment extended. Time spent on diversion is widely experienced as a punitive intervention in itself, and it often adds substantially to the total time under court supervision: in my field site, the median time that people spend in diversion before they are returned to court is 343 days, or nearly a year.[23]

The assertion that diversion can be understood as a punishment requires some discussion. Proponents and practitioners frame it as an *alternative* to punitive action. And because it happens before conviction, pretrial diversion is not a punishment in the legal sense. The US Supreme Court has repeatedly indicated that punishment is defined by explicit punitive intent:[24]

it is a formal legal sanction as defined in a statute and handed down by a judge. This definition of punishment, which dominates case law in the United States, specifically excludes many of the harms inflicted by the criminal legal system, including abusive prison and jail conditions such as beatings at the hands of guards;[25] civil processes that can be triggered by criminal legal contact, such as deportation proceedings;[26] and, perhaps most notably, pretrial incarceration. In *U.S. v. Salerno* (1987), the Court ruled that incarceration prior to conviction was not punishment, since it was intended to manage risks rather than to punish.[27] The Court's definition is often taken up by sociolegal scholars. In his classic book *Punishment and Modern Society*, for instance, David Garland defines punishment as "the legal process whereby violators of the criminal law are condemned and sanctioned in accordance with specified legal categories and procedures."[28]

And yet, everyone I spent time with in diversion described the experience as punishment. When group therapists asked their clients to reflect on their time in the program and what it meant to them, the most common response was a brief "I'm just taking my lick." That characterization of the program as a sanction to be endured came up everywhere. A common question between participants meeting each other for the first time was, "How much time did you get in here?" as though they were discussing criminal sentences. In every interview I asked people where they would place diversion on a spectrum from punishment (1) to services (10). I expected deliberation and some reflection on the blurred lines between punishment and services often theorized in scholarship on alternative legal interventions.[29] At the very least, I expected variation, assuming that the healthy, middle-class people who had made it through the program and exited with clean criminal records would differ from those who had found themselves back in jail. Instead, nearly all of them answered without pausing to think, "It's punishment."

An alternative to the legal definition of punishment is one that focuses on the specific pains inflicted on people by the state in response to acts it classifies as criminal, without reference to intent. Criminologist Todd Clear, for instance, defines punishment as *penal harm*, or "a government's organized infliction of harm" on a person who is thought to have broken its laws.[30] Penal harm explicitly includes the indirect consequences of legal sanctions, such as the deprivations and violence that people can experience in prison and the pains of living under criminal legal control outside of it.[31] Definitions akin to this one have been taken up by scholars like Malcolm Feeley and Nicole Van Cleve, who describe pretrial court processes themselves as punishment,[32] and Sarah Lageson, who conceives of the public availability of digital criminal records such as mug shots as "digital punishment."[33] These broader conceptions of punishment recognize that the intent of the government matters little to the person suffering the pain of criminal legal control.

Assessment of penal harm requires a close look at the consequences, for people's mental and material well-being, of the state's responses to what it sees as criminal behavior.[34] Diversion participants in my field site experienced several main forms of harm, including social stigma, the daily humiliations of subjection, physical pain, and financial burdens.

STIGMA

Nina was a woman in her forties who had lost her home and job when she and her husband were arrested together and jailed for pill possession. They had been living in a tent under a highway overpass ever since their release from jail into diversion. Because she had been given post-plea diversion, her record now reflected a felony conviction that would be removed only if she reached the end of the two-year program. For months during the time I knew her, Nina searched for work, attending job programs and taking her résumé around to dozens of businesses as part of that program, but no one even interviewed her. As she described the experience: "Whether or not we're homeless, addicted to drugs, we're still people. And they treat us like we're not people. First time being in trouble, and I'm being treated like garbage. I can't find a job nowhere. . . . When I'm done my record's gonna be wiped off. Why put me through that right now? Because now on every job application, yes, I'm a convicted felony [sic]. Just on pills. But nobody's going to hire me. . . . So now I have to stay home and suffer. Well, not stay home, but stay out here and suffer." Nina finally gave up on her job search. She and her husband continued to live under the overpass, where drug use was ubiquitous and temptations to relapse were everywhere. She clung to the hope that she could make it through the program and that her luck would change on the other side.

Criminal legal involvement is a key source of stigma,[35] or—as sociologist Erving Goffman famously defined it—an attribute that reduces an individual in others' minds "from a whole and usual person to a tainted and discounted one."[36] The stigma associated with diversion shapes people's lives in a range of ways, beginning with the criminal record. All of the pretrial diversion programs in my national sample maintain court supervision—with the public black marks it entails—until participants have completed their requirements, which can take years. Among all urban diversion programs, an estimated 94 percent bring criminal charges always or sometimes before diverting people into treatment, and about half operate only post-plea or post-conviction.[37]

As a result, their participants typically carry charges or convictions on their records during their time in treatment and often beyond.

People with criminal records encounter both civil penalties and informal discrimination in essential areas of life, including housing, education, welfare, and work.[38] Exclusion from the workforce can be particularly harmful, since it threatens the ability of people like Nina to meet their basic needs. Criminal convictions lock people out of hundreds of kinds of jobs, by law. Employers also discriminate against people with even minor involvement in the criminal legal system: researchers have found that they are less likely to call job applicants with arrests or criminal charges (even without convictions) on their records.[39]

The stigma associated with criminal legal involvement also shapes everyday social interactions for people in diversion. Participants from social environments in which legal system involvement was unusual felt this particularly acutely. One young White woman who ran an organic farm, Charlotte, reflected on the shame she felt whenever she had to mention that she was in diversion: "It's really degrading, honestly. I mean, it's embarrassing to, like, briefly synopsis my life as of recently. You bring up, like, 'The reason for this is, like, probation' [sic; diversion] and then suddenly you can see the other person's gears starting to turn, like, 'criminal.'" Charlotte's sentiments were especially common among middle-class participants. They often tried to avoid telling people that they were in a court-mandated program, inventing other excuses for their absences from evening events, the frequent trips to the courthouse or drug testing sites, or their inability to travel because of their program obligations. Even years after their cases had been closed, middle-class people who agreed to be interviewed usually asked to meet me in places where they were sure they wouldn't run into anyone they knew. They didn't want anyone to find out that they had once been in diversion.

Subjection

The pains of diversion extended beyond the public stigma that triggered or threatened social exclusion. They also included the daily humiliations associated with subjection to the power of the state, even those with no direct bearing on financial security or social relationships. The experience of drug testing is a particularly clear illustration.

Every few days, diversion participants in my field site traveled to the criminal courthouse to be drug tested. Pushing through the heavy metal doors at the entrance, they walked through a metal detector and put their belongings through an X-ray machine. No phones or other electronics, no food, and no liquids are allowed inside, and there are no lockers. When they forgot to leave their phones behind, those with access to cars could walk back out to stash them there. Those who arrived by public transportation, by bicycle, or on foot just had to leave again.

On the other side of the metal detector, a long hallway leads to an open space with a large sign reading "Collections Department and Drug Screening. Monday–Friday 8:00–5:00." It instructs new arrivals to check in at the window. One at a time, people walk up to a glass window to talk with the attendant, who asks them to loudly say (and often spell) their names for everyone to hear. She writes down each name, takes the payment for the test, and sends the person to sit on the long unpadded wooden benches. On most days, four or five people are there at once, waiting and staring down at their hands, stripped of their cell phones. Across from the benches is a wide marble staircase leading up to the courtrooms on the second floor. Men in suits eye the people waiting as they walk down the stairs and past them toward the exit.

People are called back, one at a time, to pass through the doors into the screening area. Once inside, each one is handed a cup and asked to sit to urinate into it, facing a court official who watches from a few feet away. This moment requires careful preparation. Particularly if hydration is low, nerves can be a formidable obstacle. Brooke, for instance, left her nine-to-five job a little early on days when she had to go in for drug testing, so she usually arrived not long before the center closed at 5 p.m. Once, she was too nervous to produce any urine, and the testing center closed before she could finish the ritual of drinking water and waiting. The program penalized her for missing her test day. Anxious to avoid repeating that experience, the next time she went she drank so much water beforehand that her test came back as "dilute." Because people sometimes overhydrate in attempts to cover what would be positive results, dilutes are even worse: at best they are treated as a non-result and require that the client return to the testing center, and at worst they are counted as missed or positive tests.

The office can also close early without giving notice, often putting people in difficult positions. One high schooler, Eason, walked three miles from his house to take each drug test. On one blistering July day, I walked into group session to find him already in the room, head down on the table. He sat up when the therapists walked in but kept his eyes closed throughout a lot of the meeting and mostly grunted in response to any questions. Outside after the session, I asked him how he was doing and he said he was "drove" (angry). He had walked down to the courthouse the day before for a test only to be told the center was closing and would not screen him. He had returned early that afternoon to find that they had already closed for the day. The next day was the Fourth of July, so the courthouse would be closed for the rest of the week. Because he had missed his window to test, he would have a negative mark on his paperwork and his time in the program would be extended by at least another month. Eason was devastated by this news.

The frequent humiliations of the drug test—its placement inside the courthouse, the metal detector, the loud recitation of names, the physical exposure before a stranger, the unpredictable closures—might be dismissed simply as accidents of a thoughtless and underfunded bureaucracy. But as anthropologist Akhil Gupta has observed, the meaning of the state to its citizens matters, and that meaning is constituted by "the humdrum routines of bureaucracies and bureaucrats' encounters with citizens."[40] Even the wait time for a test, or the necessary returns to wait again, communicate a disregard for people's time. Sociologist Javier Auyero argues that that disregard, which forces poor people perpetually to wait in their interactions with the state, is an expression of domination.[41] Each of these moments of subjection becomes a painful part of the state's punitive project.

PHYSICAL PAIN

A third penal harm, often experienced by people who are sick, is physical pain. Abstinence from a long list of prohibited substances was essential to success in diversion. Positive tests could have serious consequences, including removal from the program altogether. That abstinence became a source of suffering not only for people with substance use disorders and those who relied on cannabis to treat symptoms of PTSD—as chapter 5 illustrates in more detail—but also for people who had been prescribed medications to manage pain. Chronic pain is not uncommon among those involved in the criminal legal system. Rates are high in the general US population and even higher among people who are poor and those who have suffered gunshot injuries, both groups that are overrepresented in the legal system.[42] But painkillers are prohibited in my field site, even with valid prescriptions, and interviews with programs in other places indicate that that prohibition is common. For people who lived with physical pain, giving up their medications could mean tremendous suffering and changes to their daily lives.

Steve, for instance, was an older White man with piercing blue eyes and an old injury to one leg that caused constant pain. He had been forced to stop taking his prescription medications for the leg when he entered the program, and the pain now prevented him from walking further than a block or two and from biking at all. He was unhoused and did not have a car, so he had to move to a place just two blocks away from the diversion office so that he could limp to his appointments. He talked often about how much he missed his bicycle, which had been not only his means of transportation but also a constant source of joy. The first time he saw my bike he touched it longingly, recalling, "I used to have one of those little short-frame beachcombers. That thing was like a Mustang. I'd get all over the place, like you." For Steve, as for many others, drug tests had forced major changes in his life and left him in nearly constant physical pain.

FINANCIAL BURDENS

Involvement in court-mandated treatment, like almost all forms of involvement with the courts, involves a financial burden. People are usually required to pay fees for program enrollment, drug testing, and/or additional treatment. They also have to find the resources to get transportation to their appointments and drug tests, cover childcare, and get time off work, often daily or weekly for years.

For people with limited financial resources, that burden was heavy. A growing body of research finds that legal financial obligations can become acute and chronic health stressors, and those obligations in the diversion context were no exception.[43] In my field site, nearly all participants had to work extra hours or rely on family members or friends for help in meeting the financial demands of the program, and payments were a constant source of stress. Pearl, a Black woman in her fifties, recalled her years of reliance on the people in her network as she struggled every month to come up with the money for diversion. Tearing up even years later, in a conversation with me on her front porch, she remembered, "And if I wouldn't have been paying the court cost, I was gonna do two years in jail. So that's like these years all up under me, just stressing me out, pressed. You know. And I'm just saying I'm going through all this here and I was just like crying a whole lot. I was more depressed trying to get off the program than I was before I got on the program. It was really depressing, ma'am. I ain't lying." For Pearl, the stress of asking her equally cash-strapped family for money every month was among the most acute of her time in diversion. For others, it was possible to find additional work or to work longer hours to meet programs' financial demands, but that often took its own toll on relationships. Asia and Bianca, for instance, were a long-term couple who entered the program together and struggled to meet its financial demands. They both took on a slew of extra shifts. Bianca, a nursing assistant, had previously worked seven days on, seven days off, but she started working fourteen days straight. Asia, a bartender, picked up as much overtime as she could. Asia eventually told me that the exhaustion and stress about money was beginning to damage what had been a happy relationship. They broke up before the program ended. As Asia reflected afterward, "We started to kind of, not blame each other, but distance each other. . . . The program, it destroyed everything."

The financial burdens associated with court-mandated treatment not only added new material stressors to participants' lives, but also reinforced their perceptions that it was designed to take advantage of rather than to help them. When I asked interview respondents what they thought the purpose of diversion was, a majority said they thought it was intended to make money off of them or to keep them in poverty. Roseanne, a young woman who had lost her job as a legal assistant following her arrest and had been unable to find another position because of the pending criminal charges on her record, described what she saw as the financial transaction at the heart of the program she was struggling to finish: "It's horrible. It's horrible. You're, and I say this all the time, you're basically buying back your reputation and your freedom. Because if you don't buy it back for the amount that they say, under the restrictions they say, then you're either stuck with a charge that you can't get rid of, that will block you from being employed, or you're serving jail time. . . . It's a means to keep, you know, people suffering from poverty, in poverty." Perceptions that the program was intended to make them suffer by stripping them of financial resources only contributed to the psychological toll of supervision. Over and over, people told me that they thought their treatment providers were trying to find problems with their behavior that could keep them in the program longer, because they wanted them to continue to pay.

In sum: although case law does not treat the criminal legal involvement that accompanies diversion as punishment, participants experience it that way. In one courtroom exchange (described in chapter 2), a judge asked a roomful of people on diversion, "How many of you spend time thinking about *when* am I gonna get off paper [court supervision]?" Every hand went up. "But you're still going to be living the same lives, just without our support!" she retorted. "What's really going to be different when you're off paper?" The question was largely rhetorical, part of a broader admonition to the defendants to appreciate the program. But after that, I told each person I interviewed about the judge's speech and asked them how they would answer her question. The responses included some of the only rude words I heard in any of my interviews. As one older Black man, Andre, answered succinctly, "Yeah she's, for lack of a better term, to me she's an asshole."

Conclusion

Diversion into treatment is widely understood as a "golden ticket" out of the court system that can only help a defendant's case. But in practice, it can extend and intensify the punishment people face, even as it moves the allocation of additional punishment out of view. People who are unable to finish their programs not only lose the chance to exit the legal system without criminal convictions but also often face additional sanctions. First, they have often had to sacrifice legal protections in order to enter diversion, up to and including pleading guilty as charged, exposing them to harsher sanctions if they do not complete treatment. Second, courtroom decision-makers assess performance in diversion as a key indicator of people's characters and likely future behavior, and prosecutors tend to pursue more punitive plea deals for people who don't complete treatment. Finally, time spent in diversion programs is typically not credited toward people's ultimate sentences, so their exposure to punishment is extended when they spend time in those programs before returning to court for formal adjudication and sentencing.

Shifting the allocation of criminal punishment to the treatment site can further unmoor it from law and evidence. Certainly, most outcomes in the traditional criminal court system are not the result of careful consideration of the legal merits of cases by a judge or jury. Nearly all criminal convictions in the United States result from guilty pleas rather than from trials.[44] And racial, gendered, and class-based biases influence every stage of the legal process. Still, the strongest predictors of felony case outcomes in the traditional court system are the legal characteristics of a criminal case: the type and severity of the arrest charges, the relevant sentencing laws and guidelines, and the criminal legal history of the defendants.[45] These case characteristics become entirely irrelevant in the treatment context. Instead, punishment outcomes are shaped or even determined by people's capacities to attend appointments, pass drug tests, and make financial payments. Expansion of diversion programs is likely creating an even wider gulf between legal criteria and the punishments people are receiving.

This chapter also highlights a particularly important pathway by which therapeutic alternatives are shaping people's legal outcomes: prosecutorial decision-making. Research on the factors that affect prosecutors' plea-bargaining decisions usually focuses on defendant and case characteristics. Studies find, for instance, that prosecutors tend to offer less generous plea deals when the evidence against the defendant is stronger, witnesses are cooperating, the alleged offense is more severe, and the defendant has a longer history of criminal legal involvement.[46] They also offer harsher terms, on average, when defendants are Black, Latine, and/or male.[47] Previous work has told us very little about whether or how prosecutors consider defendants' performances within the court system itself when making plea offers. The findings laid out here suggest that prosecutors do take those performances seriously and are inclined to be more punitive toward defendants who do not meet the requirements the court places on them.

The costs often associated with diversion are not equally distributed. People who are Black and poor are dramatically overrepresented in the criminal courts, and they constitute an even larger share of people who are returned to court from treatment.[48] In my field site, 75 percent of defendants who return from diversion without completing it are Black, compared to 63 percent at entry.[49] People represented by public defenders rather than private attorneys are also markedly overrepresented among those who return.[50] Those disparities are not unique to my site; they align with those recorded in drug courts around the country.[51] When courtroom actors talk about individuals who "lack motivation to change," they are talking about a group of defendants who are even more deeply marginalized than the rest; when diversion programs require people to enter guilty pleas as a condition of entry, the resulting convictions will be concentrated within that group; and when the courts punish people who have already spent months or years in diversion, they are punishing that same group.

Reforms can obfuscate the traditional work of their adopting institutions by perpetuating it in less recognizable forms. They may do that both by changing the venue in which work is carried out and by giving it new rationales. The allocation and administration of punishment is shifted largely out of view when people are moved out of the traditional court system and into diversion. People experience their time in diversion as punishment, but its punitive pains are almost entirely hidden: they are not discussed in courtrooms, and information about what a diversion program entails is rarely available to the public. For people who are required to enter guilty pleas before entering treatment, the decisions that leave them with criminal convictions on their records are made behind closed doors, when therapists decide to return their cases to court. Treatment-based reforms also give ideological cover to the punishment of victimless acts by people who are poor, Black, and ill. Even if it is hard to justify sanctions for the charges themselves, decision-makers can point to treatment noncompletion as a signal that people deserve to be placed under more punitive forms of control. If they have been offered a way to change their situations and refused it, proving themselves unable or unwilling to govern their own lives—the narrative goes—then the state's coercive intervention can only be warranted.

Conclusion

Elaine went into diversion in 1997, following an arrest for possession of drug paraphernalia and forty-seven days in the county jail. "Forty-seven days," she said several times during our interview, shuddering visibly as she talked about how terrified she had been of death in there. Like most people, she had jumped at the chance to get out when they offered her diversion. At first the program placed her with a White counselor whom Elaine described as "military style." She knew so little about Black people like Elaine that she had cut off a piece of another participant's weave to run a hair drug test, a memory that still made Elaine double over with laughter. But later they switched her to a therapist who was Black and around Elaine's age. She chuckled a little, remembering her. "Just, we just had fun. I mean everything we talked about, whatever we talked about! And me, I love to laugh, so I had her laughing . . . I wanted to stay her friend forever." Elaine made it through her year on diversion without a positive drug test and was released from the program on time.

She raised her young kids and lived in her little house in peace after that. She went back to using crack cocaine a week before the program was over, right after her last test—"You do that for a year and you just can't wait for that day to be over with!" she recalled—but she had managed to steer clear of the police ever since. She didn't want another diversion program, she said. "No paper. Paper or jail. 'You gonna do this or you going to jail.' I don't want to do that." She was still in the same place when I went to see her, a little Section 8 house on a tree-lined street. The living room was decorated all over in red mosaic art that matched her lipstick, and a grown son came in once to say hi and bring her more bottled water.

But she did wish she could stop using. Over the hours we sat in her little red living room, she told stories about a long list of things she had tried over the past two decades, beginning with psychiatry. She described serious childhood trauma and what she referred to as a "mental thing" in its aftermath. "I think a lot of drugs is dealing with people's mental-ness, to me," she reflected. "Things that happened and you don't feel worthy and some shit." I asked if the psychiatrist helped, and she didn't even hesitate: "Hell, no. She just give me some damn medicine and then that's it. But I can't take the medicine—I was taking it, I did take it, and I wind up going back on the other medicine.... I just think once you on the street medicine you just on the street medicine. No matter what medicine they give you, you gonna go find the street medicine." Once she tried getting a ride out to an inpatient drug treatment center, but they wouldn't admit her. "'Okay, the crack smoking, we don't take those. You gotta be on heroin, pills, alcohol.' If you smoke crack, they can't help you. You gotta be on I guess stuff that you have to get medicine for," she reflected. She had tried a few times to quit by detoxing at home. Laughing, she told me about the liver water and seven-day cleanses she had tried. "God, I took those things. And it wasn't working. Okay. It wasn't working. Man, then I'm coming in my house and it started working! And I was like in the bathroom, girl. I was like 'nooooooo!'"

At some point toward the end of the visit, I asked Elaine why she wanted to quit. She got quiet for a minute and squinted at the window. "I mean I'd like to stop because I would like to feel some things and do—but the world is just, people just so cruel and cold and you just want to just stay in your little corner, your little sandbox. And play by your damn self. You know what I mean?"

Mental illness is thorny. We don't understand what causes most of it or why some people get better and others don't. In part because we still don't understand many of their pathogeneses, we don't have very effective treatments for most of those illnesses. The success rate for treatment of schizophrenia is only around 30 percent, for instance, and most of the available treatments for substance use disorder have no basis in science at all. Many of the treatments for mental disorder have not advanced substantially since the 1960s.[1]

Even when effective mental health treatments exist, they often do not reach the people who need them: most people with mental illness in the United States today are not receiving any treatment at all.[2] Medical care is expensive, and tens of millions of people in the United States are uninsured.[3] Mental health services can also be hard to access even for people with the means to pay for them. Public services are severely underfunded, producing persistent shortages of mental health professionals across the board and particularly for treatment of substance use disorders.[4] Waiting lists are often long. In poor and rural areas, services are often not available at all.[5] And particularly for people without reliable transportation and for those receiving treatments that require them to go in to a clinic very frequently, like methadone, traveling long distances for care can be out of the question.[6]

Further complicating our responses to mental illness are the blurred boundaries between individual health and other social problems. Poverty can trigger and exacerbate mental illness, and mental illness can lead to poverty. Mental illness is criminalized, and criminalization contributes to mental illness. Criminalization causes poverty, and poverty is criminalized. Our images of poverty, criminality, and illness are superimposed until we can't tell where one starts and another begins. But all of them are seen as problems of the individual who needs to be fixed, and fixed by way of coercion. People like Elaine, we're told, should not be left in charge of their own lives.[7]

Therapeutic Alternatives to Punishment

The management of mental illness in the United States, particularly at the bottom of the social hierarchy, is deeply entangled with the criminal legal system. Changes in legislation and policing practices over the last several decades have markedly increased arrests and incarcerations for drug possession and other offenses that often stem from illness, and people with substance use or other mental disorders now constitute a majority of those held in US jails and prisons.[8] Now, as public pressure for reform grows, elected officials around the country are expanding efforts to divert people out of court and into treatment. All told, hundreds of thousands of people now enter court-mandated mental health treatment every year, and a criminal legal mandate has become the modal pathway into publicly funded drug treatment in the United States.[9] The expansion of diversion programs that promise treatment-based alternatives to punishment is widely celebrated as a step toward improving health and reducing the broad reach of the penal system. But in this book, I have argued that we have misunderstood the impacts of such programs. I find that they do not simply replace processes of judgment and punishment with healthcare. Rather, they extend those processes into new and hidden sites and reshape them in ways that tend to amplify inequality and, paradoxically, *intensify* coercive control over the most vulnerable people. They do this via three main processes.

First, the expansion of diversion lends legitimacy to the ongoing punishment of mental illness. In policy debates, diversion helps to justify the continued criminalization of behaviors common among people who are ill, such as drug use. The invisibility of diversion programs allows them to be everything to everyone: liberal advocates can picture generous social services, while conservatives can emphasize that they protect public safety by making tough demands for accountability. Groups across the political spectrum can imagine interventions that are highly effective in transforming people's behavior for the long term. By legitimizing criminal legal intervention, diversion also encourages frontline decision-makers to intervene more widely and into more corners of people's lives. Previous research on diversion does not account for this expansion, which tends to expose more people to more punishment, meaning that it has not been able to capture its real impacts.

Second, treatment situated within the court system assimilates punitive logics.[10] Under pressure to show that they can be trusted to manage people who are widely understood as risky, treatment providers structure their programs around a set of practices common to criminal legal supervision in a variety of forms. Many of those practices are directly at odds with effective mental healthcare. Complicating matters further, therapists are tasked with monitoring their clients' compliance with program rules and making decisions that can send them back to court to be punished. Those enforcement duties inexorably alter the daily interactions between clients and their therapists and make it difficult for them to establish trusting and productive relationships.

Finally, diversion obfuscates processes of judgment and punishment. Treatment programs sort their participants, marking as many as half—and disproportionately those who are poor, Black, and ill—as noncompliant with treatment and returning them to the traditional courts for sanctions. This sorting process means that studies that find better outcomes among people who complete diversion may be measuring *not* the impacts of treatment programs themselves but preexisting differences between people who do and do not complete. Those who are unable to finish their programs, in fact, find themselves even worse off: those who return to court are exposed to more punishment than they would have faced had they never been diverted. But that allocation of punishment is veiled both materially and ideologically. Not only are people sorted and marked for punishment behind closed doors in diversion, but those sent back to court are widely viewed as fundamentally intransigent and therefore in need of more coercive control.

Institutional Entrenchment

The study of treatment-based reforms in the criminal legal system can help us to answer broader questions about when and how reform works to further entrench institutions' power in the social world. Social theorists have long observed that reform can amplify the social processes it promised to change. Michel Foucault famously described the birth of the prison—emblem of a broader apparatus of surveillance and control—as a response to public outcry against the violent and public displays of punishment that had previously dominated. It was a strategy, he wrote, designed "not to punish less, but to punish better; to punish with an attenuated severity perhaps, but in order to punish with more universality and necessity; to insert the power to punish more deeply into the social body."[11] Others have written about subsequent reforms with similar effects.[12] And these ideas circulate beyond the academic sphere: abolitionist activists often point to the dangers of "reformist reforms," which ultimately increase the reach of the criminal legal system, for instance.[13] But our understanding of what differentiates the reforms these theorists describe from the rest remains incomplete. As legal scholar Jamelia Morgan recently put it, "clear lines between reformist and nonreformist reforms are often hard to find."[14]

A few key bodies of scholarship have shed some light on those lines. One documents a kind of reform that legal scholar Lauren Edelman calls "symbolic compliance."[15] Organizations rely heavily on legitimacy for survival, and they tend to adopt new practices primarily as a means to shore up that legitimacy.[16] As a result, organizations often adopt practices that publicly signal commitments to desirable values without producing any substantive changes to their daily work. Corporations may embrace structures such as grievance and evaluation procedures or antiharassment policies as toothless demonstrations of commitments to preventing discrimination, for instance. These reforms may actually make it harder for people to seek justice when those corporations do discriminate: Judges deciding employment discrimination cases tend to infer nondiscrimination from the presence of these formal procedures.[17]

A second literature highlights reforms that serve as political distractions. These reforms may have the desired effects they promise, but those effects are small and can distract from more important trends in the opposite direction. Many criminal legal reforms, for instance, target only low-level, nonviolent offenses—or what Marie Gottschalk calls the "non, non, nons" (people with nonviolent, nonserious, and nonsexual charges or convictions).[18] Those reforms often come in tandem with more severe punishments for other kinds of offenses: legislators can justify their support for very modest reforms in terms of generating increased capacity to punish other people more severely, and they often increase the punitiveness of laws aimed at more serious offenses even as they enact decarcerative reforms for lower-level charges.[19]

A third body of work focuses on net-widening reforms—those that promise to decarcerate but in fact increase the overall rates and intensity of criminal legal intervention.[20] A long list of studies have found that the number of people under legal supervision has increased following implementation of reforms that offer alternatives to prison.[21] A few have offered some insights into the forces driving those effects. Criminologist Stanley Cohen points to legal professionals' commitment to classifying people into "more and more elaborate categories" of good, bad, treatable, and untreatable, expanding the penal net as they assign an ever wider range of interventions across those categories.[22] Sociologist Michelle Phelps has found that the specific state-level policies and procedures surrounding probation shape the degree to which it contributes to net widening.[23] And sociologist Forrest Stuart has examined the paternalistic patterns of thought that drive police officers to pull more people into the legal system in an effort to improve their behavior and thus pull them out of poverty.[24]

The kind of reform that emerges from the findings in this book might be thought of as an *entrenching reform*. This kind of reform gives new tools—new forms of discretion, new programs, new practices—to the same organizations or institutional actors. Although they may be operated by new workers, they ultimately consolidate power and discretion within the institutions that implement them. Entrenching reforms share points of contact with each of the kinds of reform outlined above. Like symbolic compliance, they help organizations to shore up their legitimacy. Like distracting reforms, they can satisfy calls for change without making the kinds of large-scale or structural changes that would be needed to transform an area of social life. Like net-widening reforms, they can broaden the reach of an organization. But entrenching reforms are not just symbolic: The changes they make to an organization's daily work are the source of their power. By making that work less easily recognizable, they can help organizations to sidestep established systems of accountability and transparency and avoid public contestation. They also do more than distract from more pressing political problems: They actually strengthen the position of an institution and its hold over a set of social problems. And they do more than draw more people into the legal system: They also alter the processes by which that system assigns punishment, creating more room for the (re)production of inequality as they do.

The inequalities in punishment that emerge in the context of diversion are not incidental to the broader process of institutional entrenchment. Previous research indicates that racialized laws and unequal distributions of resources are enforced by institutions through their constituent organizations.[25] Reform can operate as one aspect of that enforcement. Systems of accountability and oversight designed to counteract or control the production of inequality by organizations are often fought for over years or even decades. An entrenching reform like diversion can allow an organization to dramatically alter the way it carries out its work, allowing it to sidestep systems of oversight—such as legal constraints or transparency requirements—that may have been built painstakingly over a long period of time. The public may not be able to see what is happening clearly enough even to know what new kinds of controls might need to be established. Organizations can then find themselves free to exercise discretion unhampered by previous constraints, with very real implications for the production of social inequalities.

ENTRENCHMENT IN OTHER DOMAINS

This book has shown how one prominent set of reforms has helped to expand the reach of an institution rather than producing the fundamental changes it promised. But the framework of institutional entrenchment may help to make sense of other recent reforms and their consequences.

Police have increasingly come under fire for their responses to mental health emergencies, for instance, and activists have proposed that local governments should fund trained, unarmed professionals to respond instead. They note that an estimated 60 percent of all police contacts in the United States, and around a quarter of fatal police shootings, involve people with serious mental illness.[26] One response from the police has been to expand the use of crisis intervention teams (CITs), units within police forces whose officers receive additional training in responding to mental health crises. There are now at least 2,700 CIT units around the country.[27] The units may be understood as a kind of entrenching reform: they have helped to *legitimize* police as first responders to mental health crises, drawing praise from liberal advocates and more funding for police forces.[28] Once in place, they *assimilate* the logics of the institution: police officers trained as mental health responders still arrive at scenes with the training, mentalities, weapons, and legal powers of police. As a result, their traditional work continues, obfuscated by the banner of the CIT. Researchers have found no evidence that CIT training reduces arrests, civilian injuries, or police use of force.[29]

In another sphere altogether, private corporations have come under fire for racial and gender bias in hiring and promotion. In response, many have introduced job tests and formal performance reviews. Both tools are touted as means to achieve fairness in the workplace: corporations can simply stipulate that managers hire or promote from among the people with the highest scores on tests or reviews. The reform successfully legitimizes the institution: the companies' use of these quantitative rating systems leads judges to presume that they do not discriminate, for instance, protecting firms from lawsuits and increasing public legitimacy.[30] But the tools assimilate dominant logics. The managerial position is characterized by hierarchical power and discretion, which shapes managers' use of reformist practices: they unilaterally exempt favored candidates from tests, fake test results, or interpret numbers in ways that confirm their prior beliefs.[31] The reforms ultimately help to obfuscate the ongoing exercise of discretion, obscuring it behind a screen of objective, empirical measurement. That screen gives managers even more freedom. On average, introducing job tests and performance evaluations actually reduces the share of management jobs held by women and people of color.[32]

Studies of corporate sustainability reforms reveal similar patterns. Under pressure to assuage public concerns about industry impacts on public health and the environment, a wide range of companies has committed to initiatives designed to prevent environmental pollution. The Responsible Care program, launched in 1985 and since adopted by ninety-six of the one hundred largest chemical producers in the world, is a prominent example of such initiatives. Its widespread adoption has helped to legitimize the operations of such companies with limited government oversight.[33] But the program has assimilated profit logics, consistently prioritizing shareholder interests when they conflict with commitments to reduce emissions or improve safety measures. The adoption of Responsible Care ultimately obfuscates companies' negative impacts on public health and the environment, and adopters have consistently higher toxic emissions than do others that did not adopt the reforms.[34]

Police forces have also introduced reforms that use big data to target their interventions. In the face of heavy criticisms of racism in "proactive" policing, writes sociologist Sarah Brayne, big data was introduced as a tool to increase objectivity and reduce bias. Use of that data to decide whom to target legitimizes police patrol, allowing them to tell the public—and the courts, in case of legal contestation—that their decisions are, in the words of one captain Brayne quotes, "just math."[35] But data use assimilates dominant logics, and it comes to reflect the biases that already define the policing institution. Police do not conduct point-driven surveillance in wealthy neighborhoods, meaning that the neighborhoods that were already most heavily policed are those where people are most likely to be assigned risk scores. And risk scores are higher for people who have already been targeted more often by police—typically those in neighborhoods where most people are poor and Black—flagging them for additional intervention. Ultimately, police targeting of race- and class-subjugated neighborhoods is obfuscated. The introduction of big data allows deeper and likely even more unequal forms of surveillance.[36]

Each of these cases offers an illustration of entrenching reform—a new practice that is reshaped and put to work in service of the adopting institution, helping to entrench its power and social influence.

Improving Alternatives

What should be done in response to the criminal legal institutional entrenchment documented here? The answers to this question are not simple, but in the rest of this concluding chapter, I offer a few ideas. First, the data in this book do not tell us that diversion should never be used or that it cannot be improved. In some contexts, diversion may be the best or only reform that is politically possible. As Gottschalk observes, "The necessary policy changes if we are serious about dismantling the carceral state are fairly straightforward. But the politics are not."[37] And for people who would otherwise have been subjected to traditional criminal sanctions and who are able to complete diversion, it is almost certainly better than the alternative. There are a lot of things that might be done, within the context of existing diversion programs, to reduce the harms documented in part III of this book. Jurisdictions could eliminate drug testing and fees, provide transportation, and make treatment voluntary. Even small moves in that direction could reduce harm by increasing completion rates and reducing the painful aspects of program participation.

The harms associated with the net widening documented in part I might also be reduced by diverting people earlier in the legal process.[38] The earlier the diversion happens, the fewer marks appear on people's records. Police diversion and pre-filing diversion by prosecutors can protect people from some of the consequences of entering the criminal court system. Still, net widening is probably never benign, since research suggests that any contact with police or the courts can carry negative consequences. And net-widening effects themselves are hard to control, since police and prosecutors exercise tremendous discretion with minimal oversight. Police choose where to patrol and when to intervene. Prosecutors make their charging and plea-bargaining decisions in complicated and uncertain contexts that would be difficult to regulate. The changes they make in the context of diversion are likely subconscious, so it may be difficult to legislate, train, or regulate net widening out of existence.

One crucial step toward improving diversion programs as they currently exist would be to increase their transparency. As these programs currently operate, there is almost no way to know with certainty what kinds of treatment participants are receiving, what kinds of requirements are placed on them, how their legal outcomes are decided, or what their ultimate legal outcomes look like. In most jurisdictions we can't know whether there are inequalities in who is being selected for diversion or who is completing treatment. In some, we don't even know whether diversion programs exist. Without this and other information, the public is not well situated to make informed decisions about whether and how much to invest in diversion programs. This lack of transparency about the basic characteristics of diversion programs is also a tremendous obstacle for defendants who are deciding whether to enter those programs or not. In my field site, I found that people very rarely knew what they were signing up for when they accepted a diversion offer. Since official information is often impossible to come by, they were left to rely on the judge or their defense lawyers to tell them about what will happen if they enter diversion. Often those professionals did not have accurate information either. Information transparency would allow all of us to make clear-eyed evaluations of the role diversion plays—and should play—in our legal system.

Beyond Alternatives

As the term *alternative* is used in the contemporary legal system, it usually refers to alternative approaches that could be taken by the same agencies or even the same individual decision-makers. But the findings in this book suggest that it's time to rethink our use of the criminal courts to manage mental illness. Even if the issues documented here could be resolved within the court system, we would still be asking prosecutors, judges, and defense attorneys to spend untold hours every day navigating decisions about mental health treatment that are well outside of their traditional scope of work and training. Most of those state workers are severely overworked and underpaid. Below, I briefly consider some medical, legal, and economic policy changes that could help to move people who are sick off of overburdened caseloads and dockets entirely.

HEALTHCARE

Provision of accessible, high-quality healthcare outside of the legal system could alleviate a lot of the suffering associated with mental illness. Public mental healthcare services, including trained providers, are severely underfunded and in short supply.[39] The limited services that do exist are often difficult to access, both because people have to travel to get to them and because of the administrative obstacles to enrollment.[40] Making healthcare more accessible could have an enormous impact on people's lives. Even though research on mental illness has a long way to go, there are plenty of treatments that can help. Psychiatric medications used to treat forms of mania and psychotic disorders—both common among incarcerated people—reduce and even eliminate symptoms of illness for many people.[41]

Both pharmaceutical and therapy-based treatments have also had some success in treating substance use disorders. Opioid and methamphetamine use disorders, for instance, can be treated with medications that reduce withdrawal symptoms, cravings, and the effects of the drugs themselves.[42] Medications such as buprenorphine and methadone are particularly well supported for treatment of opioid use disorder: a number of high-quality randomized controlled trials have shown that they substantially reduce mortality and improve health among people with that disorder.[43] Cognitive behavioral therapy may also help people reduce drug use and change higher-risk behaviors.[44]

Practices often referred to as "harm reduction"—which focus on reducing the immediate health risks associated with drug use—are also effective in saving the lives and improving the health of people who use drugs.[45] Increasingly, nonprofits and government agencies are adopting these practices from grassroots groups around the United States, which have used them for many years, often under the leadership of people who use or have used drugs themselves. In the city where I conducted the fieldwork for this book, for instance, a group of volunteers offers harm-reduction services in various locations around the city.[46] On one evening every week, they can be found in the parking lot outside of a community center in one of the poorest neighborhoods in the area. On the ground outside, a circle of people bag and hand out supplies to anyone who walks up and asks for them, without asking for names or identification. In the bags are bandages, alcohol pads, sterile water, and clean syringes, which help people who inject drugs to prevent new cases of HIV, hepatitis C, and other infections. They also give out naloxone (Narcan), which can save a life in the event of an overdose. Inside the center, paramedics and doctors set up stations at folding tables and offer free medical care for the wounds that often result from using adulterated street drugs, buprenorphine prescriptions for people who are trying to get off opioids, and any other basic care that people need. Groups like these don't conduct randomized trials to measure their impacts. But we know that sterile equipment is effective at preventing infection and medical care at treating it. And when the volunteers handing out the Narcan ask each person whether they have used it on anyone to reverse an overdose in the last few weeks, almost all of them say yes.

Another key harm-reduction practice is the creation of safe injection facilities (SIFs), places where drug users can inject themselves under the supervision of trained professionals. The first of these sites in North America was established in Vancouver, Canada, as the result of a powerful organizing effort by people who used drugs.[47] Now publicly funded and open eighteen hours a day, the site has been rigorously evaluated and found to be highly cost-effective:[48] it has reduced infectious disease transmission,[49] overdose,[50] and public disorder,[51] and it has not increased crime in the surrounding area or the number of people who inject drugs.[52] It also refers individuals to a range of external programs, including drug detoxification and treatment,[53] and studies indicate that people who visit the site regularly are more likely to seek treatment and ultimately stop using injection drugs.[54] At least ten countries around the world have established similar sites, to similar effect.[55]

LEGAL STRUCTURES

Even universal, high-quality mental healthcare would likely not eliminate all of the behaviors that are currently criminalized. To relieve police and the courts of responsibility for illness, we will also need to roll back laws that criminalize sick people. Among people who receive public mental healthcare, the most common arrest charges are often classified as "public disorder." These are largely victimless acts such as camping; sleeping, sitting, or lying down in public; living in vehicles; dumpster diving; urinating; "begging"; "loitering"; "loafing"; and "vagrancy."[56] Criminalizing behaviors that flow from homelessness, which is often connected to mental illness, produces a vicious cycle: Involvement in the criminal legal system can disqualify people both from subsidized housing and from mental health treatment.[57] Even when a police encounter does not result in an arrest, police harassment, move-along orders, and evictions—all justified by laws on the books—can exacerbate mental health problems by causing intense stress and significant disruptions to people's lives.[58]

One of the highest-impact legal changes we could make is to legalize and regulate all drugs. Not only is drug possession still the most common arrest charge nationwide and a frequent cause of arrest for people with mental illness,[59] but it carries the most severe legal consequences among the prohibitions mentioned here: it can lead to felony convictions in forty-five states and result in significant time behind bars.[60] Because drug criminalization is the primary pathway by which people with mental illness are pulled deeper into the criminal system, and because legalization is still so seldom seriously discussed, I will spend some time on this idea here.

Although we often think of the criminalization of drugs as a natural and immovable fact of life, in fact it is relatively recent. As recently as the early twentieth century, opiates and cocaine were still widely available in drug stores and mail-order catalogs.[61] It was only with the 1914 Harrison Narcotic Act that the federal government functionally banned both drugs. Changes elsewhere in the world began around the same time. The US State Department convened an international conference on the drug trade that resulted in an agreement among many countries not to export drugs to places where they were prohibited. The agreement came into force a few years later when it was written into peace treaties at the end of World War I. Since then, the United States has added myriad items to its list of prohibited substances and has led the way in pushing countries around the world to adopt and maintain drug prohibitions.[62]

The devastating effects of drug prohibition are now well documented. Contact with the criminal legal system, and especially time spent in prison or jail, has a wide range of long-term negative impacts on people's lives.[63] Drug criminalization has also had other serious consequences for public health. The first of these is the absence of any regulation over potentially lethal substances that are in widespread use. The global ban on trade in most drugs has produced a massive underground market, which involves a quarter of a billion people and hundreds of billions in US dollars every year.[64] Because there is no organized testing and labeling of the products sold in that market, users have no way to know their dosage or content before they ingest them. As one group of prominent public policy and public health scholars explain the issue:

> People overdose because they don't know what they are getting; they don't know if the heroin is four percent or forty percent, or if it is cut with bad stuff, or if it is heroin at all—it may be a synthetic opiate or an amphetamine-type substance. Just imagine if every time you picked up a bottle of wine, you didn't know whether it was eight percent alcohol or eighty percent alcohol, or whether it was ethyl alcohol or methyl alcohol. Imagine if every time you took an aspirin, you didn't know if it was five milligrams or 500 milligrams.[65]

Dosage varies widely, since dealers often cut drugs with other substances to increase their supply. Sometimes those other substances are stronger drugs, since they can produce similar effects more cheaply. Heroin was increasingly laced with fentanyl, for instance, producing a surge in overdoses. Now the cheaper and stronger xylazine, often referred to as tranq dope, is infiltrating other street drugs, to terrible effect.[66] Adulterated drugs, the direct result of an unregulated drug market, are responsible for a majority of fatal overdoses in the United States.[67]

Criminalizing drug use also makes drug injection itself less safe. When police presence increases, users tend to become more reluctant to carry their own injecting equipment. That means that they are less likely to have clean syringes on them and more likely to borrow or find used syringes, which raises their risk of HIV and other blood-borne diseases. Serious overdoses have resulted from people swallowing their stashes when they encounter police. Criminalization drives people to carry out dangerous procedures without medical help, often hastily and in hiding. People tend to use less safe injection practices when they are injecting quickly because of anxiety about being caught; and when they hide to ingest drugs, they are less likely to be found if they overdose.[68]

Finally, drug prohibition is driving a bloody global war that is responsible for torture, human trafficking, and hundreds of thousands of homicides in the last two decades alone.[69] The violence of the drug trade is produced not by anything special about the product being sold, but by the way the exchange is governed.[70] The criminalization of drug markets prevents participants from turning to the state to regulate trade, enforce contracts, and resolve grievances in an industry that moves hundreds of billions of dollars every year. In addition, police and other state agents actively intervene to disrupt markets and keep them unstable. Every time they displace a drug market organization or arrest or kill a leader, organizations are more likely to reorganize hierarchies, splinter, change norms and patterns of trade, relocate, and compete with new groups for contested territories. Organizational disruptions often produce conflict between market groups that is settled by violence, since it cannot be resolved by state regulatory agencies. By contrast, underground drug markets in places where the state does not intervene in the industry often develop stable routines and norms and operate for years without violence.[71]

What exactly would happen if all drugs were legalized and regulated is something of an unknown, since many of them have been prohibited around the world for nearly a century. But a couple of policies that have been tried may be instructive. Switzerland, for instance, put in place a new national drug policy in the early 1990s that included the free provision of heroin to people with opioid use disorders. Concerned about growing numbers of drug users and cases of HIV, leaders decided to shift away from abstinence-oriented approaches to incorporate some elements of harm reduction. Public clinics began providing free, unadulterated heroin in controlled doses to people who were not responding to the available drug treatments. People could receive those doses for as long as they needed them, without facing pressure to taper off.[72]

The results were striking. The heroin clinics dramatically reduced overdose deaths, HIV infections, mental and physical illness, use of street heroin and cocaine, drug use overall, and property crimes.[73] They freed people of the desperate need to find money for the next dose, giving them back their time so that they could stabilize their lives, find jobs, and put themselves in better positions to recover from their illnesses. They resulted in "an almost complete disappearance of public visibility of drug problems."[74] And they reduced the number of people who began using heroin for the first time by 80 percent, likely because they reduced street heroin dealing and use and the social life that revolves around it. The same kinds of clinics have since been tried in the Netherlands and Germany, with similar results.[75]

The experiment with heroin-assisted treatment offers some clues as to what a future in which drugs are legalized could look like. Providing people with measured doses of unadulterated drugs, in a safe environment, eliminates many of the health risks of illegal drug use. It could also reduce use in general, as it did in Switzerland, by allowing people with substance use disorders to stabilize their lives and by reducing the development of social dynamics that draw new people into using. Provision of drugs to people who need them also reduces their need to come up with money for the next dose, reducing the suffering that often spreads out within communities when they become desperate.[76] (As of 2009, about one in five people serving sentences in state prisons or jails reported that their most serious current offense was committed in an attempt to obtain drugs.[77]) And although establishing clinics for the free dispensation of drugs would be expensive, ending enforcement of a drug prohibition would save the US government an estimated forty-seven billion dollars a year.[78]

The regulation of tobacco may offer some additional insights into how drug legalization might work. Tobacco has always been legal in the United States, even though it is deadlier than and at least as addictive as cocaine or heroin.[79] The US government has made huge strides in eliminating cigarette use without criminalizing tobacco, even though at its peak it was far more widespread than illegal drug use is today. In the early 1960s nearly half of the adult population regularly smoked cigarettes, three and a half times the share of the population who currently use illegal drugs.[80] (An estimated 14 percent of adults today engage in illegal drug use.[81]) By 2020 only about 12 percent of adults were cigarette smokers.[82] And younger generations are even less likely to smoke than their elders. Use of both cigarettes and e-cigarettes is declining rapidly among middle and high school students.[83] Research indicates that the decline in smoking overall can be attributed to the widespread dissemination of information about health risks related to smoking, restrictions on smoking in public places and workplaces, comprehensive bans on advertising and promotion, and cheaper and more accessible smoking-cessation treatments.[84]

A note on the decriminalization of drug possession, which is gaining some popularity as a policy intervention. Under decriminalization, drugs remain illegal, but the government no longer prosecutes people for possession of small amounts of drugs. This policy addresses some of the harms associated with drug criminalization, but it leaves many others unaddressed. It still leaves dealers vulnerable to arrest and punishment, for instance, and there is substantial overlap between dealers and users.[85] It also leaves users vulnerable to all of the harms associated with unregulated drugs: the inability to control dosage and the risk of adulteration, with the concomitant risks of illness and overdose. And it does nothing to address the bloody global drug war and the violence and death associated with it. The available research certainly indicates that decriminalization is better for society than the legal structure that currently dominates most of the world. But questions about its political impacts are hard to answer. If decriminalization reduces the stigma surrounding drug use, it could have positive long-term effects. If it causes disillusionment about loosening drug laws by failing to solve some of the fundamental problems surrounding drug trade and use—in the state of Oregon, for instance, lawmakers recriminalized drug possession in large part because of concerns about overdose deaths[86]—then it could slow positive change.

STRUCTURAL CHANGE

Substance use and mental illness will likely never disappear, but both increase under difficult structural conditions. To alleviate more of the suffering associated with mental illness, we may need to begin to define healthcare more broadly. Permanent supportive housing, with no mandated compliance with performance requirements, can help people with severe mental illness to live better lives and stabilize their health. Preventing the most severe forms of poverty by protecting affordable rental housing and expanding social services would also help to keep people healthier.[87] Poverty and trauma are triggers for severe mental illness. And though there are many reasons that people use substances, some are external.[88] Drug and alcohol use can offer temporary respite from stress, strain, pain, and boredom. If a person has few other prospects for relief—including positive or meaningful aspects of their life—then frequent substance use can become the most appealing option. Health could be improved by redistributive economic policies that reduce poverty, promote healthy communities, and ensure that everyone has the means to live a flourishing life.

Conclusion

The reforms that institutional members themselves put forward, in response to demands for change, often keep power and resources in the same hands. Ceding control can be risky for them. But those reforms can easily be shaped by dominant institutional logics and become new tools with which to carry out the same old work. More meaningful change can require shifting resources and control around. Doing that is hard: It requires disrupting existing organizations, which can mean disrupting people's lives. It requires doing the difficult political work to try new ideas without knowing for sure what's on the other side, which requires a lot more work and risk-taking from elected officials and the public. It requires new metrics to evaluate success. Before any of that, it requires us to think more broadly about what is possible. As political scientist E. E. Schattschneider reminds us, "The definition of the alternatives is the supreme instrument of power."[89]

Acknowledgments

This book could not have come into being without the generous support of innumerable people. I won't be able to do justice to the many ways they have all shaped this project over the past several years, but at the risk of forgetting some of them and selling all of their contributions short, I will do my best.

First and foremost, I am profoundly grateful to all of the people who gave their time and energy to participate in this study. You can't be named here, but you made this project what it is. Thank you for sharing some of your lives with me, for your wisdom, and for the generosity and commitments to positive change in the world that led you to contribute to this project. I did my best to do justice to the experiences and insights you shared with me, but my debts to you can never be repaid.

This book would also not exist without the phenomenal group of scholars who have guided and trained me since the start of graduate school. Becky Pettit has offered unwavering support and incisive feedback from my first semester of grad school to the present. At every juncture, she has pushed me to think about the broader implications of my work, sharpening my research and writing by challenging me to look beyond narrow intellectual debates to the impacts social science can have on the world. Javier Auyero taught me to do ethnography and to think like a sociologist, and his unparalleled kindness and enthusiasm continue to keep me excited about the work we do. He also somehow answers every email within the hour, even when that involves reading a draft and sending feedback. Sarah Brayne taught me to generalize from the specific to the theoretical and can somehow immediately see what needs to be done to save every piece of writing I show her. Ben Carrington taught me to read *everything* and introduced me to a world of ideas that continues to shape my thinking. Mary Rose has pushed me toward precision in my research design and writing at every stage and encouraged me to write work that people will read and understand. Each of you has left your unique mark on this project and strengthened it at every step along the way with your ideas, critiques, and encouragement. Your steady guidance and insights made me into a sociologist, and your warmth and support made me *want* to be a sociologist.

Many of the ideas in this book took shape during the two years I spent as a doctoral fellow at the American Bar Foundation in Chicago with the support of the National Science Foundation. That fellowship gave me the gifts of time and the influence of a vibrant group of people dedicated to the study of law and society. I learned so much from the faculty there, the other doctoral fellows, and the wider community of scholars who welcomed me in. Thank you especially to John Hagan, Terry Halliday, Carol Heimer, Ajay Mehrotra, Beth Mertz, Janice Nadler, Laura Beth Nielsen, Jothie Rajah, and Chris Schmidt. And thank you to Evelyn Atkinson, Kyla Bourne, Magda Boutros, Anya Degenshein, Gabriela Kirk-Werner, Jessica López-Espino, Tova Markenson, Margot Moinester, Robert Manduca, Asad Rahim, Anna Reosti, Georg Rilinger, Roseanna Sommers, and Arielle Tolman for your friendship, feedback, and warm intellectual community. I was so lucky to find you all.

To all of the other friends who have lent support over the course of this project, including Felix Amankona-Diawuo, Marvin Arnold, Riad Azar, John Bardes, Kasha Bornstein, Clemmy Brown, Julien Burns, Kendall Calyen, Jesse Chanin, Faith Deckard, Erik Elshire, Jeanne Firth, Will Flagle, Maricarmen Hernández, Jed Horne, Tiffany Huang, Katie Jensen, Taya Kitaysky, Janick Lewis, Alfred Marshall, Vann Miller, Callie Millington, Lizzie Mytty, Katie Sobering, Alex Stokes, Brandon Washington, Jane Wholey, Amy Wolfe, Tom Wooten, and Aaron Zagory: thank you. Each of you contributed to this book in different ways. You advised me on the big decisions, read drafts of my work, wrote with me, helped me move, talked through ideas with me, made me laugh at myself, gave me airport rides, honed my research questions and analysis, taught me about the legal system, talked through ethical and logistical questions while I was in the field, took me shopping for professional clothes, let me stay on your couches, did political work with me, made sure I took breaks, and picked me up every time I fell flat on my face. It takes a village, and you have been an unbeatable village.

I am deeply indebted to the research assistants who helped me with the research for this book. In particular, Hsiao-Jan Huang did a tremendous amount of work on the data collection and analysis of the national survey of diversion programs. I was floored by her creative problem-solving, dedication to finding answers, and brilliant analytic mind. Many others also made invaluable contributions to this project along the way, including Sean Asaeda, Jillian Benedict, Ren Biel, Benisha Pierre-Louis, Caitlin Udas, Benjunior Udogwo, Jocelyn Vititow, and Gina Zhen. I could not have dreamed up a more insightful and enjoyable group of students. The time I spent working with each of you consistently made my day.

To all of my colleagues and graduate students at the University at Albany, SUNY—you are the best anyone could have asked for. Thank you for welcoming me in the middle of a pandemic and doing so much to ease my way through the roughest possible start, and thank you for your ongoing support, feedback, humor, advice, and great company. I am deeply grateful to all of you, but I want to extend special thanks to David Hureau, Julie Novkov, Dana Peterson, Justin Pickett, Bill Pridemore, Matt Vogel, Teddy Wilson, and Alissa Worden. I would not have been able to write this book without your mentorship, encouragement, and concerted efforts to protect my time and ensure that I had the resources I needed.

I am also grateful to the broader community of scholars who offered insights and ideas that shaped this work, including—but not limited to—Ian Carrillo, Liz Chiarello, Erin Eife, Chris Herring, Kelley Fong, Andrew Le, Marisa Omori, Chiara Packard, Theresa Rocha Beardall, Jamie Rowen, and Loïc Wacquant. Conversations with or feedback from each of you made this book stronger.

I received generous funding for the research in this book from the National Science Foundation, the American Bar Foundation, P.E.O. International, the Horowitz Foundation for Social Policy, the Donald D. Harrington Fellows Program, the Rapoport Centennial Dissertation Support Award, the Institute for Humane Studies, and Oak Ridge Associated Universities. That support made this project possible.

My wonderful editor, Sara Doskow, believed in this book from the start and guided me through the writing and publication process with warmth and insight. Thanks to her, what could have been an arduous process was a true pleasure. The anonymous reviewers also strengthened this manuscript with their deeply thoughtful and generous feedback. And I'm thankful to the incredible production team at the University of Chicago Press— including Rosemary Frehe, Barbara Norton, Stephen Twilley, and others— for their commitment to this project and for doing all the hard work needed to see it through.

I am profoundly grateful to my family. Thank you to my parents for teaching me to let my curiosity lead me and for believing in me wholeheartedly from the beginning. Thank you to my sisters for picking up the phone every time I called and telling me exactly what to do and always being right. Thank you for making me laugh at everything, especially myself. I don't know what I would do without any of you. Thank you to Sam for inspiring me every day with your determination and fierce fight for justice, for making me laugh, for reminding me to keep my priorities straight, for picking up the slack when I was glued to my laptop, for reading every word I wrote, and for being this project's biggest cheerleader from beginning to end. You are the best partner and friend I could have asked for. Finally: this book is dedicated to Al, who helped me start this project, and to Cal, who made me finish it.

Methodological Appendix A

In the summer of 2017 I was having lunch with a friend named Eugene who was giving me an update on another friend named Myron. Myron used heroin and was enrolled in the court-mandated treatment program that Eugene had been through years before. "Diversion's a scam," Eugene told me, shaking his head. "It's set up to fail. He should have just took the jail time." I did a double take. I had been involved in various sorts of work related to the criminal legal system for years by then, but I had never heard anyone say anything like that before. I had voted religiously for the candidates for judge and district attorney who promised to expand diversion programs and assumed those programs were an unequivocal good.

I was surprised and troubled enough that I started to look around for more information. Over the weeks that followed, I found very little clarity. On one hand, my dive into the research on pretrial diversion turned up scores of journal articles with unequivocally positive findings. Study after study reported truly amazing reductions in recidivism rates among people who were diverted into therapeutic programs,[1] and experts in the field were convinced. One recent academic book on criminal legal reform declared, "One of the primary research findings of the past twenty years or so . . . is the efficacy of diversion from traditional criminal prosecution, adjudication, sentencing, and punishment."[2]

On the other hand, as I asked around, I was running into more and more people who described diversion as one of the worst experiences of their lives. Most had had their charges dismissed and were deeply grateful for that—but they talked about their assigned treatment programs as gauntlets they had run, not as services. Others had spent months or years taking drug tests, paying fees, and attending frequent appointments, only to fail out of the program and find themselves back where they had started or even worse off.

I suspected that one cause of the disjuncture between the published literature and the experiences I was hearing about might be the nature of the research on pretrial diversion. The available studies nearly all used the same study design: they compared the recidivism rates among people who were diverted to the rates among people who stayed in the traditional court system. Most of them also limited the first group to people who had *completed* diversion and dropped from their analyses the people who had not. So the effects they were finding could have reflected preexisting differences between people who were diverted and people who weren't, and between people who finished diversion and people who didn't. The studies also couldn't distinguish between the effects on people's lives of being released from the legal system and the effects of the therapeutic programs themselves.[3]

As I continued the search for information, I found that the limitations of the available research reflected deep limitations to the available data. There is no centralized dataset on pretrial diversion, so researchers have to get data directly from each jurisdiction individually. But as I'll discuss in more detail later in this appendix, jurisdictions usually only record partial information, if they record any at all. The data they do have are hard to access. The diversion programs themselves are also closed to public access. Unlike criminal courtrooms, they don't allow anyone to walk in and observe what is happening. Often there isn't any contact information available for their offices online, but even when there is a way to call or email them, they rarely return messages asking for information.

It took me six years of digging to gather the data for this book. A lot of that time was spent fighting for access to it. I called DAs, judges, court clerks, and diversion offices over and over, and over, to ask for interviews, observation access, and administrative data. I filed dozens of public-records requests and followed up on them for years. I asked for favors from journalists, elected officials, friends, friends of friends, and friends of friends of friends. All told, I spent nine months participating in a court-mandated treatment program; collected court records and administrative data; observed criminal courtroom proceedings; interviewed 130 people, including prosecutors, judges, diversion program directors, defense attorneys, and people who had been diverted out of court; conducted a national survey of pretrial diversion programs; collected relevant legislation from six states; and fielded a vignette experiment on working prosecutors. Drawing on these varied data sources, I slowly pieced together how diversion operates in daily practice and the role it plays in criminal courts and in the lives of defendants. In the process, I took away some larger insights about institutional reform. In the rest of this appendix, I describe each form of data collection and present some additional details about my findings.

The Therapeutic Environment
PARTICIPANT OBSERVATION IN
MANDATED TREATMENT

There were some aspects of diversion that I knew I could never understand unless I saw them in action. So one of the first things I did was work to get access to observe inside a program. I identified a pretrial diversion program that used best practices identified by the National Association of Pretrial Services Agencies—such as charging minimal fees and employing only counselors with graduate degrees[4]—and had eligibility and program requirements that the available research indicated were common to programs around the country.[5] The program operated in a city in the South.[6] (To protect the confidentiality of study participants, some of whom would be recognizable to anyone familiar with the field site, I do not identify the site in this book.) After months of emailing and calling, I finally got through to the program director and was able to sit down with her for an interview. At the end of our two-hour conversation, she agreed to allow me to observe their program in action if therapists and participants consented. She put me in touch with one of the lead treatment providers in the office, Eric.

Eric immediately sent me his cell phone number, said he was glad to have me join, and told me what time to show up for the first session. Assuming that we would start by meeting to discuss my special role as an observer, I checked in at the front desk to let him know that I had arrived. But there was no word from Eric until he came out to the waiting room to hold the door open to the back room for me and a dozen other people, and he just gave me a warm smile and a hug along with everybody else as I filed past him. I hovered uncertainly in one corner of the room while he and the other group therapist, Carli, pulled in extra chairs and greeted each of the group participants with jokes and questions about their new jobs or their children. When the chairs were in place, Eric gestured to me to sit down in the circle with the others. Beyond giving me time to introduce myself and ask for everyone's consent to be in the study, he treated me like any other group participant: he called on me directly to answer questions or share stories no more or less often than he called on anyone else, he handed me a worksheet to fill out along with the rest of the group, and when I hovered as he was cleaning up at the end of the night in case he wanted to check in, he just smiled and said he would see me next week.

The following week Eric introduced me to the therapists who facilitated the other group sessions, and I joined all of those sessions during the nine months that followed. Apart from giving me time for my introductions and study consent, the therapists all followed Eric's lead in treating me as a member of the group who just had a different reason for being there. So I participated in all the discussions and activities and jotted down fieldnotes only occasionally, to get important quotes down verbatim or to remind myself to write about something later. When we were assigned worksheets, I finished them quickly and then used the time to take longer notes to flesh things out. I wrote the rest of the notes after the sessions ended each night, usually by dictating into my phone on the drive home and then starting to type as soon as I got there.

The therapists' decision to treat me like a program participant rather than a special observer threw me together with the other program participants before and after, as well as during, our sessions. I usually spent an hour or so on either end hanging out with the other group members on the front steps of the building while they waited for the session to start and then for buses or rides to show up. It also placed me in their social category as far as the program was concerned. The counselors encouraged all of us to spend time together outside of sessions, in the understanding that we could provide positive support for and influences on each other. Cutting loose from old social connections was a big part of the process of "recovery," they emphasized, and spending time with people who lived the way you were trying to live was a central part of making positive change. So I went to other participants' houses when they invited me for meals or cookouts or parties, met up for coffee, gave them rides home, and just talked for long stretches outside the treatment center, braving the heat to avoid the eerily silent waiting room. When those interactions helped me understand their experiences in treatment, I asked again for consent to write about them for the study.

My hybrid status as a program participant and researcher raised a tangle of questions about ethics and power dynamics. On one hand, I was careful to remember and remind everyone else that I was there as an observer, not a regular participant. Since the group sessions were really not supposed to be there to help me, I kept my contributions succinct and only spoke when it was my turn or when there was an awkward silence after a therapist had posed a question to the group. I also made sure that everyone remembered I was there as a researcher, which people sometimes forgot despite my regular reintroductions and requests for consent. Once in a while, when we were hanging out outside of the sessions, for instance, people asked me things like what I was "in for" or what my "drug of choice" was, and I reminded them. But most of the time it was a running joke that I was the only one ridiculous enough to join the program voluntarily. Carli once asked the group, "How many of you made the choice to be here this evening?" as she was trying to make a point about how we were all constantly choosing to do the right thing or the wrong thing, even if we felt like things (such as the diversion program) were just forced on us. My hand was the only one that went up, and everybody laughed while Carli protested that *everyone* had chosen to be there and the rest of the group shook their heads.

On the other hand, I made an effort to lean into my role as a participant when it was my turn to share in the group sessions. As group members sometimes pointed out, there was a steep power differential at the heart of mandated therapy: the therapists asked participants to share intimate details about themselves, but they told us very little about their own lives. In one exchange, a young Black man named Donavan reflected on this dynamic in a session. He had just answered a string of questions about his family life and finally asked the White therapist, Marly, about her own family:

> DONAVAN: The question that you just asked, it sounds like there's no boundaries, like you go back and forth with your mom?
> MARLY: Um, well no! I was just asking you, to put it back on you.
> DONAVAN: It's not on me. It's on you.
> MARLY: Well, I would say, sometimes you do challenge a lot in group. And that's okay! Because that's what we're here to do.
> DONAVAN: I'm saying, we trying to find out about everybody. And you're not telling about you. We just telling y'all about us.
> MARLY: That's how we're trained. We're trained to focus on y'all's experiences, because it's not about us.
> DONAVAN: But it's about everybody, if it's group!

Another group member, Dalton, interjected: "I think he trying to say, like, we reveal a lot to y'all but y'all not giving us nothing back." Donavan nodded. "If we ask you anything about you, y'all put a wall up and hide it and reverse it back to us." "If y'all opened up to us—" Dalton started to say. Donavan jumped back in, his voice rising: "Y'all ain't showing no type of trust! Y'all just want to know everybody's stories. That's what y'all doing, you don't want to show us nothing about you.... We don't even know if y'all have went through *any* of this."

The power disparity in court-mandated therapy is stark, and it's loaded with race and class dynamics. The clients were forced to be present and then pressured to make themselves emotionally vulnerable, while therapists tended to say nothing about themselves. Two-thirds of the clients in my field site were Black and most were poor, while more than half of the therapists were White and all had graduate degrees. Like the therapists, I was a White woman with a lot of years of higher education and was there voluntarily. To offset that inevitable power imbalance in one of the few ways I could, I made an effort to "show trust" by talking openly about the kinds of experiences and struggles that therapists were asking us to share. Even though I didn't have anything to say about drug use, a lot of my history was directly relevant to the other topics that therapists raised. I grew up below the poverty line in the South and have family members who have struggled with substance use disorders and have been in and out of the legal system. I had also lived for much of my life in a neighborhood with high rates of violence and had several experiences that left me with ongoing symptoms of PTSD. So it wasn't hard for me to participate fully in response to most of the prompts we were given. I will never know exactly how this participation shaped my relationships with other people in the group, but my impression was that it helped to build trust and contributed to their openness with me when we spent time together outside of sessions.

But Donavan's observation points not just to imbalances in emotional vulnerability but also to the thornier issue of extraction. As he said to Marly, "Y'all just want to know everybody's stories." This is, of course, exactly what I was doing as a researcher. I won't wade into any larger debates here about the value or the ethics of that endeavor. In the immediate term, I just wanted to be sure that I only collected people's stories if and when they wanted me to. Fieldwork in court-mandated treatment is doubly complicated by the sensitivity of the site—participants are sharing information with their mental healthcare providers and also still have open legal cases—and by the coerced nature of people's presence there. I navigated this complex terrain as best I could, largely by asking for consent before every new interaction. It was hard to know whether everyone felt free to refuse in the group setting— no one ever refused or even expressed reservations—but I was reassured when nearly half of the group members did withhold consent and choose to leave the room when journalists came to observe a session. Although they drew the line at news stories, outside of treatment most participants talked about the sessions as though they were relatively public. Many of them assumed that treatment providers could report anything they said back to prosecutors and that it might be used against them in court. Some also indicated that they didn't trust other program participants not to share their secrets. They indicated that an academic study in which everything would be kept anonymous, in a site that they did not consider private, gave them little additional cause for concern. But I did emphasize that everyone was free to choose not to be observed or written about and that I could easily leave or avoid putting them in my notes.

A related risk is that what I write might inadvertently cause harm to people who had consented to participate. To protect against harms to individuals as best I could, I gave everyone pseudonyms in my fieldnotes and omitted any details that I thought could identify them. I also took the additional step of anonymizing the field site. The program was small enough that the counselors who worked in it, and likely some of its participants, could be identified if I were to name the city where it operates—or even the state, since that information, alongside my descriptions of the site, would make it possible for a knowledgeable reader to identify the specific jurisdiction. To protect against group-based harms, I also tried to avoid writing about anything that was unrelated to my central research questions and might bring negative attention to the vulnerable groups of people in this study. Additional details about people and their lives can bring depth to our writing and make study participants more three-dimensional, but the lines between benign details and those that might be used to reinforce negative narratives can be blurry. Because people who use drugs, who are under criminal legal supervision, who are Black, and who are poor constitute most of my ethnographic study participants, and all contend with social stigma, I tried when in doubt to err on the side of writing about their experiences narrowly in relation to my research questions.

In all, I interacted regularly with ninety-two treatment program participants. Those ninety-two who came to sessions regularly represented just over one in five of the 419 participants who exited the pretrial diversion program that year (which is the best number I have to estimate the number of people enrolled during my fieldwork). Some of the program participants attended group sessions only sporadically, so I didn't see them often, and some had been released from the treatment sessions by their therapists altogether and were only taking drug tests and paying off program fees. Others had disappeared from the program entirely and would exit the program due to noncompliance and be returned to court. I spent time outside of treatment sessions with thirty-four of the participants, and with nine of them I developed closer relationships and spent time consistently over the course of my fieldwork. These ethnographic study participants reflected the racial and gender distribution of the program as a whole (see tables 1a and 1b).

ADMINISTRATIVE DATA

To situate my observations in the field site within broader patterns of program entry and exit, I requested public-record administrative data on pretrial diversion program participants from the diversion office in my field site. The office denied the request, but I eventually received the data from an elected representative who had been able to obtain it from them. They consist of deidentified individual-level data ($N = 1447$) on the dates of pretrial diversion program entry and exit, criminal charges, race, gender, age, diversion type or "track," and completion status for every felony and misdemeanor defendant who entered diversion between 2014 and 2017. Descriptive statistics are shown in table 1a.

INTERVIEWS WITH DIVERSION PROGRAM PARTICIPANTS

I also interviewed fifty people who had already exited diversion with or without completing the program. Talking to people who had already exited was a useful supplement to my fieldwork with people still in the program. For one thing, interviews in general can give information on things that can't always be observed, like people's interpretations of their own actions, their aims and concerns, and their emotional experiences.[7] For another, people who had already exited diversion could reflect on the process of being removed (or disappearing) from the program and on the events that followed. They were also freer to take risks, since they didn't have to worry about being kicked out of the program if something they said got back to the diversion staff, and they were also talking to someone they would never see again. People in interviews talked more often than the current participants about drug use, past trauma, and the ways they had tried to circumnavigate diversion program requirements, for instance. They also tended to be more open in their criticisms of the program and treatment providers.

I recruited past program participants via flyers in public places and social-services agencies, Craigslist ads, and social networks. We met up for interviews wherever was convenient for them, including parks, fast food restaurants, coffee shops, shelters, my car, people's porches, meeting rooms in public libraries, and the meeting room in a shared office that I rented for this purpose. Although I only advertised these interviews in my primary jurisdiction, I decided to open them to people who had been through diversion in the neighboring jurisdiction as well. Both jurisdictions were part of the same urban area, and people were often arrested across the county line from where they lived. The pretrial diversion programs in the two jurisdictions were also very similar. About a third of the people I ultimately interviewed had been through diversion in the neighboring jurisdiction and two-thirds in the primary field site. Each person was compensated $25 for their time. The interviews were semi-structured, so each was different from the others, and the questions I asked differed accordingly in order, phrasing, and content. I asked a lot of follow-up questions that differed along with people's initial answers. But these are the standard questions that I brought in with me to guide each interview:

Could you start by walking me through how you decided to participate in the diversion from the program?
    Did they give you a choice between diversion and something else?
        What did your lawyer tell you would happen if you didn't take diversion?
        Did you have a public or private defense lawyer?
    Did you take diversion pre-plea or post-plea? What did they tell you would happen to you if you didn't finish the program?
    So did you have any doubts about taking the diversion option? Why or why not?
So then walk me through a month of your life in diversion. What did you have to do to stay in the program?
[For each of the program requirements] What was your experience with [ ] like?
    Was there anything useful to you about [ ]? If so, what was it?
    Was there anything not useful about it? If so, what?
[If applicable] What was your counselor like?
[If applicable] What were the [group and/or individual] sessions like?
How much did they ask you to pay toward the program?
    Were there other financial costs associated with your participation?
        Like transportation to appointments or to court? More or less how much did that amount to?
Were there any other restrictions on you during the program?
How long were you in the program?
    Did you end up finishing, or did you leave early?
    [If they left early] Do you remember what the reasons were for that?
    [If they left early] What happened then to your case?
Overall, what would you say the main impacts of diversion were on you?
    On your family?
If you were back in that same place and your lawyer told you that you could take diversion or keep going with your case, would you still go for diversion?
If you were put in charge of the diversion program in *[this county]*, what elements would you keep the same and what would you change?
Is there anything else you want to add or that I should know?

At the end of each interview, I asked each person to fill out a short survey asking about their race, ethnicity, age, gender, years of formal education, vocation and current employment status, household income, and number of people in their household, either verbally or on paper. The results are

TABLE 1A. Demographic characteristics of diversion participants from administrative data in fieldsite, 2014–17 (N = 1447)

RACE		
Black	62.5%	902
White	35.6%	514
Asian	1.0%	15
Hispanic	0.9%	13
Other	1.2%	9
SEX		
Female	30.0%	433
Male	70.0%	1,011
Age, range	17 to 71	
CHARGE TYPE		
Drug possession (other than marijuana charges, which are not handled by this program)	47.5%	687
Property	22.9%	332
Other (including "public order" offenses; 92% of charges in this category are misdemeanors)	29.6%	428
CHARGE LEVEL		
Felony	52.9%	680
Misdemeanor	47.1%	763

shown in table 1c. Among interview participants, half identified as Black and half as White, and half identified as men and half as women. Although class is a complex and contested category, and my sample included enormous variation, I use the terms *middle-class*, *working-class*, and *poor* as rough approximations for class identity here. For each participant, I assigned a class status based on per-person household income, employment, and years of formal education. With exceptions for participants in more complex or unusual economic situations, I followed the approach used by sociologist Matt Clair in a recent study of criminal defendants, using *middle-class* to refer to people with at least a four-year college degree, *working-class* to refer to those with less than a four-year college degree and with stable work, and *poor* to refer to those with less than a four-year college degree and no stable income.[8] According to my classification, roughly one-fifth of interview respondents were middle-class, just over two-fifths were poor, and the rest were working-class.

TABLE 1B. Diversion participants, ethnographic study participants (N = 92)

RACE, AS READ BY RESEARCHER		
Black	65%	60
White	35%	32
GENDER, AS READ BY RESEARCHER		
Woman	25%	23
Man	75%	69
CLASS, BASED ON INCOME AND EDUCATION, WHERE KNOWN (N = 61)		
Middle-class	24%	15
Working-class	56%	34
Poor	20%	12

TABLE 1C. Diversion participants, interview respondents (N = 50)

RACE, SELF-REPORTED		
White	46%	23
Black	52%	26
Asian American	2%	1
GENDER, SELF-REPORTED		
Woman	50%	25
Man	50%	25
CLASS, BASED ON INCOME AND EDUCATION		
Middle-class	21%	11
Working-class	37%	18
Poor	42%	21
Mentioned a mental illness diagnosis (other than substance use disorder), unprompted, during interview	32%	16
Age, self-reported: range	21–70	

Interviews with Treatment Providers

I also wanted to understand how treatment providers understood their therapeutic work with mandated clients. Those providers are central to the treatment environment. They facilitate the mandatory therapeutic group sessions related to substance use and other mental health concerns; they meet with clients individually to discuss their progress; and they decide when and how much to increase program requirements if a client has positive drug tests or misses appointments. Their heavy caseloads mean that they usually don't have time to "chase the clients," as they put it, when they don't show up for treatment sessions, but they do occasionally check in on them by phone. Program directors supervise and check in with treatment providers and usually take responsibility for the final decisions about returning cases to court. They are also typically the people with the power to set and change program policies and practices.

I interviewed forty-seven mental health professionals in total (for details about this sample, see table 2), including twenty-three pretrial diversion–program directors, twenty therapists who worked with court-mandated clients, and four directors of private facilities that provide treatment to court-mandated clients. (A slew of nonprofits in my field site received mandated clients not only from pretrial diversion—when therapists referred them out for additional treatment—but also from the drug court, the mental health court, probation and parole, pretrial services, and individual judges who mandated people into treatment as a condition of release.) Like my interviews with diversion participants, these interviews were semi-structured and varied widely. Depending on the role a given program director played and their clinical background, I often asked them some of the questions from the therapist interview guide as well. But below are the lists of questions I took in with me to guide the interviews with therapists and program directors.

THERAPISTS

Could you start by walking me through what led you to become a therapist, initially?
How did you come to work at this particular program?
    How long have you been working here?
Do you see both court-mandated and non-court-mandated clients, or only the former?
    [If relevant] What's the percentage of each, more or less?
Do you notice any differences between the two groups in terms of what they're like to work with in therapy?
    [If they mention challenges with mandated clients] What are the main ways you've found to navigate those challenges?
How long is a typical appointment with each client?
    What kind of therapeutic approach do you use?

What are the requirements for them to complete the program
 successfully?
   Passing drug tests?
   Demonstrating progress in therapy?
   How do you generally gauge progress?
   Complying with daily phone calls?
   Showing up for appointments?
   Other?
How often and to whom do you have to report on your client's progress?
What goes in the reports?
Do you have a sense of which of those things is most important to *[the
 entity to whom you report]*?
What usually happens if people aren't able to pay?
   For the weekly sessions?
   For drug testing *[if applicable]*?
   The program fee at the end, to exit the program?
How often do you have to send clients' cases back to the courts?
What are the main reasons that cases get sent back?
   What is the process through which that happens?
   What are the criteria? Who sets those?
   Who is involved in the discussion? Who makes the final decision?
[If you are the sole decision-maker] Has anyone ever challenged your
 decision to send a case back or not to?
With mandated clients, do you strictly provide talk therapy, or do you also
 do other things *[like refer people out to other agencies or providers or call
 them if they stop coming to appointments, for instance]*?
For yourself, what are the metrics by which you gauge success? How do
 you know if your clients are making progress?
What percentage of your mandated clients would you say meet those
 goals?
   What do you think makes the difference between those who do and
    who don't meet those goals?
   Do any examples come to mind?
If they were to put you in charge of the program, is there anything you
 would change?
What are your favorite things about your job?
What are the hardest things?
What do you see as the primary purposes of diversion?
Anything else I should know?

DIVERSION PROGRAM DIRECTORS

What's the process by which people come to the diversion program? What happens first?
Do prosecutors ever send you too many or too few cases?
What are the requirements for the mandated clients to complete the program successfully?
    Passing drug tests?
        What are they tested for?
            Is methadone allowed? What about other medical treatments for substance use disorders?
            Marijuana?
            Prescription painkillers (with prescriptions)?
    Participating in therapy?
        Do you have therapists in-house, or do you refer participants out?
        Do they just need to be in therapy, or is there a requirement that they also demonstrate progress? (If the latter, how do you generally gauge progress?)
    Complying with daily phone calls?
    Fees?
    Other?
How does the program keep track of clients' compliance with the requirements?
How often and to whom do you have to report on your clients' progress?
    What details do you report?
What happens if clients are out of compliance with one or more of the requirements?
    What is the process by which cases get sent back to the courts? (Who is involved in the discussion? Who makes the final decision?)
What would you say makes the difference between people who finish diversion and people who don't?
Have there been any changes to program structure or guidelines—or any discussion of possible changes—since you've been there?
    If so, what were they?
    What motivated the discussion or the change?
    How did you all decide to go in the direction you did?
What do you see as the overarching purpose of the diversion program?
Anything else I should know?

I recruited providers for interviews in a few different ways. I recruited individual therapists inside the office where I was observing treatment,

TABLE 2. Treatment providers, interview respondents (N = 47)

RACE, AS READ BY INTERVIEWER		
White	66%	31
Black	26%	12
Latine	4%	2
Asian American	4%	2
GENDER, AS READ BY INTERVIEWER		
Woman	64%	30
Man	36%	17

through social networks, and via snowball sampling. Fifteen of the twenty worked in the city where I did my ethnographic fieldwork, and five worked in neighboring jurisdictions. I recruited private facility directors and pretrial diversion program directors by emailing and making repeated cold calls to their offices. To understand why the structures of diversion programs were so similar around the country despite their structural autonomy, I recruited program directors from beyond my field site. The twenty-three directors I interviewed worked in twenty-one different jurisdictions (six in the Northeast, seven in the South, three in the Midwest, and five in the West[9]).

LIMITATIONS AND FUTURE RESEARCH

A few additional details about my field site may clarify the limitations of the research I describe above and signal directions for future work. First, the diversion program where I did my observations employed in-house therapists to provide treatment to all participants. This is a common practice that protects people from the fees or insurance required to cover treatment at private facilities. The structure was helpful for research because it meant that the action was centralized rather than dispersed among different organizations. Other diversion programs refer all of their clients to external outpatient facilities for treatment, and future research on those facilities might unearth different patterns of action. Financial and bureaucratic burdens may be different, for instance, in facilities that rely entirely on client fees or insurance rather than on funding from a district attorney's office. The stories I heard from interviewees about what sounded to me like provider malpractice were also all related to these external facilities. It could be that the quality of care can vary more widely in those sites. Overall, though, the former clients I interviewed also described similar experiences across facility types. My interviews with private treatment providers also suggested that the dynamics in those facilities were very similar to the ones that I observed. Often nearly all of their clients are mandated to be there, and the programs work closely with the criminal courts and (like in-house providers) rely on their referrals for their survival.

Second, the demographics of my field site likely shape my findings. According to the 2020 census, nearly two-thirds of the residents in the jurisdiction where I conducted my ethnographic fieldwork are Black, under 10 percent are Hispanic or Latine, and nearly all of the rest are White. About a quarter live below the poverty line. Of those who enter the criminal court system, roughly 85 percent are assessed as indigent and represented by public defenders (a figure just slightly higher than the 80 percent of defendants assessed as indigent nationally at the last count[10]). The local court told me that neither they nor any other entity collected data on the racial demographics of criminal defendants, but administrative data from the diversion program indicated that about 63 percent of participants were identified in their system as Black, about 36 percent as White, and the rest as either "Hispanic," "Asian," or "Other." Seventy-five percent were identified as men, 25 percent as women, and none as nonbinary. Those demographics are reflected in my ethnographic study participants (see tables 1a and 1b). And although I oversampled women among my interviewees, I was able to spend only limited time in the field with women with young children or other demanding caregiving duties. Research studies including more people of other ethnicities, races, genders, and nationalities could shed more light on how things like language barriers, religious discrimination, gendered duties, or threats to residency status might shape the dynamics of mandated treatment.

The Courtroom

OBSERVATIONS

The other side of court-mandated treatment is the criminal courtroom itself. People who are diverted have to attend public court dates before, and often during and after, their time in treatment. Judges mandate people into treatment programs at a variety of stages and for many different reasons. Prosecutors, defense attorneys, and judges confer in open court about program entry and—for some forms of treatment—the specific requirements that should be placed on people and what to do when they miss their assigned sessions or turn in positive drug tests. More broadly, the norms and logics developed in the courtroom influence decisions made in private by all of the actors involved.[11] In-court interactions thus offer important insights into the use and impacts of treatment-based reforms.

I conducted about 380 hours of observations of criminal courtroom proceedings in my field site. I rotated among courtrooms within the courthouse, where all felony and state misdemeanor cases are handled from the setting of bail to the final disposition. I took notes on paper, since the courthouse did not allow electronic devices. During those observations, I paid particular attention to the ways prosecutors and judges interacted with and talked about defendants entering and exiting diversion. I also took careful notes on when and how judges mandated treatment and drug testing and on courtroom decision-makers' conversations about defendants' mental health and justifications for punishing behaviors related to illness.

INTERVIEWS

I interviewed legal professionals to learn about things I could not observe in court, including their interpretations of their own actions, their aims and concerns, and their emotional experiences.[12] In total, I conducted thirty-three interviews with those professionals, including thirteen prosecutors, thirteen defense attorneys (eleven public defenders and two private attorneys), and seven judges. Basic demographic information about these interview respondents is shown in table 3, below. I recruited prosecutors primarily through social connections and snowball sampling, judges mainly by calling and emailing their offices, and public defenders in person in their office, in a process facilitated by the head defender. Interviews explored the meanings these professionals attributed to diversion and its role in the court system, to compliance or noncompliance with treatment, to substance use and diagnoses of mental illness, and to legal punishment. Their patterns of thought have material consequences for the distribution of punishment. Prosecutors decide whether and how to charge criminal cases, whether to divert them, and what plea offers to make or sentences to ask for when they return to court. Judges can mandate people into treatment or drug testing and then use their outcomes as reasons to remand them to jail pretrial, revoke their probation or parole, or hold them in contempt of court and fine them. They can also require diverted defendants to appear for frequent court hearings, and they have the power to accept or reject plea deals, including those made at the point of entry into a diversion program or following defendants' return from such a program. As the people in charge

TABLE 3. Courtroom decision-makers, interview respondents ($N = 33$)

RACE, AS READ BY INTERVIEWER		
White	73%	24
Black	18%	6
Asian American	9%	3
GENDER, AS READ BY INTERVIEWER		
Woman	33%	11
Man	67%	22

of courtroom proceedings, judges also do the vast majority of the talking during those proceedings and so play an outsized role in shaping courtroom norms and logics. Finally, defense attorneys advise their clients on whether to accept diversion or not, and they participate in the daily interactions that produce shared understandings of mental illness and punishment.[13]

QUALITATIVE DATA ANALYSIS

I used the same approaches to analysis for all of the qualitative data I collected. I typed all of my fieldnotes and transcribed the interview recordings, giving participants pseudonyms as I went to protect anonymity. I read back over all of the transcripts, fieldnotes, and memos multiple times and wrote down the themes that emerged repeatedly. Then I used MaxQDA, a qualitative data-analysis software, to code everything. I started with the themes I had identified as I read through the data and applied codes related to those themes, including the challenges defendants faced as they progressed through the diversion program; the disjuncture between participants' understandings of program rules and enforcement and their operations in practice; decision-makers' evaluations of "compliant" and "noncompliant" defendants and the meanings attributed to those markers; and the range of legal and processual factors that shaped case outcomes. I refined, combined, and added to those codes inductively as I identified patterns across the data.[14] Wherever possible, I also triangulated participants' accounts of their legal cases with information drawn from court dockets, which give detailed accounts of court hearings and legal decisions for past and current defendants. Throughout the process, I applied the evidentiary criteria typically used in ethnographic research, searching for patterns across events that occurred repeatedly over the course of my fieldwork.[15]

COURT DOCKETS

To trace the flow of defendants through the court system and diversion, I collected case-history data for 394 defendants who had both entered and exited diversion between 2014 and 2017. Using case numbers that a journalist had obtained from the pretrial diversion program through a public-records request followed by legal action, I made a painstaking search of past court docket entries to compile full case histories for each of those individuals. There is a docket entry for every hearing and every motion filed in the case, describing the legal question or event and the judge's decision. In all, I gathered 2590 pages of court documents, which included information on defendants' race, gender, age, time spent in jail, bond amount, events and outcomes at every individual court date, any subsequent arrests, periods of disappearance, court fees and/or restitution amounts paid, charges added or dropped, and ultimate legal outcomes (such as time on probation or in prison for those returned from diversion). I read and coded these pages by hand to produce an anonymized dataset that I could use to look at patterns in the progression of diverted cases through the system and their outcomes.

EXPERIMENTAL SURVEY

Prosecutors play a central role in deciding punishment outcomes for everyone who enters the criminal courts, including those who are diverted. But decision-making among local prosecutors is almost entirely hidden from view, since prosecutors are not required to provide the court with any documentation of, or justifications for, their charging decisions or plea offers. Their decisions happen almost entirely behind closed doors and are very rarely subject to judicial review.[16] And even if we had good data on prosecutorial decision-making, it would still be hard to know whether their decisions were influenced by the availability of diversion. Prosecutors in offices with diversion might charge low-level cases more often, for instance, but that might be because of some other aspect of their offices or locations that made them more likely *both* to use diversion programs *and* to intervene more widely. Research indicates that factors such as agency culture and jurisdiction demographics powerfully shape prosecutorial practices.[17] In order to isolate the influence of diversion itself on decision-making, I fielded a vignette-based experiment on active state prosecutors. I presented prosecutors with case vignettes and asked them to make charging and plea-bargaining decisions about those cases. Half were randomly selected into a condition that also told them the cases were eligible for diversion. Any differences in outcomes between the two groups should thus be attributable to the diversion variable. For a detailed description of the survey design, participant recruitment, and full results, see methodological appendix B.

The National Landscape

PROGRAM STRUCTURE

Each diversion program operates with near-total autonomy. The National Association of Pretrial Services Agencies publishes best practices for pretrial diversion and offers some training for practitioners at its annual conferences, but programs are free to follow their guidance or not to. Directors never mentioned legal constraints as factors in their decisions about program structure. With the help of research assistants, I made a systematic search of legislation in six states—New York, Washington, Illinois, Pennsylvania, and Louisiana—with a number of active pretrial diversion programs that turned up only one statute related to internal operations of pretrial diversion programs. Even that statute (from Washington State) does not dictate specific program rules or requirements; it only specifies that programs should treat medications prescribed to treat heroin use disorder like any other prescription medication when responding to positive drug test results.

When I began my research, there was no available database documenting the prevalence or structures of pretrial diversion programs nationally. To situate my research within the national landscape, I created a new dataset. I began by taking a random sample of 20 percent of US cities with populations of over 100,000,[18] since more than 80 percent of the US population is concentrated in urban jurisdictions.[19] With the help of research assistants, I set out to find out a few basic facts about each of the sixty-four cities in the sample, including how many diversion programs they or the counties in which they were situated were currently operating, who was eligible for them, what their requirements looked like, and what happened to people's criminal cases if they completed the programs.

For each jurisdiction, we made a thorough internet search for official information about active adult diversion programs that promised alternatives to arrest or conviction or reduced sentences and that operated in the criminal courts (and outside of carceral settings). Every jurisdiction in our sample made mention of at least one diversion program on a government website or in an official report. But any information beyond the names of the programs was more difficult to come by. What information we did find was saved and processed into a large spreadsheet.

We then focused on gathering more detailed information about pretrial diversion programs operated by prosecutors' offices. In an effort to fill in the blanks in our dataset, we called and emailed each jurisdiction directly. Some of their websites listed phone numbers, email addresses, and names of individuals to contact. Others gave only generic information email or contact options, from which messages were almost never answered. When we were able to get through to an office at all, we often had to call or email multiple times and be passed around to multiple people—sometimes over weeks or months—before successfully reaching someone who could answer any of our questions. We contacted each of the jurisdictions in our sample an average of 2.9 times, and 33 percent of those jurisdictions eventually gave us basic information about at least some of their diversion programs.

Once we got someone on the phone, the depth of the information they could give us varied widely. Some staff members were knowledgeable and allocated plenty of time to explain the operations of their programs; others gave brief or less informative answers. But we added whatever we learned to our database. Two other members of the research team then returned to each of the jurisdictions to recheck the accuracy of the information in the database against any call notes and against the government websites and reports we had saved. Key results are shown in table 4.

PROGRAM DEMOGRAPHICS AND OUTCOMES

Information about how pretrial diversion programs operate still tells us nothing about the number, demographics, or legal outcomes of the people they enroll. To gather that information, I submitted public-records requests to agencies in each jurisdiction in the sample, requesting deidentified individual-level data on the age, race, sex, criminal charges, length of time in the program, program outcome, and final disposition of each person who had entered pretrial diversion over the previous five years. I also requested the number of people charged with felonies in the jurisdiction for each of those years. None of the jurisdictions provided enough of the requested data to allow me to estimate basic data points such as the percentage of defendants diverted in any given year or to track the ultimate legal outcomes of diversion participants. Agencies invariably told me that they did not track cases between diversion and the courts, meaning that they had no information about anyone's final legal outcomes. Many did not even track program completion, so they had no estimates of how often diversion was successful. One of the largest urban offices in the country—run by a progressive DA

TABLE 4. Adult diversion program characteristics from a random national sample of urban jurisdictions

Eligible charge types	Pretrial diversion programs, prosecutor-led (N = 98)	Specialty courts (N = 126)	All other diversion programs (N = 11)	Total: all programs (N = 235)
Substance use or sale	18.4%	29.4%	27.3%	24.7%
Other specific (e.g., sex work or other "quality-of-life" offenses)	22.5%	5.6%	9.1%	12.8%
Any low-level, nonviolent charge	38.8%	31.8%	54.6%	35.7%
Unspecified; discretionary	20.4%	33.3%	9.1%	26.8%
Total	100%	100%	100%	100%
Missing information	6.7%	11.9%	35.3%	11.3%

Legal stage	Pretrial diversion programs, prosecutor-led (N = 98)	Specialty courts (N = 123)	All other diversion programs (N = 14)	Total: all programs (N = 235)
Pre-booking	0%	0%	21.4%	1.3%
Pre-filing	10.2%	0%	0%	4.3%
Pre-plea	66.3%	22.0%	7.1%	39.6%
Post-plea	21.4%	38.2%	14.3%	29.8%
Post-conviction	0%	33.3%	35.7%	19.6%
Varies	2.0%	6.5%	21.4%	5.5%
Total	100%	100%	100%	100%
Missing information	6.7%	14.0%	17.7%	11.3%

with a professed commitment to data transparency and an active "data dashboard" on their website—responded as follows to our records request: "We may know that a case went into [a] diversion program, but not specifically how/if a program was successfully completed (*i.e.* like when a case is dismissed—we don't have the reason for the dismissal . . .)." And some programs claimed to collect no information at all about people entering

TABLE 4. *(continued)*

Other eligibility	Pretrial diversion programs, prosecutor-led (N = 105)	Specialty courts (N = 143)	All other diversion programs (N = 17)	Total: all programs (N = 265)
Limited criminal legal history	65.7%	44.1%	29.4%	51.7%
Diagnosis of mental disorder, including substance use disorder	16.2%	69.2%	41.2%	46.4%
Veteran	5.7%	18.2%	5.9%	12.5%
Unhoused	1.0%	4.2%	11.8%	3.4%
Other (e.g., women, parents, or under 25 only)	9.5%	12.6%	5.9%	10.9%
None specified or missing information	25.7%	28.0%	47.1%	28.3%

or exiting their diversion programs. Another of the largest counties in the country, run by another progressive DA three years into his term, sent a one-line email in response to our request: "Unfortunately, our office has not started tracking data on adult pretrial diversion programs."

PROGRESSIVE PROSECUTORS AND REFORM POLICIES

Finally, to situate diversion within the national political landscape, in a moment in which progressive prosecutors are winning elections in growing numbers of cities around the country, I created a dataset on the current practices and promises of district attorneys. In 2021 a research assistant and I created a comprehensive list of active DAs who had run on explicitly progressive platforms. We included all of those who had been endorsed by Real Justice, an organization at the forefront of promotion and campaign funding for progressive DA candidates; those endorsed by the progressive Color of Change PAC; and those listed in a 2020 journal article by two legal scholars who made a comprehensive survey and mapped progressive prosecutors around the country between 2016 and 2020. Our final list included fifty-three district attorneys.

We then conducted exhaustive internet searches for campaign websites, government websites, and reputable news stories on each of the district attorneys in our dataset. We downloaded everything we could find on the policies that they had promised to implement or that they implemented publicly once in office, including the information published on their official websites and 647 articles from major newspapers covering their campaigns and administrations. We then coded all of that information, identifying thirty-nine distinct types of policies and practices that they had either promised to implement or announced publicly that they had implemented. Most of those thirty-nine policy approaches fell into broader categories of transparency, procedural justice, accountability for the powerful, witness support, and reduced punishment. Ninety-eight percent of them (all but one) had explicitly promised to expand or start new pretrial diversion programs or reported having done so.

Methodological Appendix B
Experimental Survey

To understand whether and how the availability of pretrial diversion affects prosecutorial decision-making, I fielded an experimental survey on state prosecutors. Below I describe in detail the design of the study and its experimental conditions, the content of the vignettes that were shown to respondents, respondent recruitment, data analysis, and results.

Experimental Procedure

I conducted a between-subjects experimental study to test (1) whether prosecutors who are told that pretrial diversion is available are more or less inclined to accept felony charges and (2) whether prosecutors tend to select more or less punitive plea deals for defendants who return to court without completing diversion. Study participants, who were all active state prosecutors, were asked to review two case vignettes—a felony drug case and a felony check fraud case—and to draw on their experiences to make charging and plea-bargaining decisions about them. The vignettes reviewed by all prosecutors were identical except for two factors, which varied independently of one other.

The primary axis of variation was the availability of diversion: Half of all prosecutors, selected at random, were told before making a charging decision that the case would be eligible for pretrial diversion. They were then told, before selecting a plea deal to offer, to imagine that the diverted defendant had returned to court without completing diversion. The rest of the participants were not given that information. Because prosecutors were randomly assigned to diversion and nondiversion conditions, any differences in charging or plea-bargaining patterns between the two conditions could then be attributed to that factor.

A secondary axis of variation was the race of the suspect and defendant: Half of all prosecutors, again randomly selected, were told that the

TABLE 5. Experimental study design

	NO DIVERSION	DIVERSION
White individual	Condition 1 (no diversion option, White individual)	Condition 3 (diversion option, White individual)
Black individual	Condition 2 (no diversion option, Black individual)	Condition 4 (diversion option, Black individual)

individuals in question were White, while the other half were told that they were Black. Because the state exercises more intensive and punitive control over the lives of Black people,[1] I hypothesized that prosecutors would be more likely to take advantage of a new means and justification to expand criminal legal control—pretrial diversion—when the individual in question was described as Black.

Each prosecutor saw two vignettes with the same independent variables, such that any individual respondent could not know what factors were manipulated across conditions. Again, random assignment was used to place each prosecutor in one of the four conditions. Table 5 shows the four conditions into which prosecutors were randomly assigned.

Survey Content

Each prosecutor was randomly assigned to one of the four conditions by Qualtrics, the survey platform, when they opened the survey. They were given a standard consent form telling them that their participation was anonymous and voluntary and asking for their consent to continue. Those who agreed were asked whether they were active state prosecuting attorneys, and only those who answered "yes" were permitted to continue. Prosecutors were then presented with two case vignettes and a series of questions about them, which I created and edited with the help of nine prosecutors and criminal defense attorneys from six different jurisdictions, to maximize ecological validity. The full survey text is shown below, with the suspect's race indicated in brackets to signal that it was varied across conditions.

CASE 1

Imagine that you have been assigned the following case for screening:

A twenty-year-old [white/black] male with no previous arrest record was arrested for check fraud—a felony offense in your jurisdiction—after attempting to cash a $2500 personal check written out to him from a bank account that had been closed the previous year. The suspect told the arresting officer that he had accepted the check as payment for construction work for a neighbor, whose name matched that on the closed account. The neighbor informed the investigating officer that he had closed the account in question after his checkbook had disappeared and that he had paid the suspect in cash for the construction work. The same neighbor has one prior conviction for check fraud.

[*Conditions 3 and 4 only*: Assume that if the case is accepted, the suspect will be eligible for a pretrial diversion program run by your office, in which he would be evaluated by a social worker and assigned to an appropriate course of treatment, drug testing, and/or classes. If he completed the program successfully, charges against him would be dropped.]

Based on the information above, how likely would you be to accept this case for prosecution?

- Very likely
- Somewhat likely
- Somewhat unlikely
- Very unlikely

A twenty-year-old [white/black] male with no previous arrest record was arrested for check fraud—a felony offense in your jurisdiction—after attempting to cash a $2500 personal check written out to him from a bank account that had been closed the previous year. The suspect told the arresting officer that he had accepted the check as payment for construction work for a neighbor, whose name matched that on the closed account. The neighbor informed the investigating officer that he had closed the account in question after his checkbook had disappeared and that he had paid the suspect in cash for the construction work. The same neighbor has one prior conviction for check fraud.

[*Conditions 1 and 3 only*: Assuming the case had been accepted, what kind of plea deal would you most likely be able to offer the defendant?]

[*Conditions 2 and 4 only*: Assuming the case had been accepted and the defendant had entered diversion but failed to comply with program requirements, so that the case was returned to you for prosecution, what kind of plea deal would you most likely be able to offer the defendant?]

Three drop-down menus:

CHARGE TYPE	SENTENCE TYPE	SENTENCE LENGTH	
Misdemeanor	Inactive/ unsupervised probation	0 year	0 month
Felony	Active/supervised probation	1 year	1 month
	Prison or jail time	2 years	2 months
	Deferred probation	3 years	3 months
		4 years	4 months
		5 years	5 months
		Other____	6 months
			7 months
			8 months
			9 months
			Under a month

Following another page break, respondents were presented with a second case to evaluate. The questions are identical. The vignette is below.

CASE 2

Imagine that you have been assigned the following case for screening:

A nineteen-year-old [white/black] male with no previous arrest record was arrested for possession of prescription drugs without a valid prescription, a felony offense in your jurisdiction. The arresting officer had stopped the suspect for driving with a broken headlight and reports that he acted suspicious as the officer approached the vehicle. The suspect consented to a search, and a plastic bag containing thirty loose pills was found under the passenger's seat. The suspect produced a prescription in his name for the pills, five months past its expiration date. Laboratory analysis of the pills proved positive for opiates.

Finally, each respondent was asked to estimate the number of cases on their current caseload and to indicate whether their jurisdiction had a felony pretrial diversion program. They were thanked for their participation and offered an Amazon credit where applicable. They were not asked to give demographic information, since that information was not related to the study hypotheses and could have compromised respondent anonymity within the relatively small participating offices.

Recruitment

The two district attorneys' offices that distributed the survey to the prosecuting attorneys on staff were urban offices in the US South and Midwest, respectively. Both agreed to distribute the survey after I made contact through acquaintances who worked with them. Prosecutors in the office in the South were offered incentives in the form of $20 in Amazon credit for each respondent. Those in the Midwestern office were not offered incentives, at the request of the supervising attorney who sent out the survey. Both participating offices emailed the survey link inviting prosecuting attorneys to participate in an anonymous study that would examine how actors in the criminal justice system process information and make decisions. Roughly 63 percent of all invited attorneys consented to participate. (This rate of uptake is substantially higher than is typical for web-based surveys, whose response rates tend to range between 2 and 33 percent.[2]) Ninety-three percent of the respondents who began the survey completed it.

COVID-19 was declared a pandemic and a national emergency as prosecutors from the second office were still taking the survey. On March 11, 2020, efforts began to reduce jail populations in their jurisdiction, in part by deprioritizing prosecution of low-level charges. Because the eight respondents who took the survey after that date were working in a very different context from the rest, I excluded their responses from my analyses. (Inclusion of those responses does not alter results.) I also paused survey recruitment, since the emergency directives being issued to police and prosecutors around the country meant that any new responses might not be representative of typical charging practices. I was left with just seventy responses, well short of the two hundred that I had calculated would be needed for statistically significant results.

Analysis

Prosecutors were given four options for rating the likelihood of charging a case: very likely (coded as 3) somewhat likely, somewhat unlikely, and very unlikely (coded as 0). Responses to both vignettes were aggregated, giving each respondent a total possible score of 6. For plea offers, felony/misdemeanor offers were coded as 0/1 and aggregated across vignettes, so that a total score of 0 would indicate that a respondent had selected misdemeanor plea deals for both case vignettes, while a 2 would indicate that she had selected felony plea deals for both.

Because study respondents are randomly assigned to experimental conditions, the research design allows estimation of the treatment effect without inclusion of control variables in the statistical models.[3] In fact, adjusting for respondent characteristics when working with "clean data," or data for which random assignment can be stipulated, can invalidate findings.[4] I thus use a two-tailed t-test and Mann-Whitney U test to compare means between conditions to measure the effects of the parameter of interest: here, the availability of diversion. Statistical tests show that the assumption of equal variance in the two groups holds. Table 6 shows the means, and differences between means, on the primary dependent variables across conditions (diversion and nondiversion).

Results: Main Effects

To assess the main effects of diversion on prosecutorial decision-making, I combined data from conditions 1 and 2 and compared it to data from conditions 3 and 4 (see table 5). I find that prosecutors are more likely to bring charges when they are told they can divert the case in question and that they select more punitive plea-deal offers when they are told that a defendant has returned from diversion without completing it. In other words, pretrial diversion tends to widen the penal net, encouraging prosecutors to draw more people into the court system and to punish them more severely once they are there. These main effects are presented in the body of this book in bar graphs and in table 6, below.

Results: Race and Interaction Effects

Descriptively, the effects associated with diversion availability are in the same directions across race conditions, and they are statistically significant in the context of charging decisions. I was not able to test for interaction

TABLE 6. Means and differences across conditions

	Nondiversion condition	Diversion condition	Mean difference across conditions	Significance of difference
Mean likelihood of case acceptance (scale: 0–6)	2.24 (1.62)	3.19 (1.74)	0.95**	$p < 0.01$
Mean frequency of felony plea-deal offer (scale: 0–2)	0.68 (0.85)	1.00 (0.87)	0.32*	$p < 0.05$

effects because the study was so underpowered (that is, the sample was smaller than it needed to be to detect statistically significant effects). But below and in table 7, I outline some descriptive findings that could be useful to inform future studies.

The difference in likelihood of case acceptance between diversion and nondiversion conditions is significant (at $p < 0.05$) when I include in the model only responses from conditions in which suspects are described as White and the same for those in which defendants are described as Black. Descriptively, the increase in the likelihood of charging a case when diversion is available is 10 percent greater for Black than for White suspects (1.02, compared with 0.93).

The differences in likely plea-bargain offers between diversion and nondiversion conditions are not significant when the dataset is divided in half by race condition. Effects are in the same directions across conditions, however: Likelihood of a charge reduction appears lower in the diversion conditions than in the nondiversion conditions. Descriptively, the penalty for treatment noncompletion may also be greater for Black defendants. The difference across diversion conditions in frequency of felony (rather than misdemeanor) plea offers is 68 percent greater for Black than for White defendants (0.42, compared with 0.25).

As shown in table 7, the baseline likelihood of case acceptance and frequency of felony plea-deal offer are lower for Black individuals, which is inconsistent with previous research indicating that Black individuals are no less likely to have their cases accepted and that prosecutors seek harsher sentences for them.[5] Overall, findings present some evidence of social desirability,

TABLE 7. Means and differences across conditions, by defendant race

	WHITE INDIVIDUALS ($N = 35$)			BLACK INDIVIDUALS ($N = 35$)		
	Nondiversion condition	Diversion condition	Difference	Nondiversion condition	Diversion condition	Difference
Mean likelihood of case acceptance (scale: 0–6)	2.55 (1.64)	3.48 (1.89)	0.93*	1.88 (1.58)	2.9 (1.55)	1.02*
Mean frequency of felony plea-deal offer (scale: 0–1)	0.80 (0.89)	1.05 (0.80)	0.25	0.53 (0.80)	0.95 (0.95)	0.42

Standard deviation in parentheses
*$p < 0.05$

or "the tendency of research subjects to choose responses they believe are more socially desirable or acceptable rather than choosing responses that are reflective of their true thoughts or feelings."[6] This tendency has been widely documented in research on racism, including research using experimental designs: Respondents often report more generous behavior or attitudes toward Black people than would be observed in the real world, for instance.[7] Across conditions, prosecutors reported lower likelihood of charging Black suspects and higher likelihood of offering Black suspects charge reductions in the plea-bargaining process. Those responses are in direct contradiction to a large body of evidence that prosecutors are more punitive toward Black suspects at both of those decision-making junctures.[8]

Taken together, my findings indicate that net-widening effects are present for both Black and White individuals and that they may be larger when the accused individuals are described as Black. These findings are consistent with a large body of literature about state control over people who are Black. If these results were confirmed in a larger study, they would have important implications for punishment and inequality.

Methodological Appendix C

Cities in National Sample

1. Abilene, Texas
2. Allen, Texas
3. Anaheim, California
4. Arlington, Texas
5. Aurora, Colorado
6. Austin, Texas
7. Bridgeport, Connecticut
8. Cambridge, Massachusetts
9. Carmel, Indiana
10. Cedar Rapids, Iowa
11. Centennial, Colorado
12. Charleston, South Carolina
13. Clarksville, Tennessee
14. Clovis, California
15. Dallas, Texas
16. Davie, Florida
17. El Monte, California
18. Elizabeth, New Jersey
19. Eugene, Oregon
20. Fairfield, California
21. Fayetteville, North Carolina
22. Fort Wayne, Indiana
23. Garland, Texas
24. Greeley, Colorado
25. Green Bay, Wisconsin
26. Greensboro, North Carolina
27. Hialeah, Florida
28. Inglewood, California
29. Jersey City, New Jersey

30. Lansing, Michigan
31. Laredo, Texas
32. Las Cruces, New Mexico
33. Lincoln, Nebraska
34. Long Beach, California
35. Los Angeles, California
36. Lubbock, Texas
37. Mesa, Arizona
38. New Haven, Connecticut
39. New Orleans, Louisiana
40. North Las Vegas, Nevada
41. Norwalk, California
42. Odessa, Texas
43. Oklahoma City, Oklahoma
44. Olathe, Kansas
45. Omaha, Nebraska
46. Oxnard, California
47. Pomona, California
48. Port St. Lucie, Florida
49. Rochester, New York
50. Rockford, Illinois
51. Roseville, California
52. San Buenaventura, California
53. Sandy Springs, Georgia
54. Simi Valley, California
55. Sparks, Nevada
56. St. Louis, Missouri
57. Stamford, Connecticut
58. Syracuse, New York
59. Tampa, Florida
60. Toledo, Ohio
61. Tulsa, Oklahoma
62. Vallejo, California
63. Virginia Beach, Virginia
64. Worcester, Massachusetts

Notes

INTRODUCTION

1. Vera Institute of Justice, "Diversion Programs, Explained," 2022, https://www.vera.org/inline-downloads/diversion-programs-explained.pdf; American Civil Liberties Union, "Blueprint for Smart Justice," ACLU: Smart Justice, 2019, https://50stateblueprint.aclu.org/assets/reports/SJ-Blueprint-IN.pdf; Brennan Center for Justice, "Right on Crime," https://rightoncrime.com/about/; Rick Perry, "Follow the Texas Model," in *Solutions: American Leaders Speak Out on Criminal Justice*, ed. Inimai Chettiar and Michael Waldman (New York: Brennan Center for Justice, 2015), 89–92; Johns Hopkins Bloomberg School of Public Health, "Criminal Justice Diversion Programs: Policy Recommendations for Maryland," 2015," https://www.jhsph.edu/research/centers-and-institutes/institute-for-health-and-social-policy/award-programs/lipitz-award/past-awardees/_documents/Criminal-Justice-Diversion.pdf (page discontinued); Texas Criminal Justice Coalition, "Interim Testimony 2016: Senate Committee on Criminal Justice," 2016, https://www.texascjc.org/system/files/publications/Senate CJ Interim Testimony %28Pretrial Diversion %26 Treatment%29.pdf.

2. The 4 percent rearrest rate among people who completed this pretrial diversion program is dramatically lower than that seen elsewhere in the criminal legal system. An estimated 66 percent of state prisoners are rearrested within three years, for instance. Bureau of Justice Statistics, "Recidivism of Prisoners Released in 24 States in 2008: A 10-Year Follow-Up Period (2008–2018)" (US Department of Justice, 2021), https://bjs.ojp.gov/sites/g/files/xyckuh236/files/media/document/rpr24s0810yfup0818_sum.pdf.

3. National Center on Addiction and Substance Abuse at Columbia University, "Behind Bars II: Substance Abuse and America's Prison Population," 2010, https://www.centeronaddiction.org/addiction-research/reports/behind-bars-ii-substance-abuse-and-america's-prison-population.

4. SAMHSA [Substance Abuse and Mental Health Services Administration], *Treatment Episode Data Set (TEDS): Admissions to and Discharges from Publicly Funded Substance Use Treatment* (Rockville, MD: Substance Abuse and Mental Health Services Administration, 2019), https://www.samhsa.gov/data/data-we-collect/teds-treatment-episode-data-set.

5. Many state and federal funds are allocated specifically to diversion programs, and many more fund substance use treatment programs that provide services to both voluntary and court-mandated clients (court-mandated clients constitute about 27 percent of the total). SAMHSA, *Treatment Episode Data Set (TEDS)*; SAMHSA

[Substance Abuse and Mental Health Services Administration], *Justification of Estimates for Appropriations Committees, Fiscal Year 2024*, https://www.samhsa.gov/sites/default/files/samhsa-fy-2024-cj.pdf; US Department of Health and Human Services, "Biden-Harris Administration Announces $28 Million in Funding Opportunities for Grants Expanding Treatment Services for Substance Use Disorder," 2024, https://www.samhsa.gov/newsroom/press-announcements/20240202/biden-harris-administration-announces-28-million-funding-opportunities-grants-expanding-treatment-services-substance-use-disorder.

6. Inimai Chettiar and Michael Waldman, eds., *Solutions: American Leaders Speak Out on Criminal Justice* (New York: Brennan Center for Justice, 2015); Heritage Foundation, "Rogue U.S. Attorneys Coming to a City near You?," 2020, https://www.heritage.org/node/24579251/print-display; Critical Resistance, "Urgent! Take Action Against Proposed New SF Jail," 2017, http://criticalresistance.org/take-action-jail-11-17/; Catherine Camilletti, "Pretrial Diversion Programs: Research Summary," Bureau of Justice Assistance, 2010, https://bja.ojp.gov/sites/g/files/xyckuh186/files/media/document/PretrialDiversionResearchSummary.pdf; Johns Hopkins Bloomberg School of Public Health, "Criminal Justice Diversion Programs"; Texas Criminal Justice Coalition, "Interim Testimony 2016: Senate Committee on Criminal Justice"; American Civil Liberties Union, "Blueprint for Smart Justice"; Vera Institute of Justice, "Diversion Programs, Explained."

7. Analysis of explicitly "progressive" prosecutors' campaign promises is based on a dataset described in methodological appendix A. Information about other candidates for DA is based on an analysis of news articles (from a Google alert for "pretrial diversion" from 2017 to the present). See, e.g., Ann Montgomery, "Candidate Questionnaire—DA Incumbent," *Waxahachie Sun*, 2024, https://www.waxahachiesun.com/candidate-questionnaire-ann-montgomery-da-incumbent/article_de920ef8cf59-11ee-82b3-eba82213b869.html; Charles Ramo, "The DA Needs to Be an Active Role," *The Auburn Plainsman*, 2020, https://www.theplainsman.com/article/2020/02/the-da-needs-to-be-an-active-role; Chris Caraveo, "2020 Elections Q&A: Maricopa County Attorney," *Daily Independent*, 2020, https://yourvalley.net/stories/2020-elections-qa-maricopa-county-attorney,171452; "Candidate Q&A: Kostiha Hopes to Remain County Attorney," *Mineral Wells Index*, 2020, https://www.mineralwellsindex.com/news/candidate-q-a-kostiha-hopes-to-remain-county-attorney/article_fef5432e-5012-11ea-bbfc-5f521ccbe343.html; Erin Kelly, "Grace, Coleman Discuss Pre-Trial Diversion, Safety in Race for District Attorney," *The Meridian Star*, 2019, 600, https://www.meridianstar.com/news/local_news/grace-coleman-discuss-pre-trial-diversion-safety-in-race-for/article_f8e531b4-2da9-5197-bbdd-122c8314f91e.html; Samantha Serbin, "Columbus Attorney Challenges Incumbent for District Attorney of the Chattahoochee Judicial Circuit," WTVM, 2020, https://www.wtvm.com/2020/03/11/columbus-attorney-challenges-incumbent-district-attorney-chattahoochee-judicial-circuit/; Staff Report, "Cooke Co. DA Seeking 2nd Term in 2020," *Gainesville Register*, 2020, https://www.gainesvilleregister.com/news/local_news/cooke-co-da-seeking-nd-term-in/article_a1791d38-0a53-11ea-bfc5-73573c5ca69e.html; Leon Stafford, "Henry DA Pattillo Receives Justice Award from County Branch of NAACP," *The Atlanta Journal-Constitution*, 2020, https://www.ajc.com/news/local/henry-pattillo-receives-justice-award-from-county-branch-naacp/JTe6OHgktSb1j7wCxHrp7K/; Tyler Estep, "Gwinnett's Longtime DA Considering Running as a Democrat in 2020," *The Atlanta*

Journal-Constitution, 2019, https://www.ajc.com/news/local/gwinnett-longtime-considering-running-democrat-2020/wL3ocEtEgVObxzcGjdmGAM/.

8. SAMHSA, "Key Substance Use and Mental Health Indicators in the United States: Results from the 2017 National Survey on Drug Use and Health" (Center for Behavioral Health Statistics and Quality, Substance Abuse and Mental Health Services Administration, 2018), https://www.samhsa.gov/data/sites/default/files/cbhsq-reports/NSDUHFFR2017/NSDUHFFR2017.htm.

9. The definition of "mental illness" here is taken from US Department of Health and Human Services, *Mental Health: A Report of the Surgeon General* (Rockville, MD: DHHS, 1999), 5. Estimates of the prevalence of mental disorders are taken from National Center on Addiction and Substance Abuse at Columbia University, "Behind Bars II," and Doris J. James and Lauren E. Glaze, "Bureau of Justice Statistics Special Report: Mental Health Problems of Prison and Jail Inmates," Bureau of Justice Statistics, 2006. It should be noted that measuring rates of mental illness is complicated. The category of "mental illness" itself is contested, and definitions of madness in general and of particular diagnoses have shifted over time and have always been biased by racialized, classed, and gendered logics. Michael Rembis, "The New Asylums: Madness and Mass Incarceration in the Neoliberal Era," in *Disability Incarcerated: Imprisonment and Disability in the United States and Canada*, ed. Liat Ben-Moshe, Chris Chapman, and Allison C. Carey (New York: Palgrave Macmillan, 2014), 139–59; Owen Whooley, "Nosological Reflections: The Failure of *DSM-5*, the Emergence of RDoC, and the Decontextualization of Mental Distress," *Society and Mental Health* 4, no. 2 (2014): 92–110; Jonathan M. Metzl, *The Protest Psychosis: How Schizophrenia Became a Black Disease* (Boston: Beacon Press, 2009). The *DSM-5* also provides broad categories for diagnosis of illnesses and leaves treatment providers with wide discretion in their diagnosis and treatment. Providers' decisions are often biased across race, class, and gender. American Psychiatric Association, *Diagnostic and Statistical Manual of Mental Disorders*, 5th ed., 2022, https://doi.org/10.1176/appi.books.9780890425787 (hereafter *DSM-5*); Howard N. Garb, "Race Bias and Gender Bias in the Diagnosis of Psychological Disorders," *Clinical Psychology Review* 90 (2021): 102087–102087. Estimates of the prevalence of mental disorder in carceral settings vary across studies. See, e.g., Seena Fazel, Parveen Bains, and Helen Doll, "Substance Abuse and Dependence in Prisoners: A Systematic Review," *Addiction* 101, no. 2 (February 2006): 181–91.

10. Antoine Bechara, "Decision Making, Impulse Control and Loss of Willpower to Resist Drugs: A Neurocognitive Perspective," *Nature Neuroscience* 8, no. 11 (November 2005): 1458–63; Keith Humphreys and Warren K. Bickel, "Toward a Neuroscience of Long-Term Recovery from Addiction," *JAMA Psychiatry* 75, no. 9 (2018): 875–76; National Institute on Drug Abuse, "The Science of Drug Use and Addiction: The Basics," National Institute of Health, 2021; American Psychiatric Association, *DSM-5*.

11. National Center on Addiction and Substance Abuse at Columbia University, "Behind Bars II."

12. Many people with co-occurring disorders are arrested on minor charges multiple times every year. See analyses of 2017 to 2019 data from the National Survey on Drug Use and Health: Pew Charitable Trusts, "More than 1 in 9 People with Co-Occurring Mental Illness and Substance Use Disorders Are Arrested Annually," 2023, https://www.pewtrusts.org/en/research-and-analysis/issue-briefs/2023/02/over-1-in-9-people-with-co-occurring-mental-illness-and-substance-use-disorders-arrested-annually#:~:text=Adults

%20with%20co%2Doccurring%20disorders%20made%20up%202%25%20of%20the,as%20the%20most%20serious%20charge; Alexi Jones and Wendy Sawyer, "Arrest, Release, Repeat: How Police and Jails Are Misused to Respond to Social Problems," Prison Policy Initiative, 2019, https://www.prisonpolicy.org/reports/repeatarrests.html. As of 2010, an estimated 24.4 percent of incarcerated people met medical criteria for co-occurring disorders. National Center on Addiction and Substance Abuse at Columbia University, "Behind Bars II."

13. SAMHSA, "Behavioral Health Trends in the United States: Results from the 2014 National Survey on Drug Use and Health," Substance Abuse and Mental Health Services Administration, 2015, https://www.samhsa.gov/data/sites/default/files/NSDUH-FRR1-2014/NSDUH-FRR1-2014.pdf; National Institute on Drug Abuse, "Common Comorbidities with Substance Use Disorders Research Report," 2020, https://www.ncbi.nlm.nih.gov/books/NBK571451/.

14. The Pew Charitable Trusts, "Drug Arrests Stayed High Even as Imprisonment Fell from 2009 to 2019," February 15, 2022, https://www.pewtrusts.org/en/research-and-analysis/issue-briefs/2022/02/drug-arrests-stayed-high-even-as-imprisonment-fell-from-2009-to-2019; Bureau of Justice Statistics, "Drugs and Crime Facts (NCJ 165148)," 2002, https://bjs.ojp.gov/content/pub/pdf/dcf.pdf; Federal Bureau of Investigation, "Crime in the United States, 2019," https://ucr.fbi.gov/crime-in-the-u.s/2019/crime-in-the-u.s.-2019/topic-pages/offenses-known-to-law-enforcement.

15. Brian Elderbroom and Julia Durnan, "Reclassified: State Drug Law Reforms to Reduce Felony Convictions and Increase Second Chances" (Urban Institute, 2018), https://www.urban.org/sites/default/files/publication/99077/reclassified_state_drug_law_reforms_to_reduce_felony_convictions_and_increase_second_chances.pdf.

16. Yvonne Zylan and Sarah A. Soule, "Ending Welfare as We Know It (Again): Welfare State Retrenchment, 1989–1995," *Social Forces* 79, no. 2 (2000): 623–52; Matthew Desmond, *Poverty, by America* (New York: Crown, 2023); Issa Kohler-Hausmann, *Misdemeanorland: Criminal Courts and Social Control in an Age of Broken Windows Policing* (Princeton, NJ: Princeton University Press, 2018).

17. Graham Thornicroft, *Shunned: Discrimination Against People with Mental Illness* (Oxford and New York: Oxford University Press, 2006); Joe Soss, Richard C. Fording, and Sanford F. Schram, *Disciplining the Poor: Neoliberal Paternalism and the Persistent Power of Race* (Chicago: University of Chicago Press, 2011).

18. Sonya Acosta and Erik Gartland, "Families Wait Years for Housing Vouchers Due to Inadequate Funding" (Center on Budget and Policy Priorities, July 22, 2021), https://www.cbpp.org/sites/default/files/7-22-21hous.pdf; Patricia Strach, Katie Zuber, and Elizabeth Perez-Chiques, "Why Policies Fail: The Illusion of Services in the Opioid Epidemic," *Journal of Health Politics, Policy and Law* 45, no. 2 (2020): 341–64; Richard G. Frank, Keith Humphreys, and Harold Pollack, "Our Other Epidemic: Addiction," *JAMA Health Forum* 2, no. 3 (2021): e210273; American Hospital Association, "Statement of the American Hospital Association to the Committee on Ways and Means of the United States House of Representatives: America's Mental Health Crisis," February 2, 2022, https://www.aha.org/system/files/media/file/2022/02/aha-house-statement-ways-and-means-committee-americas-mental-health-crisis-statement-2-2-22.pdf; Joe Soss, Richard C. Fording, and Sanford F. Schram,

Disciplining the Poor: Neoliberal Paternalism and the Persistent Power of Race (Chicago: University of Chicago Press, 2011).

It is important to note that these shifts have occurred even as spending on public healthcare has increased and that reductions in inpatient capacity in public hospitals have been driven not just by budget cuts but also because reducing that capacity was a way for local governments to receive more federal funding. See Armando Lara-Millán, *Redistributing the Poor: Jails, Hospitals, and the Crisis of Law and Fiscal Austerity* (Oxford and New York: Oxford University Press, 2021).

19. Pamela Herd and Donald P. Moynihan, *Administrative Burden: Policymaking by Other Means* (New York: Russell Sage Foundation, 2018); Julian Christensen et al., "Human Capital and Administrative Burden: The Role of Cognitive Resources in Citizen-State Interactions," *Public Administration Review* 80, no. 1 (January 2020): 127–36.

20. US Department of Housing and Urban Development, "HUD 2022 Continuum of Care Homeless Assistance Programs Homeless Populations and Subpopulations," December 6, 2022, https://files.hudexchange.info/reports/published/CoC_PopSub_NatlTerrDC_2022.pdf; Lydie A. Lebrun-Harris et al., "Health Status and Health Care Experiences Among Homeless Patients in Federally Supported Health Centers: Findings from the 2009 Patient Survey," *Health Services Research* 48, no. 3 (June 2013): 992–1017.

21. National Law Center on Homelessness & Poverty, "Housing Not Handcuffs: Ending the Criminalization of Homelessness in U.S. Cities," 2019, https://homelesslaw.org/wp-content/uploads/2019/12/HOUSING-NOT-HANDCUFFS-2019-FINAL.pdf; Roshan Abraham, "A Palantir Co-Founder Is Pushing Laws to Criminalize Homeless Encampments Nationwide," *Vice*, March 13, 2023, https://www.vice.com/en/article/qjvdmq/a-palantir-co-founder-is-pushing-laws-to-criminalize-homeless-encampments-nationwide; City of Grants Pass, Oregon v. Johnson et al., No. 23–175 (Supreme Court of the United States June 28, 2024).

22. William H. Fisher et al., "Patterns and Prevalence of Arrest in a Statewide Cohort of Mental Health Care Consumers," *Psychiatric Services* 57, no. 11 (November 2006): 1623–28.

23. Kohler-Hausmann, *Misdemeanorland*.

24. Christopher Wildeman and Emily A. Wang, "Mass Incarceration, Public Health, and Widening Inequality in the USA," *The Lancet* 389 (2017): 1464–74; Michael Massoglia and William Alex Pridemore, "Incarceration and Health," *Annual Review of Sociology* 41 (2015): 291–310; Lauren C. Porter and Laura M. Demarco, "Beyond the Dichotomy: Incarceration Dosage and Mental Health," *Criminology* 57, no. 1 (2019): 136–56; Lauren C. Porter and Meghan A. Novisky, "Pathways to Depressive Symptoms Among Former Inmates," *Justice Quarterly* 34, no. 5 (2017): 847–72; Keramet Reiter and Thomas Blair, "Punishing Mental Illness: Trans-Institutionalization and Solitary Confinement in the United States," in *Extreme Punishment: Comparative Studies in Detention, Incarceration and Solitary Confinement*, ed. Keramet Reiter and Alexa Koenig (New York: Palgrave MacMillan, 2015), 177–96; Keramet Reiter, *23/7: Pelican Bay Prison and the Rise of Long-Term Solitary Confinement* (New Haven, CT: Yale University Press, 2016).

25. Vijaya Murali and Femi Oyebode, "Poverty, Social Inequality and Mental Health," *Advances in Psychiatric Treatment* 10 (2004): 216–24.

26. Bryan L. Sykes and Michelle Maroto, "A Wealth of Inequalities: Mass Incarceration, Employment, and Racial Disparities in U.S. Household Wealth, 1996 to 2011," *RSF: The Russell Sage Foundation Journal of the Social Sciences* 2, no. 6 (2016): 129–52; Robert Apel and Gary Sweeten, "The Impact of Incarceration on Employment during the Transition to Adulthood," *Social Problems* 57, no. 3 (2010): 448–79; Bruce Western, "The Impact of Incarceration on Wage Mobility and Inequality," *American Sociological Review* 67, no. 4 (2002): 526–46; Sarah Brayne, "Surveillance and System Avoidance: Criminal Justice Contact and Institutional Attachment," *American Sociological Review* 79, no. 3 (2014): 367–91; Claire W. Herbert, Jeffrey D. Morenoff, and David J. Harding, "Homelessness and Housing Insecurity Among Former Prisoners," *RSF: The Russell Sage Foundation Journal of the Social Sciences* 1, no. 2 (2015): 44–79; Christopher Mele and Teresa Miller, eds., *Civil Penalties, Social Consequences* (New York: Routledge, 2005); National Inventory of Collateral Consequences of Conviction, "Collateral Consequences Inventory," 2023, https://niccc.nationalreentryresourcecenter.org/consequences.

27. Christopher Uggen et al., "The Edge of Stigma: An Experimental Audit of the Effects of Low-Level Criminal Records on Employment," *Criminology* 52, no. 4 (2014): 627–54; American Bar Association, "Collateral Consequences of Criminal Convictions: Judicial Bench Book," 2018, https://www.ojp.gov/pdffiles1/nij/grants/251583.pdf.

28. Doris A. Fuller et al., "Overlooked in the Undercounted: The Role of Mental Illness in Fatal Law Enforcement Encounters," 2015, https://www.treatmentadvocacycenter.org/storage/documents/overlooked-in-the-undercounted.pdf.

29. Samuel L. Dickman, David U. Himmelstein, and Steffie Woolhandler, "Inequality and the Health-Care System in the USA," *The Lancet* 389 (2017): 1431–41; SAMHSA, "Racial/Ethnic Differences in Mental Health Service Use Among Adults," Substance Abuse and Mental Health Services Administration, 2015, https://store.samhsa.gov/product/racialethnic-differences-mental-health-service-use-among-adults/sma15-4906; Jones and Sawyer, "Arrest, Release, Repeat"; Shytierra Gaston, "Producing Race Disparities: A Study of Drug Arrests Across Place and Race," *Criminology* 57, no. 3 (2019): 424–51; Katherine Beckett et al., "Drug Use, Drug Possession Arrests, and the Question of Race: Lessons from Seattle," *Social Problems* 52, no. 3 (2005): 419–41; Kohler-Hausmann, *Misdemeanorland*; Jeffrey Fagan and Garth Davies, "Street Stops and Broken Windows: Terry, Race, and Disorder in New York City," *Fordham Urban Law Journal* 28, no. 2 (2000): 457–504; Mona Lynch et al., "Policing the 'Progressive' City: The Racialized Geography of Drug Law Enforcement," *Theoretical Criminology* 17, no. 3 (2013): 335–57.

30. Michelle Alexander, *The New Jim Crow: Mass Incarceration in the Age of Colorblindness* (New York: The New Press, 2012); Doris Marie Provine, "Race and Inequality in the War on Drugs," *Annual Review of Law and Social Science* 7 (2011): 41–60; Doris Marie Provine, *Unequal Under Law: Race in the War on Drugs* (Chicago: University of Chicago Press, 2007).

31. Institute for Crime & Justice Policy Research, University of London, "World Prison Brief," 2024, https://www.prisonstudies.org/highest-to-lowest/prison

-population-total?field_region_taxonomy_tid=All; Roy Walmsley, "World Prison Population List," National Institute of Corrections, 2015, https://nicic.gov/resources/nic-library/all-library-items/world-prison-population-listeleventh-edition.

32. Deborah M. Ahrens, "Retroactive Legality: Marijuana Convictions and Restorative Justice in an Era of Criminal Justice Reform," *Journal of Criminal Law and Criminology* 110, no. 3 (2020): 379–440; Courtney Black, "Mental-Health Courts: Expanding the Model in an Era of Criminal Justice Reform," *Washington University Journal of Law and Policy* 63 (2020): 299–323.

33. Pew Research Center, "America's New Drug Policy Landscape: Two-Thirds Favor Treatment, Not Jail, for Use of Heroin, Cocaine," Pew Research Center, 2014, https://www.pewresearch.org/politics/2014/04/02/americas-new-drug-policy-landscape/; Public Opinion Strategies, "National Poll Results," January 25, 2018, https://www.politico.com/f/?id=00000161-2ccc-da2c-a963-efff82be0001.

34. Police Brutality Center, "What Does Defund the Police Mean?," 2022, https://policebrutalitycenter.org/what-does-defund-the-police-mean/#:~:text=Defunding%20the%20police%20would%20allow,and%20resources%20for%20ongoing%20care; Amistad Law Project, "Philly Rallies for Non-Police Mobile Crisis Response, Demands More Funding," March 16, 2022, https://amistadlaw.org/news/philly-rallies-non-police-mobile-crisis-response-demands-more-funding; M4BL Policy Platforms, "End the War on Drugs," 2022, https://m4bl.org/policy-platforms/end-the-war-on-drugs/; Meera Jagannathan, "As Activists Call to Defund the Police, Mental-Health Advocates Say 'The Time Is Now' to Rethink Public Safety," *MarketWatch*, 2020, https://www.marketwatch.com/story/long-before-defund-the-police-mental-health-advocates-have-been-redefining-public-safety-2020-06-11; Larry Buchanan, "Black Lives Matter May Be the Largest Movement in U.S. History," *The New York Times*, July 3, 2020, https://www.nytimes.com/interactive/2020/07/03/us/george-floyd-protests-crowd-size.html.

35. Caren Morrison, "Progressive Prosecutors Scored Big Wins in 2020 Elections, Boosting a Nationwide Trend," *The Conversation*, 2020, https://theconversation.com/progressive-prosecutors-scored-big-wins-in-2020-elections-boosting-a-nationwide-trend-149322.

36. Joycelyn Pollock, Steven Glassner, and Andrea Krajewski, "Examining the Conservative Shift from Harsh Justice," *Laws* 4 (2015): 107–24; Hadar Aviram, *Cheap on Crime: Recession-Era Politics and the Transformation of American Punishment* (Oakland: University of California Press, 2015); Wagner and Sawyer, "States of Incarceration: The Global Context 2018."

37. Julie Netherland and Helena Hansen, "White Opioids: Pharmaceutical Race and the War on Drugs That Wasn't," *BioSocieties* 12, no. 2 (2017): 217–38; Justin De Benedictis-Kessner and Michael Hankinson, "How the Identity of Substance Users Shapes Public Opinion on Opioid Policy," *Political Behavior* (December 20, 2022): 1–21; Justin De Benedictis-Kessner and Michael Hankinson, "Concentrated Burdens: How Self-Interest and Partisanship Shape Opinion on Opioid Treatment Policy," *American Political Science Review* 113, no. 4 (2019): 1078–84.

38. Christopher Seeds, "Bifurcation Nation: American Penal Policy in Late Mass Incarceration," *Punishment & Society* 19, no. 5 (2017): 590–610; "Right on Crime"; Katherine Beckett, Anna Reosti, and Emily Knaphus, "The End of an Era?

Understanding the Contradictions of Criminal Justice Reform," *The Annals of the American Academy of Political and Social Science* 664, no. 1 (2016): 238–59; Chettiar and Waldman, *Solutions: American Leaders Speak Out.*

39. Forrest Stuart, *Down, Out, and Under Arrest: Policing and Everyday Life in Skid Row* (Chicago: University of Chicago Press, 2016); Kelly Hannah-Moffat and Paula Maurutto, "Shifting and Targeted Forms of Penal Governance: Bail, Punishment and Specialized Courts," *Theoretical Criminology* 16, no. 2 (2012): 201–19; James L. Nolan, *Reinventing Justice: The American Drug Court Movement* (Princeton, NJ: Princeton University Press, 2001); Michael Rempel et al., *Changing the Role of the Prosecutor: A Multisite Evaluation of Prosecutor-Led Diversion* (New York: Center for Court Innovation, 2017).

40. Criminal legal institutions have become the largest source of referrals to publicly funded drug treatment programs (and the vast majority of treatment programs receive public funding). SAMHSA, "Treatment Episode Data Set (TEDS-A)," 2019, https://www.samhsa.gov/data/data-we-collect/teds-treatment-episode-data-set.

41. Vera Institute of Justice, "Diversion Programs, Explained"; American Civil Liberties Union, "Blueprint for Smart Justice."

42. Ninety-one percent of the prosecutors' offices in my national sample operate at least one pretrial diversion program. See methodological appendix A.

43. Only about 16 percent of the pretrial diversion programs in my national sample limited participation to people with diagnosed mental disorders. See methodological appendix A for more details.

44. Camilletti, "Pretrial Diversion Programs," 1; National Association of Pretrial Services Agencies, "Promising Practices in Pretrial Diversion," 2009, https://cjcc.doj.wi.gov/sites/default/files/subcommittee/Promising%20Practices%20in%20Pretrial%20Diversion%20%282%29.pdf; Johns Hopkins Bloomberg School of Public Health, "Criminal Justice Diversion Programs."

45. For an analysis of the widespread tendency to blame disordered substance use for a range of social ills, see Allison McKim, *Addicted to Rehab: Race, Gender, and Drugs in the Era of Mass Incarceration* (New Brunswick, NJ: Rutgers University Press, 2017).

46. See methodological appendix A.

47. American Civil Liberties Union, "Blueprint for Smart Justice," 13.

48. Other social theorists have contributed important insights into the "problem of the unanticipated consequences of purposive action," more broadly—most famously, Robert K. Merton, "The Unanticipated Consequences of Purposive Social Action," *American Sociological Review* 1, no. 6 (December 1936): 894–904, at 894.

49. Rothman, *Conscience and Convenience*, 12.

50. Dan Berger, Mariame Kaba, and David Stein, "What Abolitionists Do," *Jacobin*, August 24, 2017, https://jacobin.com/2017/08/prison-abolition-reform-mass-incarceration; Critical Resistance, "Reformist Reforms vs. Abolitionist Steps in Policing," 2021, https://criticalresistance.org/wp-content/uploads/2021/08/CR_abolitioniststeps_antiexpansion_2021_eng.pdf [perma.cc/L86J-G62X]; Interrupting Criminalization, Project Nia, and Critical Resistance, "So Is This Actually an Abolitionist Proposal or Strategy? A Collection of Resources to Aid in Evaluation and Reflection," 2022, https://criticalresistance.org/resources/actually-an-abolitionist-strategy-binder/ [https://perma.cc/NR626EV5]; Mariame Kaba, "Police 'Reforms'

You Should Always Oppose," *Truthout*, 2014, https://truthout.org/articles/police-reforms-you-should-always-oppose/; Mariame Kaba, *We Do This 'til We Free Us* (Chicago: Haymarket Books, 2021). The notion of "(non)reformist reform" originated in theorist André Gorz's 1967 book on anti-capitalist labor organizing, which defined a reformist reform as one that "subordinates its objectives to the criteria of rationality and practicability of a given system and policy," and contrasted it to a "nonreformist reform," which "bases the possibility of attaining its objective on the implementation of fundamental political and economic changes." André Gorz, *Strategy for Labor: A Radical Proposal* (Boston: Beacon Press, 1967), 7–8.

51. Amna A. Akbar, "Demands for a Democratic Political Economy," *Harvard Law Review Forum* 134 (2020): 90–118; Jamelia Morgan, "Responding to Abolition Anxieties: A Roadmap for Legal Analysis," *Michigan Law Review* 120 (2022): 1199–1224.

52. Katherine Beckett, "The Politics, Promise, and Peril of Criminal Justice Reform in the Context of Mass Incarceration," *Annual Review of Criminology* 1 (2018): 235–61.

53. Rothman, *Conscience and Convenience*, p. xii.

54. National Association of Pretrial Services Agencies, "Performance Standards and Goals for Pretrial Diversion/Intervention," 2008, https://napsa.org/eweb/DynamicPage.aspx?Site=NAPSA&WebCode=Diversion.

55. Center for Health and Justice at TASC, "No Entry: A National Survey of Criminal Justice Diversion Programs and Initiatives," 2013, www.centerforhealthandjustice.org; National Association of Pretrial Services Agencies, "Promising Practices in Pretrial Diversion," 2009, https://cjcc.doj.wi.gov/sites/default/files/subcommittee/Promising%20Practices%20in%20Pretrial%20Diversion%20%282%29.pdf.

56. Results from my national survey of diversion programs indicate that 95 percent of urban jurisdictions in the South—which I define by census region—have active pretrial diversion programs (for details on the survey, see methodological appendix A). For imprisonment rates in the region, see Bureau of Justice Statistics, "Prisoners in 2021," 2022, https://bjs.ojp.gov/library.

57. For the full vignettes, survey text, and more details about the study design and respondent recruitment and participation, see methodological appendix B.

58. Roger Friedland and Robert R. Alford, "Bringing Society Back In: Symbols, Practices, and Institutional Contradictions," in *The New Institutionalism in Organizational Analysis*, ed. Walter W. Powell and Paul J. DiMaggio (Chicago: University of Chicago Press, 1991), 232–63, at 243.

59. David J. Rothman, *Conscience and Convenience: The Asylum and Its Alternatives in Progressive America*, Revised Addition (New York: Aldine de Gruyter, 2002).

60. Definitions of schizophrenia developed in part as pathologization of Black political resistance, for instance, and many physical illnesses that afflict primarily women were defined as mental illnesses for generations before they were reclassified. Metzl, *The Protest Psychosis*; Maya Dusenbery, *Doing Harm: The Truth About How Bad Medicine and Lazy Science Leave Women Dismissed, Misdiagnosed, and Sick* (New York: HarperOne, 2018).

61. Anne Harrington, *Mind Fixers: Psychiatry's Troubled Search for the Biology of Mental Illness* (New York: W. W. Norton, 2019).

62. Alisa Roth, *Insane: America's Treatment of Mental Illness* (New York: Basic Books, 2018); Caroline Jean Acker, *Creating the American Junkie: Addiction Research in the Classic Era of Narcotic Control* (Baltimore, MD: Johns Hopkins University Press, 2002); Thornicroft, *Shunned.*

63. See above and, e.g., Meera Jagannathan, "As Activists Call to Defund the Police, Mental-Health Advocates Say 'The Time Is Now' to Rethink Public Safety"; M4BL Policy Platforms, "End the War on Drugs"; Pew Research Center, "America's New Drug Policy Landscape."

64. Social scientists increasingly recognize that the invisibilization of crisis is an important tool of governance. See, e.g., Armando Lara-Millán, *Redistributing the Poor: Jails, Hospitals, and the Crisis of Law and Fiscal Austerity* (Oxford and New York: Oxford University Press, 2021); Chris Herring, "Complaint-Oriented Policing: Regulating Homelessness in Public Space," *American Sociological Review* 84, no. 5 (2019): 769–800.

65. John W. Meyer and Brian Rowan, "Institutionalized Organizations: Formal Structure as Myth and Ceremony," *American Journal of Sociology* 83, no. 2 (1977): 340–63, at 341; see also Mary Douglas, *How Institutions Think* (Syracuse, NY: Syracuse University Press, 1986); Ronald L. Jepperson, "Institutions, Institutional Effects, and Institutionalism," in *The New Institutionalism in Organizational Analysis*, ed. Paul J. DiMaggio and Walter W. Powell (Chicago: University of Chicago Press, 1991), 143–63.

66. D. Werb et al., "The Effectiveness of Compulsory Drug Treatment: A Systematic Review," *International Journal of Drug Policy* 28 (2016): 1–9; Anh T. Vo et al., "Assessing HIV and Overdose Risks for People Who Use Drugs Exposed to Compulsory Drug Abstinence Programs (CDAP): A Systematic Review and Meta-Analysis," *International Journal of Drug Policy* 96 (October 2021): 103401.

CHAPTER ONE

1. *State v. Blake*, 481 P.3d 521 (2021).

2. Gene Johnson, "Washington State Justices Strike Down Drug Possession Law," *Associated Press*, February 25, 2021, https://apnews.com/article/spokane-washington-538035a1cf94b649861a3b3a5f8ad75a#. Mark Cooke, "The Unsettled Policy Landscape of Drug Possession Laws in Washington," *Washington State Bar News: The Official Publication of the Washington State Bar Association*, November 5, 2021, https://wabarnews.org/2021/11/05/the-unsettled-policy-landscape-of-drug-possession-laws-in-washington/; ACLU of Washington, "Q & A: The Blake Decision," 2023, https://www.aclu-wa.org/pages/q-blake-decision.

3. Nathaniel Rakich, "How Red or Blue Is Your State?," 2021, https://fivethirtyeight.com/features/how-red-or-blue-is-your-state-your-congressional-district/.

4. State of Washington, Engrossed Senate Bill 5476 (2021).

5. Noah Corrin, "Washington State Senate Passes Controversial Drug Possession Bill," *KHQ*, 2023, https://www.khq.com/news/washington-state-senate-passes-controversial-drug-possession-bill/article_13d498bc-bac3-11ed-a9d2-2b71e97e3026.html.

6. "TVW," https://tvw.org.

7. State of Washington, Second Engrossed Second Substitute Senate Bill 5536 (2023).

8. National Law Center on Homelessness & Poverty, "Housing Not Handcuffs"; Clara Harter, "Could Newsom's New Mental Health Court Be a Fix for Local Homelessness?," *Santa Monica Daily Press*, March 12, 2022, https://smdp.com/2022/03/12/could-newsoms-new-mental-health-court-be-a-fix-for-local-homelessness/; California Courts, the Judicial Branch of California, "Community/Homeless Courts," 2023, https://www.courts.ca.gov/5976.htm; "California's Compassionate Intervention Act," 2023, https://www.interventionca.org.

9. Wright Gazaway and KATU Staff, "Republicans Look to Roll Back Part of Measure 110, Seek Punishment for Drug Possession," 2023, https://ktvl.com/news/republicans-look-to-roll-back-part-of-measure-110-seek-punishment-for-drug-possession.

10. Sophie Quinton, "Oregon's Drug Decriminalization May Spread, Despite Unclear Results," 2021, https://www.pewtrusts.org/en/research-and-analysis/blogs/stateline/2021/11/03/oregons-drug-decriminalization-may-spread-despite-unclear-results.

11. State of Oregon, House Bill 4002 (2024).

12. Pew Research Center, "America's New Drug Policy Landscape."

13. Department of Justice, "Department of Justice Announces More Than $341 Million in Grants to Combat America's Addiction Crisis," 2020, https://www.justice.gov/opa/pr/department-justice-announces-more-341-million-grants-combat-america-s-addiction-crisis; Ronald F. Wright and Kay L. Levine, "Models of Prosecutor-Led Diversion Programs in the United States and Beyond," *Annual Review of Criminology* 4 (2021): 331–51; Allan Smith, "Progressive DAs Are Shaking up the Criminal Justice System. Pro-Police Groups Aren't Happy," NBC News, 2019, https://www.nbcnews.com/politics/justice-department/these-reform-prosecutors-are-shaking-system-pro-police-groups-aren-n1033286; Riley Vetterkind, "DOJ Announces Counties Set to Receive Funds to Expand or Establish Drug Courts," Madison.com, 2019, https://madison.com/news/local/govt-and-politics/doj-announces-counties-set-to-receive-funds-to-expand- or/article_b68c4e4c-3326-5b4a-aef9-d166a410d668.html; Jamie Rowen, "Worthy of Justice: A Veterans Treatment Court in Practice," *Law & Policy* 42, no. 1 (January 2020): 78–100.

14. For more detail on each of these data sources, see methodological appendix A.

15. Mental health services, and particularly treatments for substance use disorder, are understaffed and underfunded around the United States. Care is often unaffordable, especially for the tens of millions of Americans who are uninsured, and even those who can pay can struggle to access them. Services are altogether unavailable in many geographic areas, there can be many bureaucratic hurdles to entry, and waiting lists can be long. See Strach, Zuber, and Perez-Chiques, "Why Policies Fail"; Frank, Humphreys, and Pollack, "Our Other Epidemic"; American Hospital Association, "Statement of the American Hospital Association to the Committee on Ways and Means of the United States House of Representatives"; Amy E. Cha and Robin A. Cohen, "Demographic Variation in Health Insurance Coverage: United States, 2020," National Health Statistics Reports (US Department of Health and Human Services, February 11, 2022), https://www.cdc.gov/nchs/data/nhsr/nhsr169.pdf; C. Holly A.

Andrilla et al., "Geographic Variation in the Supply of Selected Behavioral Health Providers," *American Journal of Preventive Medicine* 54, no. 6 (June 2018): S199–207; SAMHSA, "Key Substance Use and Mental Health Indicators in the United States."

16. James and Glaze, "Bureau of Justice Statistics Special Report"; Jennifer C. Karberg and Doris J. James, "Substance Dependence, Abuse, and Treatment of Jail Inmates, 2002," Bureau of Justice Statistics, 2005; National Center on Addiction and Substance Abuse at Columbia University, "Behind Bars II." For a discussion of the difficulties of measuring rates of mental illness in carceral settings, see Rembis, "The New Asylums."

17. From analyses of 2017 to 2019 data from the National Survey on Drug Use and Health. Pew Charitable Trusts, "More than 1 in 9 People"; Jones and Sawyer, "Arrest, Release, Repeat."

18. Peter Conrad and Caitlin Slodden, "The Medicalization of Mental Disorder," in *Handbook of the Sociology of Mental Health*, ed. Carol S. Aneshensel, Jo C. Phelan, and Alex Bierman, 2nd ed. (Dordrecht and New York: Springer, 2013), 61–74; Allan V. Horwitz, *Creating Mental Illness* (Chicago: University of Chicago Press, 2002); Michel Foucault, *Madness and Civilization: A History of Insanity in the Age of Reason* (New York: Pantheon Books, 1965).

19. US Department of Health and Human Services, *Mental Health*, 5.

20. Horwitz, *Creating Mental Illness*; Conrad and Slodden, "The Medicalization of Mental Disorder."

21. Andrew Abbott, *The System of Professions: An Essay on the Division of Expert Labor* (Chicago: University of Chicago Press, 1988).

22. Metzl, *The Protest Psychosis*.

23. See also Whooley, "Nosological Reflections."

24. Craig Reinarman, "The Social Construction of Drug Scares," in *Constructions of Deviance: Social Power, Context, and Interaction*, ed. Patricia A. Adler and Peter Adler (Belmont, CA: Wadsworth, 1997), 97–108; Maia Szalavitz, *Unbroken Brain: A Revolutionary New Way of Understanding Addiction* (New York: St. Martin's Press, 2016); Alan I. Leshner, "Addiction Is a Brain Disease, and It Matters," *Science* 278, no. 5335 (1997): 45–47; Marc Lewis, *The Biology of Desire: Why Addiction Is Not a Disease* (New York: Public Affairs, 2015).

25. Bechara, "Decision Making, Impulse Control and Loss of Willpower"; Humphreys and Bickel, "Toward a Neuroscience of Long-Term Recovery"; National Institute on Drug Abuse, "The Science of Drug Use and Addiction."

26. American Psychiatric Association, *DSM-5*.

27. Lisa Maher and David Dixon, "The Cost of Crackdowns: Policing Cabramatta's Heroin Market," *Current Issues in Criminal Justice* 13, no. 1 (2001): 5–22; Vanila M. Singh, Thom Browne, and Joshua Montgomery, "The Emerging Role of Toxic Adulterants in Street Drugs in the US Illicit Opioid Crisis," *Public Health Reports* 135, no. 1 (January 2020): 6–10; Jennifer Ahern, Jennifer Stuber, and Sandro Galea, "Stigma, Discrimination and the Health of Illicit Drug Users," *Drug and Alcohol Dependence* 88, no. 2–3 (2007): 188–96; Gary Christian et al., "Overdose Deaths and Vancouver's Supervised Injection Facility," *The Lancet* 379, no. 9811 (January 2012): 117.

28. Thornicroft, *Shunned*.

29. Christensen et al., "Human Capital and Administrative Burden."

30. Harrington, *Mind Fixers*; Anne M. Fletcher, *Inside Rehab: The Surprising Truth About Addiction Treatment—and How to Get Help That Works* (New York: Penguin Books, 2013).

31. Fletcher, *Inside Rehab*.

32. Evelien P. M. Brouwers, "Social Stigma Is an Underestimated Contributing Factor to Unemployment in People with Mental Illness or Mental Health Issues: Position Paper and Future Directions," *BMC Psychology* 8, no. 1 (December 2020): 36; National Law Center on Homelessness & Poverty, "Housing Not Handcuffs"; Thornicroft, *Shunned*; US Department of Housing and Urban Development, "HUD 2022 Continuum of Care Homeless Assistance Programs"; Lebrun-Harris et al., "Health Status and Health Care Experiences Among Homeless Patients in Federally Supported Health Centers."

33. Dickman, Himmelstein, and Woolhandler, "Inequality and the Health-Care System in the USA"; SAMHSA, "Racial/Ethnic Differences in Mental Health Service Use Among Adults"; Jones and Sawyer, "Arrest, Release, Repeat."

34. Zylan and Soule, "Ending Welfare as We Know It (Again)"; Kohler-Hausmann, *Misdemeanorland*; Craig Reinarman and Harry G. Levine, eds., *Crack in America: Demon Drugs and Social Justice* (Berkeley and Los Angeles: University of California Press, 1997).

35. Heather Schoenfeld, *Building the Prison State: Race and the Politics of Mass Incarceration* (Chicago: University of Chicago Press, 2018); Michael C. Campbell and Heather Schoenfeld, "The Transformation of America's Penal Order: A Historicized Political Sociology of Punishment," *American Journal of Sociology* 118, no. 5 (2013): 1375–1423.

36. Gaston, "Producing Race Disparities"; Beckett et al., "Drug Use, Drug Possession Arrests, and the Question of Race"; Fagan and Davies, "Street Stops and Broken Windows."

37. John F. Pfaff, *Locked In: The True Causes of Mass Incarceration—and How to Achieve Real Reform* (New York: Basic Books, 2017).

38. States passed laws modeled on drug schedules created by the federal government in 1986 and 1988, which dramatically increased penalties for drug possession as well as distribution. Some of the harshest of these penalties were reserved for crack cocaine, which was used disproportionately by Black Americans; it was the only drug made to carry a mandatory minimum penalty for a first offense of simple possession. This mandatory minimum was adopted widely among the states. In addition, the 1990s saw the emergence of "three strikes" laws, which typically imposed mandatory life sentences on people convicted of three felony offenses, including drug possession. The federal government and twenty-four states passed legislation in this vein. Reinarman and Levine, *Crack in America*; Dimitri A. Bogazianos, *5 Grams: Crack Cocaine, Rap Music, and the War on Drugs* (New York: New York University Press, 2011); Franklin E. Zimring, Gordon Hawkins, and Sam Kamin, *Punishment and Democracy: Three Strikes and You're Out in California* (Oxford and New York: Oxford University Press, 2001).

39. The vast majority of those incarcerated on drug convictions were low-level dealers or users, not major traffickers. People convicted of low-level drug offenses still constitute a substantial share of prisoners in the United States—about 14 percent, as of 2019. Human Rights Watch, "Targeting Blacks: Drug Law Enforcement and Race in the United States," 2008, https://www.hrw.org/report/2008/05/05/targeting-blacks/drug-law-enforcement-and-race-united-states; E. Ann Carson, "Prisoners in 2019," Bureau of Justice Statistics, 2020, https://www.bjs.gov/index.cfm?ty=pbdetail&iid=7106; Marc Mauer and Ryan S. King, "A 25-Year Quagmire: The War on Drugs and Its Impact on American Society," The Sentencing Project, 2007, https://www.sentencingproject.org/publications/a-25-year-quagmire-the-war-on-drugs-and-its-impact-on-american-society/.

40. Besiki L. Kutateladze, "Tracing Charge Trajectories: A Study of the Influence of Race in Charge Changes at Case Screening, Arraignment, and Disposition," *Criminology* 56, no. 1 (2018): 123–53; Besiki L. Kutateladze et al., "Cumulative Disadvantage: Examining Racial and Ethnic Disparity in Prosecution and Sentencing," *Criminology* 52, no. 3 (2014): 514–51.

41. Federal Bureau of Investigation, "Crime in the United States," 2019, https://ucr.fbi.gov/crime-in-the-u.s/2019/crime-in-the-u.s.-2019.

42. Elderbroom and Durnan, "Reclassified: State Drug Law Reforms."

43. National Institute on Drug Abuse, "Common Comorbidities with Substance Use Disorders Research Report."

44. National Law Center on Homelessness & Poverty, "Housing Not Handcuffs."

45. Abraham, "A Palantir Co-Founder Is Pushing Laws to Criminalize Homeless Encampments Nationwide."

46. Reiter and Blair, "Punishing Mental Illness"; Reiter, *23/7*.

47. Sykes and Maroto, "A Wealth of Inequalities"; Apel and Sweeten, "The Impact of Incarceration on Employment"; Western, "The Impact of Incarceration on Wage Mobility and Inequality"; Rucker C. Johnson and Steven Raphael, "The Effects of Male Incarceration Dynamics on Acquired Immune Deficiency Syndrome: Infection Rates Among African American Women and Men," *The Journal of Law and Economics* 52, no. 2 (2009): 251–93; Massoglia and Pridemore, "Incarceration and Health"; Wildeman and Wang, "Mass Incarceration, Public Health, and Widening Inequality"; Porter and Demarco, "Beyond the Dichotomy"; Porter and Novisky, "Pathways to Depressive Symptoms Among Former Inmates"; Brayne, "Surveillance and System Avoidance"; Anna R. Haskins and Wade C. Jacobsen, "Schools as Surveilling Institutions? Paternal Incarceration, System Avoidance, and Parental Involvement in Schooling," *American Sociological Review* 82, no. 4 (2017): 657–84; Herbert, Morenoff, and Harding, "Homelessness and Housing Insecurity Among Former Prisoners"; David J. Harding, Jeffrey D. Morenoff, and Claire W. Herbert, "Home Is Hard to Find: Neighborhoods, Institutions, and the Residential Trajectories of Returning Prisoners," *The Annals of the American Academy of Political and Social Science* 647 (2013): 214–36; Holly Foster and John Hagan, "Punishment Regimes and the Multilevel Effects of Parental Incarceration: Intergenerational, Intersectional, and Interinstitutional Models of Social Inequality and Systemic Exclusion," *Annual Review of Sociology* 41, no. 1 (August 14, 2015): 135–58; Hedwig Lee et al., "A Heavy Burden: The Cardiovascular Health Consequences of Having a Family Member Incarcerated," *American Journal of Public Health* 104, no. 3

(2014): 421–28; Beth Richie, "The Social Impact of Mass Incarceration on Women," in *Invisible Punishment: The Collateral Consequences of Mass Imprisonment*, ed. Meda Chesney-Lind and Marc Mauer (New York: The New Press, 2002), 136–49.

48. Murali and Oyebode, "Poverty, Social Inequality and Mental Health."

49. Devah Pager, *Marked: Race, Crime, and Finding Work in an Era of Mass Incarceration* (Chicago: University of Chicago Press, 2007); Western, "The Impact of Incarceration on Wage Mobility and Inequality."

50. Alexander, *The New Jim Crow*; Mele and Miller, *Civil Penalties, Social Consequences*.

51. National Inventory of Collateral Consequences of Conviction, "Collateral Consequences Inventory."

52. Shervin Assari et al., "Discrimination Fully Mediates the Effects of Incarceration History on Depressive Symptoms and Psychological Distress Among African American Men," *Journal of Racial and Ethnic Health Disparities* 5 (2018): 243–52; Porter and Novisky, "Pathways to Depressive Symptoms Among Former Inmates"; Wildeman and Wang, "Mass Incarceration, Public Health, and Widening Inequality."

53. Uggen et al., "The Edge of Stigma"; American Bar Association, "Collateral Consequences of Criminal Convictions."

54. Herring, "Complaint-Oriented Policing"; Chris Herring, Dilara Yarbrough, and Lisa Marie Alatorre, "Pervasive Penality: How the Criminalization of Poverty Perpetuates Homelessness," *Social Problems* 67, no. 1 (2020): 131–49.

55. Fuller et al., "Overlooked in the Undercounted."

56. Buchanan, "Black Lives Matter May Be the Largest Movement in U.S. History."

57. M4BL Policy Platforms, "End the War on Drugs."

58. I use the term *district attorney* to refer to the chief prosecutor in a local government area, since this is the most common title for that role. Some US states or jurisdictions use other terms for this official, such as *state's attorney* or *state attorney*. For a recent list of reform-oriented DAs, see Jennifer M. Balboni and Randall Grometstein, "Prosecutorial Reform from Within: District Attorney 'Disruptors' and Other Change Agents, 2016–2020," *Contemporary Justice Review: Issues in Criminal, Social, and Restorative Justice* 23, no. 3 (2020): 261–90.

59. Bruce A. Green and Rebecca Roiphe, "When Prosecutors Politick: Progressive Law Enforcers Then and Now," *Journal of Criminal Law and Criminology* 110, no. 4 (2020): 719–68; Ian Ward, "How Progressives Are Knocking Out Local Judges Across the Country," 2021, https://www.politico.com/news/magazine/2021/09/03/robert-saleem-holbrook-conservative-judges-criminal-justice-506966.

60. Aviram, *Cheap on Crime*.

61. Seeds, "Bifurcation Nation."

62. Pollock, Glassner, and Krajewski, "Examining the Conservative Shift from Harsh Justice"; Aviram, *Cheap on Crime*; Seeds, "Bifurcation Nation."

63. Ozlem Eylem et al., "Stigma for Common Mental Disorders in Racial Minorities and Majorities a Systematic Review and Meta-Analysis," *BMC Public Health* 20, no. 1 (December 2020): 879.

64. Bernice A. Pescosolido, "The Public Stigma of Mental Illness: What Do We Think; What Do We Know; What Can We Prove?," *Journal of Health and Social Behavior* 54, no. 1 (2013): 1–21.

65. Colleen L. Barry et al., "Stigma, Discrimination, Treatment Effectiveness, and Policy: Public Views About Drug Addiction and Mental Illness," *Psychiatric Services* 65, no. 10 (October 2014): 1269–72.

66. Since 2018, Black Americans have also been overrepresented among opioid overdose deaths. For details on the numbers and rates of overdose deaths by race and ethnicity over time, see Centers for Disease Control and Prevention, "Drug Overdose Deaths," 2019, https://www.cdc.gov/drugoverdose/data/statedeaths.html; Hawre Jalal et al., "Changing Dynamics of the Drug Overdose Epidemic in the United States from 1979 through 2016," *Science* 361, no. 6408 (September 21, 2018): eaau1184.

67. De Benedictis-Kessner and Hankinson, "Concentrated Burdens"; De Benedictis-Kessner and Hankinson, "How the Identity of Substance Users Shapes Public Opinion"; Netherland and Hansen, "White Opioids."

68. Emma E. McGinty et al., "U.S. News Media Coverage of Solutions to the Opioid Crisis, 2013–2017," *Preventive Medicine* 126 (September 2019): 105771; Emma E. McGinty et al., "Criminal Activity or Treatable Health Condition? News Media Framing of Opioid Analgesic Abuse in the United States, 1998–2012," *Psychiatric Services* 67, no. 4 (April 2016): 405–11; Pescosolido, "The Public Stigma of Mental Illness."

69. Pescosolido, "The Public Stigma of Mental Illness."

70. Harrington, *Mind Fixers*.

71. Matthias C. Angermeyer et al., "Public Attitudes Towards Psychiatry and Psychiatric Treatment at the Beginning of the 21st Century: A Systematic Review and Meta-Analysis of Population Surveys," *World Psychiatry* 16, no. 1 (February 2017): 50–61.

72. Fletcher, *Inside Rehab*.

73. Pew Research Center, "America's New Drug Policy Landscape."

74. M4BL Policy Platforms, "End the War on Black Health and Black Disabled People," 2022, https://m4bl.org/policy-platforms/end-the-war-black-health/; M4BL Policy Platforms, "End the War on Drugs"; Real Justice, "Tell DA's to Drop Low Level Marijuana Arrests, Use Diversion Programs, & Expunge Criminal Records," 2018, https://act.realjusticepac.org/sign/district-attorney-petition/.

75. Pew Research Center, "America's New Drug Policy Landscape."

76. See, e.g., Frances Fox Piven and Richard A Cloward, *Regulating the Poor: The Functions of Public Welfare* (New York: Vintage Books, 1971); Alexander Hicks and Duane H. Swank, "Civil Disorder, Relief Mobilization, and AFDC Caseloads: A Reexamination of the Piven and Cloward Thesis," *American Journal of Political Science* 27, no. 4 (November 1983): 695; Mala Htun and S. Laurel Weldon, "The Civic Origins of Progressive Policy Change: Combating Violence Against Women in Global Perspective, 1975–2005," *American Political Science Review* 106, no. 3 (August 2012): 548–69.

77. David Garland, *Punishment and Modern Society: A Study in Social Theory* (Chicago: University of Chicago Press, 1990), 21. Political theorists also write about the

state's reliance on legitimacy, more broadly, and its ongoing work to justify its powers to the public. See, e.g., Richard Ashcraft, ed., *John Locke: Critical Assessments* (London: Routledge, 1991); Jürgen Habermas, *Legitimation Crisis* (Boston: Beacon Press, 1975); David Beetham, *The Legitimation of Power*, 2nd ed. (New York: Palgrave MacMillan, 2013); Daniel Bell, *The Coming of Post-Industrial Society: A Venture in Social Forecasting* (New York: Basic Books, 1999).

78. Michel Foucault, *Discipline and Punish: The Birth of the Prison* (New York: Pantheon Books, 1977).

79. District attorneys are elected in forty-seven of the fifty states. Judges are elected at least one level of the judiciary in thirty-nine states. Brennan Center for Justice, "Judicial Selection: Significant Figures," October 11, 2022, https://www.brennancenter.org/our-work/research-reports/judicial-selection-significant-figures; UNC School of Law, "The Prosecutors and Politics Project: National Study of Prosecutor Elections," February 2020, https://law.unc.edu/wp-content/uploads/2020/01/National-Study-Prosecutor-Elections-2020.pdf.

80. Carissa Byrne Hessick and Michael Morse, "Picking Prosecutors," *Iowa Law Review* 105 (2020): 1537–90.

81. Ian Ward, "How Progressives Are Knocking Out Local Judges Across the Country."

82. Angela J. Davis, *Arbitrary Justice: The Power of the American Prosecutor* (Oxford and New York: Oxford University Press, 2007).

83. Green and Roiphe, "When Prosecutors Politick."

84. Davis, *Arbitrary Justice*; Pfaff, *Locked In*.

85. President's Commission on Law Enforcement, *The Challenge of Crime in a Free Society* (Washington, DC: United States Government Printing Office, 1967).

86. Carlos Berdejó and Noam Yuchtman, "Crime, Punishment, and Politics: An Analysis of Political Cycles in Criminal Sentencing," *The Review of Economics and Statistics* 95, no. 3 (2013): 741–56; Sanford C. Gordon and Gregory A. Huber, "The Effect of Electoral Competitiveness on Incumbent Behavior," *Quarterly Journal of Political Science* 2 (2007): 107–38; Gregory A. Huber and Sanford C. Gordon, "Accountability and Coercion: Is Justice Blind When It Runs for Office?," *American Journal of Political Science* 48, no. 2 (2004): 247–63; Paul Brace and Brent D. Boyea, "State Public Opinion, the Death Penalty, and the Practice of Electing Judges," *American Journal of Political Science* 52, no. 2 (April 2008): 360–72.

87. Fair and Just Prosecution, "Joint Statement from Elected Prosecutors," July 7, 2022, https://fairandjustprosecution.org/wp-content/uploads/2022/06/FJP-Post-Dobbs-Abortion-Joint-Statement.pdf; Emily Bazelon, "The Response to Crime," *The New York Times*, April 7, 2023, https://www.nytimes.com/2023/04/07/briefing/legislators-response-to-crime.html.

88. Alexandra Berzon and Ken Bensinger, "Inside Ron DeSantis's Politicized Removal of an Elected Prosecutor," *The New York Times*, March 11, 2023, https://www.nytimes.com/2023/03/11/us/politics/desantis-andrew-warren-liberal-prosecutor.html.

89. Ellie Rushing, "DA Larry Krasner's Impeachment Trial Gets Indefinitely Postponed by the Pa. Senate," *The Philadelphia Inquirer*, January 11, 2023, https://www

.inquirer.com/news/larry-krasner-impeachment-trial-postponed-pa-senate-20230111.html; Brooke Schultz, "GOP Impeachment Effort Against Philadelphia Prosecutor Lands before Democratic-Majority Court," AP News, November 28, 2023, https://apnews.com/article/larry-krasner-philadelphia-district-attorney-impeachment-0561893995af353c49e5b11ed55b219d.

90. Harvard Law Review, "San Francisco District Attorney Chesa Boudin Recalled," *Harvard Law Review* 136 (2023): 1740–47. In Louisiana, as well, the legislature is pushing for multiple measures to limit the powers of local DAs—including by overruling them when they refuse to prosecute certain kinds of cases—in response to what legislators have referred to as the "New Orleans situation," or the election of a progressive prosecutor in that city. Julie O'Donoghue, "Louisiana's Conservative State Officials Seek to Block 'Rogue' District Attorneys," *Louisiana Illuminator*, April 17, 2024, https://lailluminator.com/2024/04/17/louisianas-conservative-state-officials-seek-to-block-rogue-district-attorneys/.

91. Davis, *Arbitrary Justice*.

92. Marco della Cava, "New, More Progressive Prosecutors Are Angering Police, Who Warn Approach Will Lead to Chaos," *USA Today*, 2020, https://www.usatoday.com/story/news/nation/2020/02/08/criminal-justice-police-progressive-prosecutors-battle-over-reform/4660796002/; Wendy N. Davis, "Progressive Prosecutors Are Encountering Pushback," 2022, https://www.abajournal.com/web/article/progressive-prosecutor-pushback.

93. Paul Butler, "The System Must Counteract Prosecutors' Natural Sympathies for Cops," *The New York Times*, April 28, 2015, https://www.nytimes.com/roomfordebate/2014/12/04/do-cases-like-eric-garners-require-a-special-prosecutor/the-system-must-counteract-prosecutors-natural-sympathies-for-cops?smid=tw-share.

94. The prevalence of pretrial diversion is hard to estimate, since programs are run by individual district attorneys, and they are not required to register or provide information to a national database. But the last count by the Bureau of Justice Statistics, in 2009, indicated that in urban jurisdictions the programs enrolled about 8 percent of all felony defendants. That survey indicates that only 72 percent of the seventy-five largest urban jurisdictions were operating pretrial diversion programs at the time, though my recent survey indicates that that percentage has risen to 100 percent. Interviews indicate that defendant enrollment within programs has also risen substantially since 2009. For a useful analysis of the 2009 BJS data, see Traci Schlesinger, "Racial Disparities in Pretrial Diversion: An Analysis of Outcomes Among Men Charged with Felonies and Processed in State Courts," *Race and Justice* 3, no. 3 (2013): 210–38.

95. President's Commission on Law Enforcement, *The Challenge of Crime in a Free Society*, 133.

96. President's Commission on Law Enforcement, *The Challenge of Crime in a Free Society*, 134.

97. The first pretrial diversion program, called the Citizen's Probation Authority Program (CPA), is thought to have been founded in Flint, Michigan, in 1965. Following release of *The Challenge of Crime in A Free Society*, several other federal initiatives encouraged other jurisdictions to begin similar programs. In 1968 the US

Department of Labor's Manpower Administration and the US Department of Justice's Law Enforcement Assistance Administration awarded funding for pretrial diversion programs to dozens of sites. In 1973 the National Advisory Commission on Criminal Justice Standards and Goals recommended that *all* jurisdictions establish such programs. In the 1970s a number of states passed legislation enabling or encouraging local jurisdictions to do so. See John P. Bellassai, *A Short History of the Pretrial Diversion of Adult Defendants from Traditional Criminal Justice Processing, Part One: The Early Years* (Washington, DC: National Association of Pretrial Service Agencies, 2010); National Association of Pretrial Services Agencies, "Pretrial Diversion in the 21st Century: A National Survey of Pretrial Diversion and Practices," 2009, https://napsa.memberclicks.net/diversion.

98. Malcolm M. Feeley, *The Process Is the Punishment: Handling Cases in a Lower Criminal Court* (New York: Russell Sage Foundation, 1979).

99. National Association of Pretrial Services Agencies, "Pretrial Diversion in the 21st Century."

100. Michael Willrich, *City of Courts: Socializing Justice in Progressive Era Chicago* (Cambridge and New York: Cambridge University Press, 2003); Rebecca Tiger, *Judging Addicts: Drug Courts and Coercion in the Justice System* (New York: New York University Press, 2013).

101. Tiger, *Judging Addicts*.

102. Stacy Lee Burns and Mark Peyrot, "Tough Love: Nurturing and Coercing Responsibility and Recovery in California Drug Courts," *Social Problems* 50, no. 3 (2003): 416–38; Nolan, *Reinventing Justice*; Michael Rempel et al., "The New York State Adult Drug Court Evaluation: Policies, Participants and Impacts," Center for Court Innovation, 2003.

103. Nolan, *Reinventing Justice*; see also Tiger, *Judging Addicts*.

104. Angela J. Thielo et al., "Prisons or Problem-Solving: Does the Public Support Specialty Courts?," *Victims & Offenders* 14, no. 3 (April 3, 2019): 267–82; Lisa N. Sacco, "Federal Support for Drug Courts: In Brief," Congressional Research Service, 2018, https://crsreports.congress.gov/product/pdf/R/R44467; but for critiques by scholars and one leftist advocacy organization, see Drug Policy Alliance, "Drug Courts Are Not the Answer: Toward a Health-Centered Approach to Drug Use," Drug Policy Alliance, 2011; Tiger, *Judging Addicts*; Kerwin Kaye, *Enforcing Freedom: Drug Courts, Therapeutic Communities, and the Intimacies of the State* (New York: Columbia University Press, 2020).

105. National Treatment Court Resource Center, "What Are Drug Courts?," https://ntcrc.org/what-are-drug-courts/; NYCourts.gov, "Mental Health Courts," Problem-Solving Courts, 2024, https://ww2.nycourts.gov/mental-health-courts-overview-27066; PTSD: National Center for PTSD, "Veterans Treatment Court," Veterans with PTSD in the Justice System, 2024, https://www.ptsd.va.gov/professional/treat/care/vets_justice_system.asp.

106. Vera Institute of Justice, "Diversion Programs, Explained"; American Civil Liberties Union, "Blueprint for Smart Justice."

107. Chettiar and Waldman, *Solutions: American Leaders Speak Out*.

108. Critical Resistance, "Urgent! Take Action Against Proposed New SF Jail."

109. See, e.g., Camilletti, "Pretrial Diversion Programs"; Johns Hopkins Bloomberg School of Public Health, "Criminal Justice Diversion Programs"; Texas Criminal Justice Coalition, "Interim Testimony 2016: Senate Committee on Criminal Justice," 2016.

110. Joe Biden, "Joe Biden for President," 2023, https://joebiden.com/justice/#; Michelle Williams, "'No One Should Be Going to Jail Because They Have a Drug Problem,' Joe Biden Says During Presidential Debate," MassLive, 2020, https://www.masslive.com/politics/2020/10/no-one-should-be-going-to-jail-because-they-have-a-drug-problem-joe-biden-says-during-presidential-debate.html.

111. Information about "progressive prosecutor" platforms is based on a dataset described in methodological appendix A.

112. Information about other candidates for DA is based on an analysis of news articles (from a Google alert for "pretrial diversion" from 2017 to the present). See, e.g., "The DA Needs to Be an Active Role"; Caraveo, "2020 Elections Q&A; "Candidate Q&A: Kostiha Hopes to Remain County Attorney"; Kelly, "Grace, Coleman Discuss Pre-Trial Diversion," 600; Serbin, "Columbus Attorney Challenges Incumbent"; Staff Report, "Cooke Co. DA Seeking 2nd Term in 2020"; Stafford, "Henry DA Pattillo Receives Justice Award"; Estep, "Gwinnett's Longtime DA Considering Running as a Democrat."

113. See methodological appendix A.

114. Nahama Broner et al., "Effects of Diversion on Adults with Co-Occurring Mental Illness and Substance Use: Outcomes from a National Multi-Site Study," *Behavioral Sciences and the Law* 22 (2004): 519–41; Louise Butler, Jane Goodman-Delahunty, and Rohan Lulham, "Effectiveness of Pretrial Community-Based Diversion in Reducing Reoffending by Adult Intrafamilial Child Sex Offenders," *Criminal Justice and Behavior* 39, no. 4 (2012): 493–513; Shannon Lange, Jürgen Rehm, and Svetlana Popova, "The Effectiveness of Criminal Justice Diversion Initiatives in North America: A Systematic Literature Review," *International Journal of Forensic Mental Health* 10 (2011): 200–214; Rempel et al., *Changing the Role of the Prosecutor*; David A. Scott et al., "Effectiveness of Criminal Justice Liaison and Diversion Services for Offenders with Mental Disorders: A Review," *Psychiatric Services* 64, no. 9 (2013): 843–49.

115. These limits on eligibility for diversion do not reflect treatment needs or to risk of future harm. Indeed, people who already have long criminal histories may be those most in need of mental healthcare, since behaviors such as drug use can quickly produce long rap sheets. More serious offenses also often stem from mental illness, and there is no evidence that treatment is less effective for people accused of those offenses. Offense type also tells us very little about the risk that a person will do harm in the future: it is a poor predictor both of the probability of rearrest and of the type of charge on which someone will be rearrested. In other words, people arrested on low-level charges are no less likely to be rearrested than someone facing a higher-level charge. People convicted of violent crimes may also be rearrested for a nonviolent offense and vice versa. See United States Sentencing Commission, "The Past Predicts the Future: Criminal History and Recidivism of Federal Offenders," 2017, https://www.ussc.gov/sites/default/files/pdf/research-and-publications/research-publications/2017/20170309_Recidivism-CH.pdf; Council on Criminal Justice, "Recidivism Rates: What You Need to Know," 2021, https://counciloncj.org/recidivism_report/; Sentencing Guidelines Commission, State of Washington, "Recidivism of Adult Felons, 2007,"

2008, https://www.cfc.wa.gov/PublicationSentencing/Recidivism/Adult_Recidivism_FY2007.pdf.

116. See table 4 in methodological appendix A.

117. Evan Sernoffsky, "SF District Attorney Chesa Boudin Launches Diversion Program for Parents Facing Criminal Charges," *San Francisco Chronicle*, January 15, 2020, https://www.sfchronicle.com/crime/article/SF-District-Attorney-Chesa-Boudin-launches-14975839.php.

118. Philippa Tomczak, "The Voluntary Sector and the Mandatory Statutory Supervision Requirement: Expanding the Carceral Net," *The British Journal of Criminology* 57, no. 1 (2017): 152–71; Janet Ransley and Lorraine Mazerolle, "Third Sector Involvement in Criminal Justice," in *The Palgrave Handbook of Australian and New Zealand Criminology, Crime and Justice*, ed. Antje Deckert and Rick Sarre (Palgrave Macmillan, 2017), 483–96; Philippa Tomczak, *The Penal Voluntary Sector* (London: Routledge, 2017); Philippa J. Tomczak, "The Penal Voluntary Sector in England and Wales: Beyond Neoliberalism?," *Criminology and Criminal Justice* 14, no. 4 (2014): 470–86; Alice Mills, Rosie Meek, and Dina Gojkovic, "Exploring the Relationship Between the Voluntary Sector and the State in Criminal Justice," *Voluntary Sector Review* 2, no. 2 (July 2011): 193–211; Philippa Tomczak and Gillian Buck, "The Penal Voluntary Sector: A Hybrid Sociology," *The British Journal of Criminology* 59, no. 4 (June 6, 2019): 898–918.

119. National Association of Pretrial Services Agencies, "Performance Standards and Goals for Pretrial Diversion/Intervention," vi; emphasis mine.

120. James A. Fields, Randall T. Ullom, and Valeda A. Slone, "Fairfield County Municipal Court, Civil—Criminal Rules," 2024, https://www.fcmcourt.org/docs/documents/56/courtrules.pdf.

121. Middlesex District Attorney's Office, "Juvenile and Young Adult Diversion Program: Description and Guidelines," 2024, https://www.middlesexda.com/sites/g/files/vyhlif11841/f/pages/diversion_program_guidelines_jan2024.pdf.

122. Information in this paragraph is taken from interviews with DAs and other key decision-makers in their offices and from a comprehensive analysis of the websites and reports published by a national sample of urban pretrial diversion programs. For more detail, see methodological appendix A.

123. National Institute of Mental Health, "Mental Health Medications," 2023, https://www.nimh.nih.gov/health/topics/mental-health-medications; A. Butler et al., "The Empirical Status of Cognitive-Behavioral Therapy: A Review of Meta-Analyses," *Clinical Psychology Review* 26, no. 1 (January 2006): 17–31; Falk Leichsenring and Sven Rabung, "Effectiveness of Long-Term Psychodynamic Psychotherapy: A Meta-Analysis," *JAMA: The Journal of the American Medical Association* 300, no. 13 (October 1, 2008): 1551; Pim Cuijpers et al., "Interpersonal Psychotherapy for Depression: A Meta-Analysis," *American Journal of Psychiatry* 168, no. 6 (June 2011): 581–92; Irvin D. Yalom, *The Theory and Practice of Group Psychotherapy*, 5th ed. (New York: Basic Books, 2005); SAMHSA, "Medications for Substance Use Disorders," 2023, https://www.samhsa.gov/medications-substance use-disorders; Amy R. Krentzman et al., "How Alcoholics Anonymous (AA) and Narcotics Anonymous (NA) Work: Cross-Disciplinary Perspectives," *Alcoholism Treatment Quarterly* 29, no. 1 (January 2011): 75–84.

124. Cory R. Lepage and Jeff D. May, "The Anchorage, Alaska Municipal Pretrial Diversion Program: An Initial Assessment," *Alaska Law Review* 34, no. 1 (2017): 1–26; R. S. Swaminath et al., "Experiments in Change: Pretrial Diversion of Offenders with Mental Illness," *Canadian Journal of Psychiatry* 47, no. 5 (2002): 450–58; Dominique E. Roe-Sepowitz et al., "Adult Prostitution Recidivism: Risk Factors and Impact of a Diversion Program," *Journal of Offender Rehabilitation* 50 (2011): 37–41; Butler, Goodman-Delahunty, and Lulham, "Effectiveness of Pretrial Community-Based Diversion"; John Orwat et al., "The Impact of the Cook County State's Attorney's Office Deferred Prosecution Program," *Journal of Offender Rehabilitation* 58, no. 2 (February 17, 2019): 133–53; Broner et al., "Effects of Diversion on Adults with Co-Occurring Mental Illness and Substance Use"; Rempel et al., *Changing the Role of the Prosecutor*.

125. Andrew Daniller, "Two-Thirds of Americans Support Marijuana Legalization," Pew Research Center, 2019, https://www.pewresearch.org/fact-tank/2019/11/14/americans-support-marijuana-legalization/; M4BL Policy Platforms, "End the War on Black Health and Black Disabled People"; M4BL Policy Platforms, "End the War on Drugs"; Pew Research Center, "America's New Drug Policy Landscape"; Real Justice, "Tell DA's to Drop Low Level Marijuana Arrests."

126. Danielle Kaeble, "Probation and Parole in the United States, 2021," Bureau of Justice Statistics, US Department of Justice, 2023, https://bjs.ojp.gov/library/publications/probation-and-parole-united-states-2021; E. Ann Carson, "Prisoners in 2022," Bureau of Justice Statistics, US Department of Justice, 2023, https://bjs.ojp.gov/library/publications/prisoners-2022-statistical-tables.

127. Maher and Dixon, "The Cost of Crackdowns"; Lisa Maher and David Dixon, "Policing and Public Health: Law Enforcement and Harm Minimization in a Street-Level Drug Market," *The British Journal of Criminology* 39, no. 4 (1999): 488–512.

128. Singh, Browne, and Montgomery, "The Emerging Role of Toxic Adulterants in Street Drugs"; Ethan A. Nadelmann and Mark A. R. Kleiman, "Should Some Illegal Drugs Be Legalized?," *Issues in Science and Technology*, 1990; Jan Hoffman, "Tranq Dope: Animal Sedative Mixed with Fentanyl Brings Fresh Horror to U.S. Drug Zones," *The New York Times*, January 7, 2023, https://www.nytimes.com/2023/01/07/health/fentanyl-xylazine-drug.html; Kavita Babu, "What Is Fentanyl and Why Is It Behind the Deadly Surge in US Drug Overdoses?," 2022, https://www.umassmed.edu/news/news-archives/2022/05/what-is-fentanyl-and-why-is-it-behind-the-deadly-surge-in-us-drug-overdoses/.

129. Gerald F. Davis and Henrich R. Greve, "Corporate Elite Networks and Governance Changes in the 1980s," *American Journal of Sociology* 103, no. 1 (1997): 1–37; Paul J. DiMaggio and Walter W. Powell, "The Iron Cage Revisited: Institutional Isomorphism and Collective Rationality in Organizational Fields," *American Sociological Review* 48, no. 2 (1983): 147–60; Friedland and Alford, "Bringing Society Back In"; Michael T. Hannan and John Freeman, *Organizational Ecology* (Cambridge, MA: Harvard University Press, 1993); Heather A. Haveman and Hayagreeva Rao, "Structuring a Theory of Moral Sentiments: Institutional and Organizational Coevolution in the Early Thrift Industry," *American Journal of Sociology* 102, no. 6 (1997): 1606–51; Cathryn Johnson, Timothy J. Ridgeway, and Cecilia L. Ridgeway, "Legitimacy as a Social Process," *Annual Review of Sociology* 32, no. 1 (2006): 53–78; Meyer and Rowan, "Institutionalized Organizations" (1977); John W. Meyer and Brian Rowan, "Institutionalized Organizations: Formal Structure as Myth and Ceremony,"

in *The New Institutionalism in Organizational Analysis*, ed. Paul J. DiMaggio and Walter W. Powell (Chicago: University of Chicago Press, 1991), 41–62; David Strang, *Learning by Example: Imitation and Innovation at a Global Bank* (Princeton, NJ: Princeton University Press, 2010); Lynne G. Zucker, "Institutional Theories of Organization," *Annual Review of Sociology* 13 (1987): 443–64.

130. Abbott, *The System of Professions*.

131. Lauren B. Edelman, "Legal Environments and Organizational Governance: The Expansion of Due Process in the American Workplace," *American Journal of Sociology* 95, no. 6 (May 1990): 1401–40; Lauren B. Edelman, "Legal Ambiguity and Symbolic Structures: Organizational Mediation of Civil Rights Law," *American Journal of Sociology* 97, no. 6 (May 1992): 1531–76; Lauren B. Edelman and Jessica Cabrera, "Sex-Based Harassment and Symbolic Compliance," *Annual Review of Law and Social Science* 16, no. 1 (October 13, 2020): 361–83; Meyer and Rowan, "Institutionalized Organizations" (1977); Philippe Nonet and Philip Selznick, *Law and Society in Transition: Toward Responsive Law* (New York: Octagon Books, 1978); Lauren B. Edelman, *Working Law: Courts, Corporations, and Symbolic Compliance* (Chicago: University of Chicago Press, 2016); Linda Hamilton Krieger, Rachel Kahn Best, and Lauren B. Edelman, "When 'Best Practices' Win, Employees Lose: Symbolic Compliance and Judicial Inference in Federal Equal Employment Opportunity Cases," *Law & Social Inquiry* 40, no. 04 (2015): 843–79; Lauren B. Edelman et al., "When Organizations Rule: Judicial Deference to Institutionalized Employment Structures," *American Journal of Sociology* 117, no. 3 (2011): 888–954.

CHAPTER TWO

1. Johns Hopkins Bloomberg School of Public Health, "Criminal Justice Diversion Programs"; Texas Criminal Justice Coalition, "Interim Testimony 2016: Senate Committee on Criminal Justice"; American Civil Liberties Union, "Blueprint for Smart Justice."

2. I estimate that nationally only 10 percent of prosecutor-led pretrial diversion programs in urban areas—and 6 percent of urban diversionary programs overall—accept participants before they have been charged. See methodological appendix A for more detail.

3. Vera Institute of Justice, "Diversion Programs, Explained."

4. Kaye, *Enforcing Freedom*; Rempel et al., *Changing the Role of the Prosecutor*; Dawn Moore, "The Benevolent Watch: Therapeutic Surveillance in Drug Treatment Court," *Theoretical Criminology* 15, no. 3 (2011): 255–68.

5. Burns and Peyrot, "Tough Love"; Ursula Castellano, "The Politics of Benchcraft: The Role of Judges in Mental Health Courts," *Law and Social Inquiry* 42, no. 2 (2017): 398–422; Nolan, *Reinventing Justice*; Hannah-Moffat and Maurutto, "Shifting and Targeted Forms of Penal Governance"; Rashmee Singh, "'Setting a Good Example for the Ladies': Example Setting as a Technique of Penal Reform in Specialized Prostitution Court," *The British Journal of Criminology* 58 (2018): 569–87; Moore, "The Benevolent Watch."

6. For an insightful examination of court officials' engagement in "the roughest form of social work" in the context of bail decisions, see Alix S. Winter and Matthew Clair,

"'The Roughest Form of Social Work': How Court Officials Justify Bail Decisions," *Criminology* 61, no. 4 (November 2023): 904–28.

7. Seismic policy shifts over the past few decades have rendered traditional public benefits more difficult to access in the United States, even as they have dramatically expanded the criminal legal system. See, e.g., Katherine Beckett and Bruce Western, "Governing Social Marginality: Welfare, Incarceration, and the Transformation of State Policy," *Punishment and Society* 3, no. 1 (2001): 43–59; Laura Tach and Kathryn Edin, "The Social Safety Net After Welfare Reform: Recent Developments and Consequences for Household Dynamics," *Annual Review of Sociology* 43 (2017): 541–61; Loïc Wacquant, *Punishing the Poor: The Neoliberal Government of Social Insecurity* (Durham, NC: Duke University Press, 2009).

8. Roth, *Insane*; Thornicroft, *Shunned*.

9. For more on the construction of "force as the best medicine" (Tiger, *Judging Addicts*, 14) in the context of drug courts, see Nolan, *Reinventing Justice*; Tiger, *Judging Addicts*.

10. See also McKim, *Addicted to Rehab*; Teresa Gowan and Sarah Whetstone, "Making the Criminal Addict: Subjectivity and Social Control in a Strong-Arm Rehab," *Punishment & Society* 14, no. 1 (2012): 69–93; Kaye, *Enforcing Freedom*.

11. Barbara Cruikshank, *The Will to Empower: Democratic Citizens and Other Subjects* (Ithaca, NY: Cornell University Press, 1999); Soss, Fording, and Schram, *Disciplining the Poor*.

12. Stuart, *Down, Out, and Under Arrest*; Andrew J. Polsky, *The Rise of the Therapeutic State* (Princeton, NJ: Princeton University Press, 1991).

13. Katheryn K. Russell-Brown, *The Color of Crime: Racial Hoaxes, White Fear, Black Protectionism, Police Harassment, and Other Macroaggression* (New York: New York University Press, 2008); Saidiya V. Hartman, *Scenes of Subjection: Terror, Slavery, and Self-Making in Nineteenth-Century America* (Oxford and New York: Oxford University Press, 1997); Schoenfeld, *Building the Prison State*; Khalil Gibran Muhammad, *The Condemnation of Blackness: Race, Crime, and the Making of Modern Urban America* (Cambridge, MA: Harvard University Press, 2010); Jennifer L. Eberhardt et al., "Seeing Black: Race, Crime, and Visual Processing," *Journal of Personality and Social Psychology* 87, no. 6 (2004): 876–93; Gaston, "Producing Race Disparities"; Charles R. Epp, Steven Maynard-Moody, and Donald Haider-Markel, *Pulled Over: How Police Stops Define Race and Citizenship* (Chicago: University of Chicago Press, 2014); Beckett et al., "Drug Use, Drug Possession Arrests, and the Question of Race"; Nicole Gonzalez Van Cleve, *Crook County: Racism and Injustice in America's Largest Criminal Court* (Stanford, CA: Stanford University Press, 2016).

14. James Eisenstein and Herbert Jacob, *Felony Justice: An Organizational Analysis of Criminal Courts* (Boston: Little, Brown, 1977); James Eisenstein, Roy B. Flemming, and Peter F. Nardulli, *The Contours of Justice: Communities and Their Courts* (Boston: Little, Brown, 1988); Jeffery T. Ulmer, *Social Worlds of Sentencing: Court Communities Under Sentencing Guidelines* (Albany: State University of New York Press, 1997); Jo Dixon, "The Organizational Context of Criminal Sentencing," *American Journal of Sociology* 100, no. 5 (1995): 1157–98.

15. From analysis of deidentified individual-level data from the primary jurisdiction on pretrial diversion participants ($N = 1447$). For more detail, see methodological appendix A.

16. SAMHSA, "Treatment Episode Data Set (TEDS-A)."

17. For data on the kinds of treatment received by court-referred participants, see SAMHSA, "Treatment Episode Data Set (TEDS-A)."

18. In an insightful study of courts' responses to domestic violence, sociolegal scholar Rashmee Singh calls these external organizations "quasi-criminal justice organizations." They are formally independent but functionally reliant on the legal system for their clients. Rashmee Singh, "When Punishment and Philanthropy Mix: Voluntary Organizations and the Governance of the Domestic Violence Offender," *Theoretical Criminology* 16, no. 3 (2011): 269–87.

19. This decision is typically made by local prosecutors following arrests or citations by police, though prosecutors can also initiate cases on their own. Some state attorneys general also have the power to initiate local prosecutions, though they do so very rarely. In some jurisdictions police can file cases directly with the courts; prosecutors then decide whether or not to dismiss those cases. See Peter Krug, "Prosecutorial Discretion and Its Limits," *The American Journal of Comparative Law* 50, no. Supplement, "American Law in a Time of Global Interdependence: U.S. National Reports to the 16th International Congress of Comparative Law" (2002): 643–64; Jeffrey Bellin, "The Power of Prosecutors," *New York University Law Review* 94, no. 2 (2019): 171–212.

20. Even when an individual is not criminally charged, they still often have an arrest record, which can bring negative long-term consequences on its own. See Naomi F. Sugie and Kristin Turney, "Beyond Incarceration: Criminal Justice Contact and Mental Health," *American Sociological Review* 82, no. 4 (2017): 719–43; Uggen et al., "The Edge of Stigma."

21. The specific charges the prosecutor chooses to bring against an individual also determine the type of conviction they are likely to receive and the relevant sentencing range, determinations whose importance has increased substantially as sentencing guidelines have placed more limits on judicial discretion: It is the prosecutor's charging decision that determines the minimum sentence a defendant will face. See Davis, *Arbitrary Justice*; Jeffery T. Ulmer, Megan C. Kurlychek, and John H. Kramer, "Prosecutorial Discretion and the Imposition of Mandatory Minimum Sentences," *Journal of Research in Crime and Delinquency* 44, no. 4 (2007): 427–58; Marie Gottschalk, *Caught: The Prison State and the Lockdown of American Politics* (Princeton, NJ: Princeton University Press, 2015).

22. Thomas H. Cohen and Tracey Kyckelhahn, "State Court Processing Statistics: Felony Defendants in Large Urban Counties, 2006," Bureau of Justice Statistics, 2010, https://www.bjs.gov/index.cfm?ty=pbdetail&iid=2193.

23. See Pfaff, *Locked In*. Pfaff finds that reported violent and property crime fell steadily between 1994 and 2008, and arrests on almost all offenses fell. But over the same period, the chance that a given arrest would lead to a felony charge roughly doubled, so that the number of felony cases filed in state court rose significantly. Once a felony case was filed, the probability of its resulting in a prison admission remained

almost perfectly unchanged. Pfaff concludes, "The primary driver of incarceration is increased prosecutorial toughness when it comes to charging people, not longer sentences" (6).

24. American Civil Liberties Union, "Diverted into Deportation: The Immigration Consequences of Diversion Programs in Maryland," 2016, https://www.aclu-md.org/en/publications/diverted-deportation-immigration-consequences-diversion programs-maryland#:~:text=Thus%2C%20participation%20in%20a%20controlled,oriented%20goals%20of%20diversion%20programs; Sarah Lageson, *Digital Punishment: Privacy, Stigma, and the Harms of Data-Driven Criminal Justice* (Oxford and New York: Oxford University Press, 2020).

25. The prosecutorial charging decision is not subject to judicial review, and courts have repeatedly rejected any attempts to place any legal constraints on this power. As the Supreme Court declared in *Bordenkircher v. Hayes* in 1978, for instance, "The decision whether or not to prosecute, and what charge to file or bring before a grand jury, generally rests entirely in his [the prosecutor's] discretion." Bordenkircher v. Hayes (United States Supreme Court 1978); see also Davis, *Arbitrary Justice*; Angela J. Davis, "Prosecution and Race: The Power and Privilege of Discretion," *Fordham Law Review* 67, no. 1 (1998): 13–68.

26. Lisa Frohmann, "Convictability and Discordant Locales: Reproducing Race, Class, and Gender Ideologies in Prosecutorial Decisionmaking," *Law & Society Review* 31, no. 3 (1997): 531–55, at 535; see also Cassia Spohn, "Reflections on the Exercise of Prosecutorial Discretion 50 Years after Publication of *The Challenge of Crime in a Free Society*," *Criminology & Public Policy* 17, no. 2 (2018): 321–40.

27. Celesta A. Albonetti, "Prosecutorial Discretion: The Effects of Uncertainty," *Law & Society Review* 21, no. 2 (1987): 291–314; Rodney F. Kingsnorth, Randall C. MacIntosh, and Jennifer Wentworth, "Sexual Assault: The Role of Prior Relationship and Victim Characteristics in Case Processing," *Justice Quarterly* 16, no. 2 (1999): 275–302; Martha A. Myers and John Hagan, "Private and Public Trouble: Prosecutors and the Allocation of Court Resources," *Social Problems* 26, no. 4 (1979): 439–51; Janell Schmidt and Ellen Hochstedler Steury, "Prosecutorial Discretion in Filing Charges in Domestic Violence Cases," *Criminology* 27, no. 3 (1989): 487–510; Cassia Spohn, Dawn Beichner, and Erika Davis-Frenzel, "Prosecutorial Justifications for Sexual Assault Case Rejection: Guarding the 'Gateway to Justice,'" *Social Problems* 48, no. 2 (2001): 206–35; Cassia Spohn and David Holleran, "The Effect of Imprisonment on Recidivism Rates of Felony Offenders: A Focus on Drug Offenders," *Criminology* 40, no. 2 (2002): 329–58.

28. Dixon, "The Organizational Context of Criminal Sentencing"; Rodney L. Engen and Sara Steen, "The Power to Punish: Discretion and Sentencing Reform in the War on Drugs," *American Journal of Sociology* 105, no. 5 (2000): 1357–95.

29. I did come across one jurisdiction in which defendants frequently opted to remain in the traditional court system rather than participating in diversion. That jurisdiction offered defendants a "trial period" of thirty days in the diversion program, during which they could decide whether to accept the diversion option or return to court. The director of that program estimated that about half of diverted defendants opted out after the trial period.

30. Cohen and Kyckelhahn, "State Court Processing Statistics."

31. Fifty-six percent of the jurisdictions in my national sample operate at least one post-plea diversionary program. In some additional jurisdictions, defendants are required to "stipulate"—or admit—to the facts in the police report prior to entering diversion, rather than entering a formal guilty plea. In practice, those stipulations typically amount to pleas. For more details on these data and findings, see methodological appendices A and C.

32. Cohen, *Visions of Social Control*, 37–38; see also Cohen, "The Punitive City."

33. National Association of Pretrial Services Agencies, "Performance Standards and Goals for Pretrial Diversion/Intervention," 15.

34. Gottschalk, *Caught*, 39.

35. Brian D. Johnson, Ryan D. King, and Cassia Spohn, "Sociolegal Approaches to the Study of Guilty Pleas and Prosecution," *Annual Review of Law and Social Science* 12 (2016): 479–95; Spohn, "Reflections on the Exercise of Prosecutorial Discretion."

36. Bruce Frederick and Don Stemen, "The Anatomy of Discretion: An Analysis of Prosecutorial Decision Making, Summary Report," *Summary Report to the National Institute of Justice* (December 2012).

37. For the full vignettes, survey text, and more details about the study design and respondent recruitment and participation, see methodological appendix B.

38. See, e.g., American Civil Liberties Union, "Blueprint for Smart Justice"; Vera Institute of Justice, "Diversion Programs, Explained."

39. Lara-Millán, *Redistributing the Poor*; Van Cleve, *Crook County*; Cohen and Kyckelhahn, "State Court Processing Statistics."

40. Lageson, *Digital Punishment*.

41. Pamela K. Lattimore et al., "Outcome Findings from the HOPE Demonstration Field Experiment: Is Swift, Certain, and Fair an Effective Supervision Strategy?," *Criminology & Public Policy* 15, no. 4 (November 2016): 1103–41; Daniel J. O'Connell, John J. Brent, and Christy A. Visher, "Decide Your Time: A Randomized Trial of a Drug Testing and Graduated Sanctions Program for Probationers," *Criminology & Public Policy* 15, no. 4 (November 2016): 1073–1102.

42. Cohen, *Visions of Social Control*. For more on the use of therapeutic alternatives in a wide variety of criminal legal sites, including prison reentry programs, policing, carceral institutions, and court-mandated residential programs, see Lynne A. Haney, *Offending Women: Power, Punishment, and the Regulation of Desire* (Berkeley and Los Angeles: University of California Press, 2010); Armando Lara-Millán and Nicole Gonzalez Van Cleve, "Interorganizational Utility of Welfare Stigma in the Criminal Justice System," *Criminology* 55, no. 1 (2017): 59–84; McKim, *Addicted to Rehab*; Stuart, *Down, Out, and Under Arrest*; Kaye, *Enforcing Freedom*; Reuben Jonathan Miller, "Devolving the Carceral State: Race, Prisoner Reentry, and the Micro-Politics of Urban Poverty Management," *Punishment & Society* 16, no. 3 (2014): 305–35; Carolyn Sufrin, *Jailcare: Finding the Safety Net for Women behind Bars* (Oakland, CA: University of California Press, 2017); Susila Gurusami, "Working for Redemption: Formerly Incarcerated Black Women and Punishment in the Labor Market," *Gender & Society* 31, no. 4 (2017): 433–56.

43. Marcelo F. Aebi, Natalia Delgrande, and Yann Marguet, "Have Community Sanctions and Measures Widened the Net of the European Criminal Justice Systems?,"

Punishment & Society 17, no. 5 (2015): 575–97; Thomas Blomberg and Karol Lucken, "Stacking the Deck by Piling Up Sanctions: Is Intermediate Punishment Destined to Fail?," *The Howard Journal of Criminal Justice* 33, no. 1 (1994): 62–80; Cohen, *Visions of Social Control*; John H. Hylton, "Rhetoric and Reality: A Critical Appraisal of Community Correctional Programs," *Crime & Delinquency* 28, no. 3 (1982): 341–73; Michael Tonry and Mary Lynch, "Intermediate Sanctions," *Crime and Justice* 20 (1996): 99–144; David R. Lilley, Megan C. Stewart, and Kasey Tucker-Gail, "Drug Courts and Net-Widening in U.S. Cities: A Reanalysis Using Propensity Score Matching," *Criminal Justice Policy Review* 31, no. 2 (March 2020): 287–308; Morris B. Hoffman, "The Denver Drug Court and Its Unintended Consequences," in *Drug Courts in Theory and in Practice* (New York: Aldine de Gruyter, 2002), 67–88; Kathy G. Padgett, William D. Bales, and Thomas G. Blomberg, "Under Surveillance: An Empirical Test of the Effectiveness and Consequences of Electronic Monitoring," *Criminology & Public Policy* 5, no. 1 (2006): 61–91; Gill McIvor, "Community Service and Custody in Scotland," *The Howard Journal* 29, no. 2 (1990): 101–13; Ken Pease, "Community Service Orders," *Crime and Justice* 6 (January 1985): 51–94; E. C. Spaans, "Community Service in the Netherlands: Its Effects on Recidivism and Net-Widening," *International Criminal Justice Review* 8 (1998): 1–14; Carol A. B. Warren, "New Forms of Social Control: The Myth of Deinstitutionalization," *American Behavioral Scientist* 24, no. 6 (July 1981): 724–40; Thomas G. Blomberg, William Bales, and Karen Reed, "Intermediate Punishment: Redistributing or Extending Social Control?," *Crime, Law and Social Change* 19 (1993): 187–201.

44. Stuart, *Down, Out, and Under Arrest*; Michelle S. Phelps, "The Paradox of Probation: Community Supervision in the Age of Mass Incarceration," *Law and Policy* 35, no. 1–2 (2013): 51–80.

CHAPTER THREE

1. National Academies of Sciences, Engineering, and Medicine, *Medications for Opioid Use Disorder Save Lives* (Washington, DC: National Academies Press, 2019).

2. A systematic search of legislation in five states—New York, Washington, Illinois, Pennsylvania, and Louisiana—turned up just over a dozen statutes related to the operations of drug and other specialty courts and no statutes related to the content or operation of pretrial diversion.

3. Bellassai, *A Short History of the Pretrial Diversion of Adult Defendants*.

4. See table 4, methodological appendix A.

5. For details on my national sample and the administrative data collected in my fieldsite, see methodological appendices A and C.

6. Michael Farrell, "Opiate Withdrawal," *Addiction* 89 (1994): 1471–75; Shane Darke, Sarah Larney, and Michael Farrell, "Yes, People Can Die from Opiate Withdrawal: Editorial," *Addiction* 112, no. 2 (February 2017): 199–200; R. Monte et al., "Analysis of the Factors Determining Survival of Alcoholic Withdrawal Syndrome Patients in a General Hospital," *Alcohol and Alcoholism* 45, no. 2 (March 1, 2010): 151–58.

7. Tami L. Mark, William N. Dowd, and Carol L. Council, "Tracking the Quality of Addiction Treatment Over Time and Across States: Using the Federal Government's 'Signs' of Higher Quality" (Research Triangle Park, NC: RTI Press, 2020).

8. Frank, Humphreys, and Pollack, "Our Other Epidemic"; Mark, Dowd, and Council, "Tracking the Quality of Addiction Treatment Over Time and Across States"; Jennifer Taylor, "The Workforce Shortage in Addiction Care Reaches a Crisis Stage," 2021, https://treatmentmagazine.com/the-workforce-shortage-in-addiction-care-reaches-a-crisis-stage/.

9. Paul Pringle, "The Trouble with Rehab, Malibu-Style," *Los Angeles Times*, 2007, https://www.latimes.com/archives/la-xpm-2007-oct-09-me-rehab9-story.html.

10. Werb et al., "The Effectiveness of Compulsory Drug Treatment."

11. Vo et al., "Assessing HIV and Overdose Risks for People Who Use Drugs."

12. Thomas Santo et al., "Association of Opioid Agonist Treatment with All-Cause Mortality and Specific Causes of Death Among People with Opioid Dependence: A Systematic Review and Meta-Analysis," *JAMA Psychiatry* 78, no. 9 (September 1, 2021): 979; Brit Long and Michael Gottlieb, "Is Opioid Agonist Treatment Associated with Reduced Risk of Overall and Cause-Specific Mortality in Opioid-Dependent People?," *Annals of Emergency Medicine* 78, no. 6 (December 2021): 776–78; Luis Sordo et al., "Mortality Risk During and After Opioid Substitution Treatment: Systematic Review and Meta-Analysis of Cohort Studies," *BMJ* 357 (April 26, 2017): 1–14; Richard S. Schottenfeld, Marek C. Chawarski, and Mahmud Mazlan, "Maintenance Treatment with Buprenorphine and Naltrexone for Heroin Dependence in Malaysia: A Randomised, Double-Blind, Placebo-Controlled Trial," *The Lancet* 371, no. 9631 (June 2008): 2192–2200; Marc A. Schuckit, "Treatment of Opioid-Use Disorders," ed. Dan L. Longo, *New England Journal of Medicine* 375, no. 4 (July 28, 2016): 357–68; Alan I. Leshner and Victor J. Dzau, "Medication-Based Treatment to Address Opioid Use Disorder," *JAMA: The Journal of the American Medical Association* 321, no. 21 (June 4, 2019): 2071; Johan Kakko et al., "1-Year Retention and Social Function After Buprenorphine-Assisted Relapse Prevention Treatment for Heroin Dependence in Sweden: A Randomised, Placebo-Controlled Trial," *The Lancet* 361, no. 9358 (February 2003): 662–68; Michael Fairley et al., "Cost-Effectiveness of Treatments for Opioid Use Disorder," *JAMA Psychiatry* 78, no. 7 (July 1, 2021): 767; Sarah E. Wakeman et al., "Comparative Effectiveness of Different Treatment Pathways for Opioid Use Disorder," *JAMA Network Open* 3, no. 2 (February 5, 2020): e1920622.

13. Enforcement against opioid agonists in court-mandated treatment is so common that at least two states have now legislated the issue: The state of Washington, one of the more progressive in the United States, passed a law in 2017 declaring that "lawfully prescribed medication for the treatment of opioid use disorder must be treated the same in judicial and administrative proceedings as . . . other lawfully prescribed medications" (RCW 71.24.587). (Other lawfully prescribed medications, such as painkillers, are also banned by some diversion programs, so this language may not protect methadone and buprenorphine use entirely.) California, another progressive state, amended its penal code in 2018 to specify that "a person who is participating in a pretrial diversion program or a preguilty plea program pursuant to this chapter is authorized under the direction of a licensed health care practitioner, to use medications including, but not limited to, methadone, buprenorphine, or levoalphacetylmethadol (LAAM) to treat substance use disorders if the participant allows release of his or her medical records to the court . . ." (California Penal Code 1000.6).

14. National Academies of Sciences, Engineering, and Medicine, *Medications for Opioid Use Disorder Save Lives*, 38; see also Hilary Smith Connery, "Medication-Assisted Treatment of Opioid Use Disorder: Review of the Evidence and Future Directions," *Harvard Review of Psychiatry* 23, no. 2 (March 2015): 63–75.

15. Buprenorphine is only a partial opioid agonist; it does not fully substitute for other opioids on the mu-receptor. Rather, it is also an agonist of another key receptor and an antagonist of a third. Like methadone, it relieves the symptoms of opioid withdrawal and reduces euphoric feelings resulting from any opioid use. See National Academies of Sciences, Engineering, and Medicine, *Medications for Opioid Use Disorder Save Lives*.

16. Programs typically run drug tests on urine samples—rather than samples of hair, blood, saliva, or fingernails, for instance—because of the convenience of sample collection and because substances are present in higher concentrations in urine than in substances like blood and remain detectable for longer periods of time. See also Karen E. Moeller et al., "Clinical Interpretation of Urine Drug Tests," *Mayo Clinic Proceedings* 92, no. 5 (May 2017): 774–96.

17. Immunoassay tests can produce false-positive results when they detect substances with similar characteristics to the target drugs and because results can be difficult to read when colors are faint or unclear. The tests are meant to be preliminary, and test kits warn users against interpreting any positive results without confirmatory testing using more accurate methods such as gas chromatography/mass spectrometry (GC-MS) testing. See Moeller et al., "Clinical Interpretation of Urine Drug Tests." The National Association of Drug Court Professionals' Adult Drug Court Best Practice Standards are equivocal on the question of confirmatory testing, noting that some appellate courts have upheld legal decisions made on the basis of immunoassay tests alone. Although some states have made moves to make confirmatory testing available in their court systems, access even in those places remains partial. Louisiana's state supreme court recently ruled that the state's drug courts must make confirmatory testing available to participants who say immunoassay test results are inaccurate, for instance, but it does not extend the requirement to other diversion or probation programs or to drug testing ordered by judges outside of the drug court context. See Bell v. State, 179 So. 3d 349 (District Court of Appeal of Florida, Fifth District 2015); Somers v. State, 368 S.W.3d 528 (Court of Criminal Appeals of Texas 2012); Moeller et al., "Clinical Interpretation of Urine Drug Tests"; National Association of Drug Court Professionals, "Adult Drug Court Best Practice Standards, Volume II," 2013, https://www.nadcp.org/standards/adult-drug-court-best-practice-standards/; Nick Chrastil, "State Supreme Court Updates Standards for Drug Courts Throughout the State to Require Confirmation Testing," *The Lens*, August 6, 2019, https://thelensnola.org/2019/08/06/state-supreme-court-updates-standards-for-drug-courts-throughout-the-state-to-require-confirmation-testing/.

18. The "10-panel" drug test used by most of the diversion programs I spoke with is designed to detect the following substances: (1) THC (tetrahydrocannabinol, the main psychoactive compound in marijuana); (2) PCP (phencyclidine), a dissociative anesthetic often called "angel dust" that was brought to the US market in the 1950s as an anesthetic but disallowed for human use in 1965; (3) cocaine; (4) amphetamines; (5) opiates; (6) benzodiazepines, a class of depressant drugs often prescribed as short-term

treatment for medical conditions such as anxiety and panic disorders; (7) barbiturates, depressants that have largely been replaced by benzodiazepines because of the high risk of overdose and other side effects associated with them; (8) propoxyphene, an opioid originally introduced in the US as a pain reliever and cough suppressant but taken off the market because of concerns about overdose and heart arrhythmias; (9) methadone, an opioid agonist commonly prescribed to treat opioid use disorder; and (10) methaqualone, a hypnotic sedative whose production was halted in the 1980s after it came into widespread recreational use in the United States. Some programs also add panels for other substances, including alcohol and buprenorphine (Suboxone), a medication prescribed to treat opioid use disorders.

19. Short-acting barbiturates such as pentobarbital can typically be detected for only about twenty-four hours; amphetamines, heroin, and codeine can usually be detected for around forty-eight hours; and morphine, methadone, hydromorphone, oxycodone, short-acting benzodiazepines, and smaller doses of marijuana (THC) or synthetic cannabinoids are often detectable for three or four days. PCP can be detected for about eight days, and long-acting barbiturates and benzodiazepines are detectable for three or four weeks. THC can linger longest: larger doses can be detectable well over a month after use. See Moeller et al., "Clinical Interpretation of Urine Drug Tests."

20. National Association of Drug Court Professionals, "Adult Drug Court Best Practice Standards, Volume II," 27–28.

21. A randomized controlled trial (RCT) is considered the gold standard for evaluating the impacts of particular programs on individuals. A brief explanation of the strengths of the RCT is in order here, since the rest of this chapter will rely heavily on them. Evaluations of interventions into people's lives aim to compare their outcomes—whether measured in terms of rearrest, drug use, or something else—to the outcomes they *would* have had in the absence of that intervention. Since that counter-positive is impossible to observe, researchers design studies to compare people who were exposed to a program or policy to similarly situated people who were not exposed. The best way to ensure that there are no systematic differences between the two groups they plan to compare is to randomly assign some people to receive the intervention and others not to. Any differences in outcomes between the groups can then be attributed to the intervention itself.

22. Angela Hawken and Mark Kleiman, "Managing Drug Involved Probationers with Swift and Certain Sanctions: Evaluating Hawaii's HOPE" (NCJRS Virtual Library, 2009); Eric Grommon et al., "Alternative Models of Instant Drug Testing: Evidence from an Experimental Trial," *Journal of Experimental Criminology* 9 (2013): 145–68. It is worth noting that, even if drug testing is not effective in improving individuals' long-term health, it may have positive effects in the short term, especially when it prevents substance use with negative impacts on public health. One high-quality study found that when counties required people who had been arrested on alcohol-related charges to take twice-daily breathalyzer tests or to wear bracelets that continuously monitored for alcohol, they saw significant reductions in repeat DUI arrests and domestic violence arrests. Beau Kilmer et al., "Efficacy of Frequent Monitoring with Swift, Certain, and Modest Sanctions for Violations: Insights from South Dakota's 24/7 Sobriety Project," *American Journal of Public Health* 103, no. 1 (January 2013): e37–43.

23. Lattimore et al., "Outcome Findings from the HOPE Demonstration Field Experiment"; O'Connell, Brent, and Visher, "Decide Your Time."

24. Jeffrey Foote et al., *Beyond Addiction: How Science and Kindness Help People Change* (New York: Simon & Schuster, 2014).

25. Keith Humphreys et al., "Brains, Environments, and Policy Responses to Addiction," *Science* 356, no. 6344 (2017): 1237–38; A. Thomas McLellan et al., "Drug Dependence, a Chronic Medical Illness: Implications for Treatment, Insurance, and Outcomes Evaluation," *JAMA: The Journal of the American Medical Association* 284, no. 13 (2000): 1689–95.

26. US Department of Health and Human Services Office of the Surgeon General, "Facing Addiction: The Surgeon General's Report on Alcohol, Drugs, and Health," 2016, https://www.ncbi.nlm.nih.gov/books/NBK424857/pdf/Bookshelf_NBK424857.pdf.

27. William R. Miller et al., "What Predicts Relapse? Prospective Testing of Antecedent Models," *Addiction* 91, Supplement (1996): S155–71.

28. Blake Farmer, "Once Pandemic Emergency Protections End, Millions Likely to Lose Medicaid," *Marketplace*, 2023, https://www.marketplace.org/2023/01/02/once-pandemic-emergency-protections-end-millions-likely-to-lose-medicaid/; Margot Sanger-Katz, "After Falling Under Obama, America's Uninsured Rate Looks to Be Rising," *The New York Times*, January 23, 2019, https://www.nytimes.com/2019/01/23/upshot/rate-of-americans-without-health-insurance-rising.html.

29. See methodological appendix A.

30. Shaila Dewan and Andrew W. Lehren, "After a Crime, the Price of a Second Chance," *The New York Times*, December 12, 2016, http://www.nytimes.com/2016/12/12/us/crime-criminal-justice-reform-diversion.html.

31. Briggs v. Montgomery, First Amended Class Action Complaint and Jury Trial Demand, No. CV-18-2684-PHX-JAS (US District Court for the District of Arizona October 12, 2018).

32. "Treatment Assessment Screening Center, Inc. (TASC)," 2023, https://www.tascsolutions.org.

33. Daniel J. Boches et al., "Monetary Sanctions and Symbiotic Harms," *RSF: The Russell Sage Foundation Journal of the Social Sciences* 8, no. 2 (January 2022): 98–115; Karin D. Martin et al., "Monetary Sanctions: Legal Financial Obligations in US Systems of Justice," *Annual Review of Criminology* 1 (2018): 471–95; Mary Pattillo et al., "Monetary Sanctions and Housing Instability," *RSF: The Russell Sage Foundation Journal of the Social Sciences* 8, no. 2 (January 2022): 57–75; Alexes Harris and Tyler Smith, "Monetary Sanctions as Chronic and Acute Health Stressors: The Emotional Strain of People Who Owe Court Fines and Fees," *RSF: The Russell Sage Foundation Journal of the Social Sciences* 8, no. 2 (January 2022): 36–56.

34. Jim Ferrell for Prosecutor, "My Top Priorities," 2022, https://www.jimferrell.org/priorities-2/; emphasis mine.

35. Amy Radil, "New Youth Program Divides Candidates for King County Prosecutor," July 21, 2022, https://www.kuow.org/stories/new-youth-program-divides-candidates-for-king-county-prosecutor.

36. MyNorthwest Staff, "KC Prosecutor Candidate: County 'Looks the Other Way' with 'Unaccountable' Restorative Justice," September 7, 2022, https://mynorthwest.com/3621828/kc-prosecutor-candidate-ferrell-restorative-justice/; Kalie Greenberg, "With Rising Gun Violence, South King County Mayors Ask to Pause Criminal Diversion Program," December 23, 2021, https://www.king5.com/article/news/local/federal-way/gun-violence-king-county-restorative-pathways-diversion-program/281-20b93973-cefd-4d22-aad9-9ac8a47063dd.

37. Radil, "New Youth Program Divides Candidates for King County Prosecutor."

38. *The Seattle Times* Editorial Board, "The *Times* Recommends: Jim Ferrell for King County Prosecuting Attorney," October 7, 2022, seattletimes.com/opinion/editorials/the-times-recommends-jim-ferrell-for-king-county-prosecuting-attorney/; King County, "Candidates, November 2022 General Election: Prosecuting Attorney," 2022, https://info.kingcounty.gov/kcelections/Vote/contests/candidates.aspx?cid=120815&candidateid=1602977&lang=en-US&pamphletson=true.

39. Friedland and Alford, "Bringing Society Back In," 243.

40. Meyer and Rowan, "Institutionalized Organizations" (1977), 341; Douglas, *How Institutions Think*; Jepperson, "Institutions, Institutional Effects, and Institutionalism."

41. Haveman and Rao, "Structuring a Theory of Moral Sentiments"; Meyer and Rowan, "Institutionalized Organizations" (1991); Jepperson, "Institutions, Institutional Effects, and Institutionalism"; Friedland and Alford, "Bringing Society Back In"; Patricia H. Thornton and William Ocasio, "Institutional Logics," in *The SAGE Handbook of Organizational Institutionalism*, ed. Royston Greenwood et al. (London: SAGE Publications, 2008), 99–128; Patricia H. Thornton, William Ocasio, and Michael Lounsbury, *The Institutional Logics Perspective: A New Approach* (Oxford and New York: Oxford University Press, 2012).

42. Paul J. DiMaggio and Walter W. Powell, "Introduction," in *The New Institutionalism in Organizational Analysis*, ed. Walter W. Powell and Paul J. DiMaggio (Chicago: University of Chicago Press, 1991), 1–40; DiMaggio and Powell, "The Iron Cage Revisited"; Meyer and Rowan, "Institutionalized Organizations" (1991); Hyunjung Ji, "Mimetic Pressure for Sustainability Efforts in a Metropolitan Area," *Academy of Management Proceedings* 2020, no. 1 (August 2020): 20506; Meyer and Rowan, "Institutionalized Organizations" (1977); Jens Beckert, "Institutional Isomorphism Revisited: Convergence and Divergence in Institutional Change," *Sociological Theory* 28, no. 2 (June 2010): 150–66.

43. Bruce Western, *Punishment and Inequality in America* (New York: Russell Sage Foundation, 2006); Loïc Wacquant, *Racial Domination* (Cambridge: Polity Press, 2024).

44. Kohler-Hausmann, *Misdemeanorland*; Malcolm M. Feeley and Jonathan Simon, "The New Penology: Notes on the Emerging Strategy of Corrections and Its Implications," *Criminology* 30, no. 4 (1992): 449–74; Wacquant, *Punishing the Poor*; Stuart, *Down, Out, and Under Arrest*.

45. Russell-Brown, *The Color of Crime*; Hartman, *Scenes of Subjection*; Muhammad, *The Condemnation of Blackness*.

46. Cruikshank, *The Will to Empower*; Vincent Lyon-Callo, *Inequality, Poverty, and Neoliberal Governance: Activist Ethnography in the Homeless Sheltering Industry*

(Peterborough: Broadview Press, 2004); Polsky, *The Rise of the Therapeutic State*; Soss, Fording, and Schram, *Disciplining the Poor*; Stuart, *Down, Out, and Under Arrest*.

47. Feeley and Simon, "The New Penology," 465; see also Jonathan Simon and Malcolm M. Feeley, "True Crime: The New Penology and Public Discourse on Crime," in *Punishment and Social Control: Essays in Honor of Sheldon Messinger*, ed. Sheldon L. Messinger, Stanley Cohen, and Thomas G. Blomberg (New York: Aldine de Gruyter, 1995), 147–80; John Pratt, "The Return of the Wheelbarrow Men; or, the Arrival of Postmodern Penality?," *The British Journal of Criminology* 40, no. 1 (2000): 127–45; Wacquant, *Punishing the Poor*.

Scholars have cautioned against black-and-white characterizations of the shift from rehabilitative to more punitive approaches to penality. The influence of the rehabilitative ideal has endured in many sites throughout the "punitive turn," perhaps especially in women's prisons and reentry programs. The shift in rhetoric and practice that began in the 1970s was also not uniform across the United States; different regions saw different developments at different times. See Philip Goodman, Joshua Page, and Michelle Phelps, *Breaking the Pendulum: The Long Struggle over Criminal Justice* (Oxford and New York: Oxford University Press, 2017); Candace Kruttschnitt and Rosemary Gartner, *Marking Time in the Golden State: Women's Imprisonment in California* (Cambridge: Cambridge University Press, 2005); Mona Lynch, *Sunbelt Justice: Arizona and the Transformation of American Punishment* (Stanford, CA: Stanford Law Books, 2009).

48. Institute for Crime & Justice Policy Research, University of London, "World Prison Brief," 2024, https://www.prisonstudies.org/highest-to-lowest/prison-population-total?field_region_taxonomy_tid=All; Roy Walmsley, "World Prison Population List," National Institute of Corrections, 2015, https://nicic.gov/resources/nic-library/all-library-items/world-prison-population-listeleventh-edition.

49. Kohler-Hausmann, *Misdemeanorland*; Kaeble, "Probation and Parole in the United States, 2021."

50. Hazel Kemshall, *Risk in Probation Practice* (New York: Routledge, 1998); Kathleen Tierney, *The Social Roots of Risk: Producing Disasters, Promoting Resilience* (Stanford, CA: Stanford University Press, 2014); David Garland, "The Rise of Risk," in *Risk and Morality*, ed. Richard V. Ericson and Aaron Doyle (Toronto: University of Toronto Press, 2003), 48–86.

51. Garland, "The Rise of Risk," 52.

52. Kelly Hannah-Moffat, Paula Maurutto, and Sarah Turnbull, "Negotiated Risk: Actuarial Illusions and Discretion in Probation," *Canadian Journal of Law and Society* 24, no. 3 (2009): 391–409.

53. Michelle S. Phelps and Ebony L. Ruhland, "Governing Marginality: Coercion and Care in Probation," *Social Problems* 69, no. 3 (2022): 799–816; Failure to Appear, "Failure to Appear Consequences," 2023, http://www.failuretoappear.org/failuretoappearconsequences.html; John Halushka, *Getting the Runaround: Formerly Incarcerated Men and the Bureaucratic Barriers to Reentry* (Berkeley and Los Angeles: University of California Press, 2023).

54. Kohler-Hausmann, *Misdemeanorland*.

55. Robert L. Dupont, Bruce A. Goldberger, and Mark S. Gold, "The Science and Clinical Uses of Drug Testing," in *The ASAM Principles of Addiction Medicine*, ed. Richard K. Ries et al., 5th ed. (Philadelphia: Lippincott Williams & Wilkins, 2014), 1717–29; Jonathan Simon, *Poor Discipline: Parole and the Social Control of the Underclass, 1890–1990* (Chicago: University of Chicago Press, 1993).

56. Alexes Harris, *A Pound of Flesh: Monetary Sanctions as Punishment for the Poor* (New York: Russell Sage Foundation, 2016); Ebony Ruhland, Bryan Holmes, and Amber Petkus, "The Role of Fines and Fees on Probation Outcomes," *Criminal Justice and Behavior* 47, no. 10 (October 2020): 1244–63.

57. Douglas, *How Institutions Think*; Jepperson, "Institutions, Institutional Effects, and Institutionalism"; Meyer and Rowan, "Institutionalized Organizations" (1991).

58. In Alaska and Delaware, local prosecutors are appointed by the state's attorney general, who is elected in Delaware and appointed in Alaska. In New Jersey, local prosecutors are appointed by the governor, with the consent of the state senate. In Connecticut, they are appointed by a state commission. In Rhode Island, all criminal cases are handled not by local prosecutors but by the state's attorney general, who is elected. See UNC School of Law, "The Prosecutors and Politics Project."

59. Berdejó and Yuchtman, "Crime, Punishment, and Politics"; Gordon and Huber, "The Effect of Electoral Competitiveness on Incumbent Behavior"; Huber and Gordon, "Accountability and Coercion"; Pfaff, *Locked In*.

60. Davis, *Arbitrary Justice*.

61. Robert Werth, "Theorizing the Performative Effects of Penal Risk Technologies: (Re)Producing the Subject Who Must Be Dangerous," *Social and Legal Studies* 28, no. 3 (2019): 327–48; Sonja Starr, "The Risk Assessment Era: An Overdue Debate," *Federal Sentencing Reporter* 27, no. 4 (2015): 205–6; Robert Werth, "Risk and Punishment: The Recent History and Uncertain Future of Actuarial, Algorithmic, and 'Evidence-Based' Penal Techniques," *Sociology Compass* 13 (2019): 1–19; Jennifer L. Skeem and Christopher T. Lowenkamp, "Risk, Race, and Recidivism: Predictive Bias and Disparate Impact," *Criminology* 54, no. 4 (2016): 680–712.

62. DiMaggio and Powell, "Introduction"; DiMaggio and Powell, "The Iron Cage Revisited"; Meyer and Rowan, "Institutionalized Organizations" (1991); Ji, "Mimetic Pressure for Sustainability Efforts in a Metropolitan Area"; Meyer and Rowan, "Institutionalized Organizations" (1977); Beckert, "Institutional Isomorphism Revisited."

63. Joan Petersilia and Susan Turner, "Intensive Probation and Parole," *Crime and Justice* 17, no. 1993 (1993): 281–335; Joan Petersilia and Susan Turner, "Comparing Intensive and Regular Supervision for High-Risk Probationers: Early Results from an Experiment in California," *Crime & Delinquency* 36, no. 1 (1990): 87–111; Susan Turner, Joan Petersilia, and Elizabeth Piper Deschenes, "Evaluating Intensive Supervision Probation/Parole (ISP) for Drug Offenders," *Crime & Delinquency* 38, no. 4 (1992): 539–56.

64. Jordan M. Hyatt and Geoffrey C. Barnes, "An Experimental Evaluation of the Impact of Intensive Supervision on the Recidivism of High-Risk Probationers," *Crime & Delinquency* 63, no. 1 (2017): 3–38.

65. See also Karol Lucken, "The Dynamics of Penal Reform," *Crime, Law & Social Change* 26 (1997): 367–84; Petersilia and Turner, "Intensive Probation and Parole"; Don Stemen and Andres F. Rengifo, "Mandating Treatment for Drug Possessors: The Impact of Senate Bill 123 on the Criminal Justice System in Kansas," *Journal of Criminal Justice* 37, no. 3 (2009): 296–304.

66. Jennifer L. Huck and Camie S. Morris, "Jail Diversion and Recidivism: A Case Study of a Municipal Court Diversion Program," *Criminal Justice Policy Review* 28, no. 9 (2016): 866–78; Scott et al., "Effectiveness of Criminal Justice Liaison and Diversion Services."

67. Broner et al., "Effects of Diversion on Adults with Co-Occurring Mental Illness and Substance Use"; Butler, Goodman-Delahunty, and Lulham, "Effectiveness of Pretrial Community-Based Diversion"; Lange, Rehm, and Popova, "The Effectiveness of Criminal Justice Diversion Initiatives in North America"; Roe-Sepowitz et al., "Adult Prostitution Recidivism"; Scott et al., "Effectiveness of Criminal Justice Liaison and Diversion Services."

68. A well-designed study of one Baltimore drug court, for instance, randomly assigned defendants either to a drug court program or to adjudication by the traditional court system. Those assigned to drug court received additional supervision, treatment for substance use disorders, and reduced incarceration time. Three years later the drug court participants self-reported less crime and substance use than did people assigned to the control group. But the researchers could not randomly assign—and thus isolate the impacts of—either the distinct elements of the program or the reduced incarceration time. See Denise C. Gottfredson et al., "How Drug Treatment Courts Work: An Analysis of Mediators," *Journal of Research in Crime and Delinquency* 44, no. 1 (2007): 3–35; Denise C. Gottfredson et al., "The Baltimore City Drug Treatment Court: 3-Year Self-Report Outcome Study," *Evaluation Review* 29, no. 1 (February 2005): 42–64.

69. Apel and Sweeten, "The Impact of Incarceration on Employment"; Christopher J. Lyons and Becky Pettit, "Compounded Disadvantage: Race, Incarceration, and Wage Growth," *Social Problems* 58, no. 2 (2011): 257–80; Pager, *Marked*; Sykes and Maroto, "A Wealth of Inequalities"; Western, "The Impact of Incarceration on Wage Mobility and Inequality."

70. Wacquant, *Punishing the Poor*.

71. Susan Dewey and Tonia St. Germain, *Women of the Street: How the Criminal Justice–Social Services Alliance Fails Women in Prostitution* (New York: New York University Press, 2016).

72. Jennifer Musto, *Control and Protect: Collaboration, Carceral Protection, And Domestic Sex Trafficking in the United States* (Oakland: University of California Press, 2016).

73. Leah Wang and Katie Rose Quandt, "Building Exits off the Highway to Mass Incarceration: Diversion Programs Explained," Prison Policy Institute, 2021, https://www.prisonpolicy.org/reports/diversion.html; Vera Institute of Justice, "Diversion Programs, Explained"; American Civil Liberties Union, "Blueprint for Smart Justice."

CHAPTER FOUR

1. Fletcher, *Inside Rehab*.

2. Heinz Kohut, *How Does Analysis Cure?* (Chicago: University of Chicago Press, 1984); National Institute on Drug Abuse, "Treatment Approaches for Drug Addiction," 2019, https://www.drugabuse.gov/publications/drugfacts/treatment-approaches-drug-addiction; G. S. Truant and J. G. Lohrenz, "Basic Principles of Psychotherapy: I. Introduction, Basic Goals, and the Therapeutic Relationship," *American Journal of Psychotherapy* 47, no. 1 (1993): 8–18.

3. Truant and Lohrenz, "Basic Principles of Psychotherapy," 8; emphasis mine.

4. Bruce E. Wampold, "How Important Are the Common Factors in Psychotherapy? An Update," *World Psychiatry* 14, no. 3 (October 2015): 270–77.

5. Sociologist Ursula Castellano has written about this tension in the context of drug courts, where she finds that counselors are forced to "ride the fence between criminal justice and social work." Ursula Castellano, "Courting Compliance: Case Managers as 'Double Agents' in the Mental Health Court," *Law and Social Inquiry* 36, no. 2 (2011): 484–514, at 489.

6. This process was typical across the jurisdictions in which I interviewed diversion practitioners. In the state of California, though, a statute dictates that the final decision to return a defendant from pretrial diversion to the traditional court system be made in a formal hearing in court (see California Code, Penal Code—PEN § 1000.3).

7. Broner et al., "Effects of Diversion on Adults with Co-Occurring Mental Illness and Substance Use"; Butler, Goodman-Delahunty, and Lulham, "Effectiveness of Pretrial Community-Based Diversion"; Lange, Rehm, and Popova, "The Effectiveness of Criminal Justice Diversion Initiatives in North America"; Ojmarrh Mitchell et al., "Assessing the Effectiveness of Drug Courts on Recidivism: A Meta-Analytic Review of Traditional and Non-Traditional Drug Courts," *Journal of Criminal Justice* 40, no. 1 (2012): 60–71; Scott et al., "Effectiveness of Criminal Justice Liaison and Diversion Services"; United States Government Accountability Office, "Adult Drug Courts: Evidence Indicates Recidivism Reductions and Mixed Results for Other Outcomes," 2005, https://www.gao.gov/products/GAO-05-219.

8. From analyses of detailed case histories of 394 defendants who both entered and exited diversion between January of 2014 and June of 2017. For more detail on these data, see methodological appendix A.

9. See also Kohler-Hausmann, *Misdemeanorland*.

10. Fletcher, *Inside Rehab*.

11. See methodological appendix A for more information on this national sample.

12. Ashley Peskoe and Stephen Stirling, "Want Heroin Treatment in N.J.? Get Arrested," NJ Advance Media for NJ.com, 2015, https://www.nj.com/healthfit/2015/01/want_heroin_treatment_in_nj_get_arrested.htm.

13. Matthew Clair, *Privilege and Punishment: How Race and Class Matter in Criminal Court* (Princeton, NJ: Princeton University Press, 2020); Matthew Clair, "Being a Disadvantaged Criminal Defendant: Mistrust and Resistance in Attorney-Client Interactions," *Social Forces* 100, no. 1 (2021): 194–217; David S. Kirk and Andrew V.

Papachristos, "Cultural Mechanisms and the Persistence of Neighborhood Violence," *American Journal of Sociology* 116, no. 4 (2011): 1190–1233.

14. Monica C. Bell, "Police Reform and the Dismantling of Legal Estrangement," *The Yale Law Journal* 126 (2017): 2054–2150; John Hagan, Carla Shedd, and Monique R. Payne, "Race, Ethnicity, and Youth Perceptions of Criminal Injustice," *American Sociological Review* 70, no. June (2005): 381–407; Vesla Weaver, Gwen Prowse, and Spencer Piston, "Too Much Knowledge, Too Little Power: An Assessment of Political Knowledge in Highly Policed Communities," *The Journal of Politics* 81, no. 3 (2019): 1153–66; Jason Sunshine and Tom R. Tyler, "The Role of Procedural Justice and Legitimacy in Shaping Public Support for Policing," *Law & Society Review* 37, no. 3 (2003): 513–48.

15. Paige L. Sweet, "The Paradox of Legibility: Domestic Violence and Institutional Survivorhood," *Social Problems* 66, no. 3 (August 1, 2019): 411–27; Paige Sweet, *The Politics of Surviving: How Women Navigate Domestic Violence and Its Aftermath* (Berkeley and Los Angeles: University of California Press, 2021).

16. Sameena Mulla, *The Violence of Care: Rape Victims, Forensic Nurses, and Sexual Assault Intervention* (New York: New York University Press, 2014), 5.

CHAPTER FIVE

1. Bureau of Justice Assistance, "Program Performance Report: Implementation Grantees of the Adult Drug Court Discretionary Grant Program, October 2012-March 2013," 2013, https://bja.ojp.gov/library/publications/program-performance-report-implementation-grantees-adult-drug-court; Huck and Morris, "Jail Diversion and Recidivism"; Douglas B. Marlowe, Carolyn D. Hardin, and Carson L. Fox, "Painting the Current Picture: A National Report on Drug Courts and Other Problem-Solving Courts in the United States," National Drug Court Institute, 2016; Mitchell et al., "Assessing the Effectiveness of Drug Courts on Recidivism."

2. For an in-depth discussion of the penalties people face when they return to court from diversion, see chapter 6. Defendants who enter diversion and then return to court typically see their punishments extended relative to those they would have received if they had never been diverted to begin with. At a minimum, they spend more time under criminal legal supervision, because the time and money spent in diversion are not credited toward returning defendants' ultimate sentences, and these are large investments: in my field site, the median time people spend in treatment before they are sent back to court is nearly a year. Many, like Isiah, have lost the opportunity to reduce the severity of their criminal convictions through plea bargaining, since they were required to plead guilty prior to entering diversion. And even those who were not made to enter guilty pleas often find themselves disadvantaged in the plea-bargaining process, since prosecutors and judges tend to penalize treatment noncompletion.

3. Bernard E. Harcourt, "Risk as a Proxy for Race: The Dangers of Risk Assessment," *Federal Sentencing Reporter* 27, no. 4 (2015): 237–43; Sandra G. Mayson, "Bias In, Bias Out," *Yale Law Journal* 128, no. 8 (2019): 2218–2300.

4. Based on administrative data from my field site (see methodological appendix A for more detail). Because the two program tiers assigned to those with more serious mental healthcare needs require at a minimum two years of program participation, while the lowest tier requires only one year, lower completion rates among those

in the top two tiers may be partly a function of greater demands on them over time. I therefore also calculated completion rates after excluding participants in the two highest tiers whose cases were returned *after* the median time to completion among those in the lowest tier. Exclusion of those defendants results in a noncompletion rate of 61 percent among people in the highest risk/need tier.

5. Clifford A. Butzin, Christine A. Saum, and Frank R. Scarpitti, "Factors Associated with Completion of a Drug Treatment Court Diversion Program," *Substance Use & Misuse* 37 (2009): 1615–33; Anne Dannerbeck et al., "Understanding and Responding to Racial Differences in Drug Court Outcomes," *Journal of Ethnicity in Substance Abuse* 5, no. 2 (2006): 1–22; Kristen E. DeVall and Christina L. Lanier, "Successful Completion: An Examination of Factors Influencing Drug Court Completion for White and Non-White Male Participants," *Substance Use & Misuse* 47 (2012): 1106–16; Daniel Howard, "Race, Neighborhood, and Drug Court Graduation," *Justice Quarterly* 33, no. 1 (2016): 159–84; Adi Jaffe et al., "Drug-Abusing Offenders with Comorbid Mental Disorders: Problem Severity, Treatment Participation, and Recidivism," *Journal of Substance Abuse Treatment* 43, no. 2 (2012): 244–50; Jerome McKean and Kiesha Warren-Gordon, "Racial Differences in Graduation Rates from Adult Drug Treatment Courts," *Journal of Ethnicity in Criminal Justice* 9 (2011): 41–55; Sanjay Shah et al., "Addiction Severity Index Scores and Urine Drug Screens at Baseline as Predictors of Graduation from Drug Court," *Crime & Delinquency* 61, no. 9 (2015): 1257–77. For one insightful analysis of these inequalities in the drug court context, see Kaye, *Enforcing Freedom*.

6. Humphreys et al., "Brains, Environments, and Policy Responses"; McLellan et al., "Drug Dependence, a Chronic Medical Illness."

7. Shah et al., "Addiction Severity Index Scores and Urine Drug Screens at Baseline."

8. National Academies of Sciences, Engineering, and Medicine, *Medications for Opioid Use Disorder Save Lives*.

9. Santo et al., "Association of Opioid Agonist Treatment with All-Cause Mortality"; Long and Gottlieb, "Is Opioid Agonist Treatment Associated with Reduced Risk of Overall and Cause-Specific Mortality in Opioid-Dependent People?"; Sordo et al., "Mortality Risk During and After Opioid Substitution Treatment"; Schottenfeld, Chawarski, and Mazlan, "Maintenance Treatment with Buprenorphine and Naltrexone"; Schuckit, "Treatment of Opioid-Use Disorders"; Leshner and Dzau, "Medication-Based Treatment to Address Opioid Use Disorder"; Kakko et al., "1-Year Retention and Social Function after Buprenorphine-Assisted Relapse Prevention Treatment"; Wakeman et al., "Comparative Effectiveness of Different Treatment Pathways for Opioid Use Disorder"; Fairley et al., "Cost-Effectiveness of Treatments for Opioid Use Disorder."

10. National Academies of Sciences, Engineering, and Medicine, *Medications for Opioid Use Disorder Save Lives*, 38; see also Connery, "Medication-Assisted Treatment of Opioid Use Disorder."

11. US Department of Justice, Drug Enforcement Administration, "Controlled Substance Schedules," 2022, https://www.deadiversion.usdoj.gov/schedules/.

12. National Institute on Drug Abuse, "Criminal Justice DrugFacts," 2020, https://nida.nih.gov/download/23025/criminal-justice-drugfacts.pdf?v=25dde14276b2fa252318f2c573407966.

13. Po Hsiu Kuo et al., "The Temporal Relationship of the Onsets of Alcohol Dependence and Major Depression: Using a Genetically Informative Study Design,"

Psychological Medicine 36, no. 8 (2006): 1153–62; Robert F. Anda et al., "Adverse Childhood Experiences and Smoking During Adolescence and Adulthood," *JAMA: The Journal of the American Medical Association* 282, no. 17 (1999); Lamya Khoury et al., "Substance Use, Childhood Traumatic Experience, and Posttraumatic Stress Disorder in an Urban Civilian Population," *Depression and Anxiety* 27 (2010): 1077–86; Giuseppe N. Giordano et al., "Unexpected Adverse Childhood Experiences and Subsequent Drug Use Disorder: A Swedish Population Study (1995–2011)," *Addiction* 109, no. 7 (2014): 1119–27; Emily M. Zarse et al., "The Adverse Childhood Experiences Questionnaire: Two Decades of Research on Childhood Trauma as a Primary Cause of Adult Mental Illness, Addiction, and Medical Diseases," ed. Udo Schumacher, *Cogent Medicine* 6, no. 1 (January 1, 2019): 1581447; Grant Sara and Julia Lappin, "Childhood Trauma: Psychiatry's Greatest Public Health Challenge?," *The Lancet Public Health* 2, no. 7 (July 2017): e300–301; A. Trotta, R. M. Murray, and H. L. Fisher, "The Impact of Childhood Adversity on the Persistence of Psychotic Symptoms: A Systematic Review and Meta-Analysis," *Psychological Medicine* 45, no. 12 (September 2015): 2481–98.

    14. Carly B. Dierkhising et al., "Trauma Histories Among Justice-Involved Youth: Findings from the National Child Traumatic Stress Network," *European Journal of Psychotraumatology* 4, no. 1 (December 1, 2013): 20274; Sachiko Donley et al., "Civilian PTSD Symptoms and Risk for Involvement in the Criminal Justice System," *Journal of the American Academy of Psychiatry and the Law* 40, no. 4 (2012): 522–29; Doreen D. Salina et al., "Rates of Traumatization and Psychopathology in Criminal Justice-Involved Women," *Journal of Trauma & Dissociation* 18, no. 2 (March 15, 2017): 174–88.

    15. See also Scott M. Hyman and Rajita Sinha, "Stress-Related Factors in Cannabis Use and Misuse: Implications for Prevention and Treatment," *Journal of Substance Abuse Treatment* 36, no. 4 (2009): 400–413; Emily R. Dworkin et al., "Daily-Level Associations Between PTSD and Cannabis Use Among Young Sexual Minority Women," *Addictive Behaviors* 74 (November 2017): 118–21; Luther Elliott et al., "PTSD and Cannabis-Related Coping Among Recent Veterans in New York City," *Contemporary Drug Problems* 42, no. 1 (March 2015): 60–76.

    16. Kaiser Family Foundation, "Latest Federal Data Show That Young People Are More Likely than Older Adults to Be Experiencing Symptoms of Anxiety or Depression," 2023, https://www.kff.org/coronavirus-covid-19/press-release/latest-federal-data-show-that-young-people-are-more-likely-than-older-adults-to-be-experiencing-symptoms-of-anxiety-or-depression/#:~:text=Nearly%204%20in%2010%20(39.3,health%20crisis%20in%20the%20U.S.

    17. Suzanne B. Cashman et al., "Patient Health Status and Appointment Keeping in an Urban Community Health Center," *Journal of Health Care for the Poor and Underserved* 15, no. 3 (2004): 474–88; Lisa Renee Miller-Matero et al., "Depression and Literacy Are Important Factors for Missed Appointments," *Psychology, Health & Medicine* 21, no. 6 (August 17, 2016): 686–95; Baligh R. Yehia et al., "Barriers and Facilitators to Patient Retention in HIV Care," *BMC Infectious Diseases* 15, no. 1 (December 2015): 246; Brian W. Pence et al., "Association of Increased Chronicity of Depression with HIV Appointment Attendance, Treatment Failure, and Mortality Among HIV-Infected Adults in the United States," *JAMA Psychiatry* 75, no. 4 (April 1, 2018): 379; Kari Campbell, Stephen P. Raffanti, and Robertson Nash, "Adverse Childhood Event Scores Associated with Likelihood of Missing Appointments

and Unsuppressed HIV in a Southeastern U.S. Urban Clinic Sample," *Journal of the Association of Nurses in AIDS Care* 30, no. 6 (November 2019): 605–6.

18. Dorothy Wallis et al., "Predicting Self-Medication with Cannabis in Young Adults with Hazardous Cannabis Use," *International Journal of Environmental Research and Public Health* 19, no. 3 (2022): 1–15.

19. Claire Nee and Clare Witt, "Public Perceptions of Risk in Criminality: The Effects of Mental Illness and Social Disadvantage," *Psychiatry Research* 209, no. 3 (October 2013): 675–83; Amy Kroska et al., "Illness Labels and Social Distance," *Society and Mental Health* 4, no. 3 (2014): 215–34; Brouwers, "Social Stigma Is an Underestimated Contributing Factor to Unemployment"; Graham Thornicroft et al., "Global Pattern of Experienced and Anticipated Discrimination Against People with Schizophrenia: A Cross-Sectional Survey," *The Lancet* 373, no. 9661 (January 2009): 408–15; M. Webber et al., "Discrimination Against People with Severe Mental Illness and Their Access to Social Capital: Findings from the Viewpoint Survey," *Epidemiology and Psychiatric Sciences* 23, no. 2 (June 2014): 155–65.

20. Bruce P. Dohrenwend et al., "Socioeconomic Status and Psychiatric Disorders: The Causation-Selection Issue," *Science* 255, no. 5047 (1992): 946–52; V. Lee Hamilton et al., "Hard Times and Vulnerable People: Initial Effects of Plant Closing on Autoworkers' Mental Health," *Journal of Health and Social Behavior* 31, no. 2 (1990): 123–40.

21. Tanya N. Aiim et al., "Trauma Exposure, Posttraumatic Stress Disorder and Depression in an African-American Primary Care Population," *Journal of the National Medical Association* 98, no. 10 (2006): 1630–36; Jooyoung Lee, "Wounded: Life After the Shooting," *The Annals of the American Academy of Political and Social Science* 642, no. 1 (2012): 244–57.

22. Dickman, Himmelstein, and Woolhandler, "Inequality and the Health-Care System in the USA."

23. Dalton Conley, *Being Black, Living in the Red: Race, Wealth, and Social Policy in America* (Berkeley and Los Angeles: University of California Press, 2010).

24. Pager, *Marked*.

25. See also Hagan, Shedd, and Payne, "Race, Ethnicity, and Youth Perceptions of Criminal Injustice"; Eric M. Uslaner, *The Moral Foundations of Trust* (Cambridge: Cambridge University Press, 2002); Weaver, Prowse, and Piston, "Too Much Knowledge, Too Little Power."

26. Bell, "Police Reform and the Dismantling of Legal Estrangement."

27. John Hagan and Celesta A. Albonetti, "Race, Class, and the Perception of Criminal Injustice in America," *American Journal of Sociology* 88, no. 2 (1982): 329–55; Martha L. Henderson et al., "The Impact of Race on Perceptions of Criminal Injustice," *Journal of Criminal Justice* 25, no. 6 (1997): 447–62; Weaver, Prowse, and Piston, "Too Much Knowledge, Too Little Power"; Joe Soss and Vesla Weaver, "Police Are Our Government: Politics, Political Science, and the Policing of Race–Class Subjugated Communities," *Annual Review of Political Science* 20, no. 1 (2017): 565–91.

28. Hagan and Albonetti, "Race, Class, and the Perception of Criminal Injustice in America"; Henderson et al., "The Impact of Race on Perceptions of Criminal Injustice."

29. Clair, *Privilege and Punishment*.

30. Annette Lareau, *Unequal Childhoods: Class, Race, and Family Life* (Berkeley and Los Angeles: University of California Press, 2003).

31. Aiim et al., "Trauma Exposure, Posttraumatic Stress Disorder and Depression"; Conley, *Being Black, Living in the Red*; Dohrenwend et al., "Socioeconomic Status and Psychiatric Disorders"; Hamilton et al., "Hard Times and Vulnerable People"; Wildeman and Wang, "Mass Incarceration, Public Health, and Widening Inequality."

32. Daniel Brice Baker and Shahidul Hassan, "Gender and Prosecutorial Discretion: An Empirical Assessment," *Journal of Public Administration Research and Theory* 31, no. 1 (2021): 73–90; Cassia Spohn, John Gruhl, and Susan Welch, "The Impact of the Ethnicity and Gender of Defendants on the Decision to Reject or Dismiss Felony Charges," *Criminology* 25, no. 1 (1987): 175–92; Cassia Spohn and David Holleran, "Prosecuting Sexual Assault: A Comparison of Charging Decisions in Sexual Assault Cases Involving Strangers, Acquaintances, and Intimate Partners," *Justice Quarterly* 18, no. 3 (2001): 652–88; David Bjerk, "Making the Crime Fit the Penalty: The Role of Prosecutorial Discretion under Mandatory Minimum Sentencing," *The Journal of Law and Economics* 48 (2005): 591–625; Ulmer, Kurlychek, and Kramer, "Prosecutorial Discretion and the Imposition of Mandatory Minimum Sentences"; Cyndy Caravelis, Ted Chiricos, and William Bales, "Static and Dynamic Indicators of Minority Threat in Sentencing Outcomes: A Multi-Level Analysis," *Journal of Quantitative Criminology* 27, no. 4 (2011): 405–25; Jill Farrell, "Mandatory Minimum Firearm Penalties: A Source of Sentencing Disparity?," *Justice Research and Policy* 5, no. 1 (2003): 95–115; Mona Lynch, "Prosecutorial Discretion, Drug Case Selection, and Inequality in Federal Court Inequality in Federal Court," *Justice Quarterly* 35, no. 7 (2018): 1309–36; Richard D. Hartley, Sean Maddan, and Cassia C. Spohn, "Prosecutorial Discretion: An Examination of Substantial Assistance Departures in Federal Crack-Cocaine and Powder-Cocaine Cases," *Justice Quarterly* 24, no. 3 (2007): 382–407; Theodore R. Curry, Gang Lee, and S. Fernando Rodriguez, "Does Victim Gender Increase Sentence Severity? Further Explorations of Gender Dynamics and Sentencing Outcomes," *Crime and Delinquency* 50, no. 3 (2004): 319–43; Timothy Griffin and John Wooldredge, "Sex-Based Disparities in Felony Dispositions Before Versus After Sentencing Reform in Ohio," *Criminology* 44, no. 4 (2006): 893–923; John H. Kramer and Jeffery T. Ulmer, "Downward Departures for Serious Violent Offenders: Local Court 'Corrections' to Pennsylvania's Sentencing Guidelines," *Criminology* 40, no. 4 (2002): 897–932; Van Cleve, *Crook County*.

33. Curry, Lee, and Rodriguez, "Does Victim Gender Increase Sentence Severity?"; Kramer and Ulmer, "Downward Departures for Serious Violent Offenders"; Kutateladze et al., "Cumulative Disadvantage"; Besiki L. Kutateladze, Nancy R. Andiloro, and Brian D. Johnson, "Opening Pandora's Box: How Does Defendant Race Influence Plea Bargaining?," *Justice Quarterly* 33, no. 3 (2016): 398–426; Terance D. Miethe, "Charging and Plea Bargaining Practices Under Determinate Sentencing: An Investigation of the Hydraulic Displacement of Discretion," *The Journal of Criminal Law and Criminology* 78, no. 1 (1987): 155–76; Jeffery T. Ulmer, Noah Painter-Davis, and Leigh Tinik, "Disproportional Imprisonment of Black and Hispanic Males: Sentencing Discretion, Processing Outcomes, and Policy Structures," *Justice Quarterly* 33, no. 4 (2016): 642–81.

34. Harcourt, "Risk as a Proxy for Race"; Mayson, "Bias In, Bias Out."

35. Kohler-Hausmann, *Misdemeanorland*, 22.

36. Jeffrey Lin, Ryken Grattet, and Joan Petersilia, "'Back-End Sentencing' and Reimprisonment: Individual, Organizational, and Community Predictors of Parole Sanctioning Decisions," *Criminology* 48, no. 3 (2010): 759–95; Pew Charitable Trusts, "Probation and Parole Systems Marked by High Stakes, Missed Opportunities," 2018, https://www.pewtrusts.org/en/research-and-analysis/issue-briefs/2018/09/probation-and-parole-systems-marked-by-high-stakes-missed-opportunities; Michelle S. Phelps, "Ending Mass Probation: Sentencing, Supervision, and Revocation," *The Future of Children* 28, no. 1 (2018): 125–46; Kohler-Hausmann, *Misdemeanorland*.

37. William R. Kelly, *Criminal Justice at the Crossroads: Transforming Crime and Punishment* (New York: Columbia University Press, 2015).

38. Broner et al., "Effects of Diversion on Adults with Co-Occurring Mental Illness and Substance Use"; Butler, Goodman-Delahunty, and Lulham, "Effectiveness of Pretrial Community-Based Diversion"; Lange, Rehm, and Popova, "The Effectiveness of Criminal Justice Diversion Initiatives in North America"; Rempel et al., *Changing the Role of the Prosecutor*; Roe-Sepowitz et al., "Adult Prostitution Recidivism."

39. Foucault, *Discipline and Punish*.

40. Wacquant, *Punishing the Poor*; Herring, "Complaint-Oriented Policing"; Lara-Millán, *Redistributing the Poor*.

41. Court Statistics Project, "State Court Caseload Digest, 2018 Data," 2018, Conference of State Court Administrators and the National Center for State Courts; Van Cleve, *Crook County*.

CHAPTER SIX

1. Bureau of Justice Statistics, "Felony Defendants in Large Urban Counties, 2009," 2009, https://www.bjs.gov/index.cfm?ty=pbdetail&iid=4845.

2. Fifty-six percent of the jurisdictions in my random national sample run a pretrial diversion program, specialty court, and/or other diversion program that operates *post-plea*. For more details on that sample, see methodological appendix A.

3. Alexandra Natapoff, *Punishment Without Crime: How Our Massive Misdemeanor System Traps the Innocent and Makes America More Unequal* (New York: Basic Books, 2018).

4. Pager, *Marked*; Uggen et al., "The Edge of Stigma; Devah Pager and Lincoln Quillian, "Walking the Talk? What Employers Say Versus What They Do," *American Sociological Review* 70 (2005): 355–80.

5. Anne Morrison Piehl and Shawn D. Bushway, "Measuring and Explaining Charge Bargaining," *Journal of Quantitative Criminology* 23, no. 2 (2007): 105–25.

6. National Institute of Justice, "Program Profile: Bronx (NY) Mental Health Court," Crime Solutions, 2016, https://crimesolutions.ojp.gov/ratedprograms/475#pd.

7. These national standards read as follows: "The pretrial diversion/intervention program should retain the right to terminate service delivery or recommend termination when the participant demonstrates unsatisfactory compliance with the intervention plan. When such a determination is made, the participant should be returned to traditional criminal justice processing without prejudice" (National

Association of Pretrial Services Agencies, "Performance Standards and Goals for Pretrial Diversion/Intervention," 24)

8. For an insightful examination of counselors' work to protect client confidentiality in their communications with the courts in the drug court context, see Nolan, *Reinventing Justice*. In the jurisdictions where I conducted in-depth interviews or observations, details about defendants' performances in treatment were not shared with the courts. But this practice may vary across states. In California, for instance, a statute dictates that the final decision to return a defendant from pretrial diversion to the traditional court system be made in a formal hearing in court (see California Code, Penal Code—PEN § 1000.3). The state of Washington also requires such a hearing and specifies that the nature of the defendant's alleged noncompliance must be considered and evidence of that noncompliance presented to the court (see Revised Code of Washington, chap. 69.50).

9. A 2003 evaluation study in New York found that defendants who did not complete drug court received longer sentences on average than similar defendants who stayed in the traditional system, although the mechanism was unclear. Rempel et al., "The New York State Adult Drug Court Evaluation."

10. Cohen and Kyckelhahn, "State Court Processing Statistics."

11. Davis, *Arbitrary Justice*; William R. Kelly and Robert Pitman, *Confronting Underground Justice: Reinventing Plea Bargaining for Effective Criminal Justice Reform* (Lanham, MD: Rowman & Littlefield, 2018).

12. Davis, *Arbitrary Justice*; Gottschalk, *Caught*; Pfaff, *Locked In*; Kelly and Pitman, *Confronting Underground Justice*.

13. Will Dobbie, Jacob Goldin, and Crystal S. Yang, "The Effects of Pre-Trial Detention on Conviction, Future Crime, and Employment: Evidence from Randomly Assigned Judges," *American Economic Review* 108, no. 2 (February 1, 2018): 201–40; Davis, *Arbitrary Justice*; Pfaff, *Locked In*; John H. Langbein, "Understanding the Short History of Plea Bargaining," *Law & Society Review* 13, no. 2 (1979): 261–72.

14. For the full vignettes, survey text, and more details about the study design and respondent recruitment and participation, see methodological appendix B.

15. Observational study of the impacts of a pretrial diversion option on prosecutorial decision-making is complicated by the fact that key factors such as prosecutorial culture and jurisdiction demographics are likely to be associated with *both* use of diversion and particular approaches to charging and other decisions. See, e.g., Frederick and Stemen, "The Anatomy of Discretion."

16. Mele and Miller, *Civil Penalties, Social Consequences*; Pager, *Marked*.

17. When analysis was limited only to respondents who had first chosen to accept the cases for prosecution, the mean likelihood of selecting a felony plea was higher in both conditions, but the size and significance of the difference between conditions was unchanged.

18. More details on the experiment are available in methodological appendix B.

19. Marisa Omori, "Spatial Dimensions of Racial Inequality: Neighborhood Racial Characteristics and Drug Sentencing," *Race and Justice* 7, no. 1 (2017): 35–58.

20. Albonetti, "Prosecutorial Discretion: The Effects of Uncertainty"; Celesta A. Albonetti, "An Integration of Theories to Explain Judicial Discretion," *Social Problems* 38, no. 2 (1991): 247–66.

21. Ulmer, Kurlychek, and Kramer, "Prosecutorial Discretion and the Imposition of Mandatory Minimum Sentences"; Bjerk, "Making the Crime Fit the Penalty"; Caravelis, Chiricos, and Bales, "Static and Dynamic Indicators of Minority Threat in Sentencing Outcomes"; Matthew S. Crow and Kathrine A. Johnson, "Race, Ethnicity, and Habitual-Offender Sentencing: A Multilevel Analysis of Individual and Contextual Threat," *Criminal Justice Policy Review* 19, no. 1 (2008): 63–83; Darrell J. Steffensmeier and Stephen Demuth, "Ethnicity and Judges' Sentencing Decisions: Hispanic-Black-White Comparisons," *Criminology* 39, no. 1 (2001): 145–78; Kutateladze, Andiloro, and Johnson, "Opening Pandora's Box"; Kutateladze et al., "Cumulative Disadvantage".

22. Marisa Omori and Nick Petersen, "Institutionalizing Inequality in the Courts: Decomposing Racial and Ethnic Disparities in Detention, Conviction, and Sentencing," *Criminology* 58, no. 4 (2020): 678–713; Baker and Hassan, "Gender and Prosecutorial Discretion: An Empirical Assessment"; Clair, *Privilege and Punishment*; Kohler-Hausmann, *Misdemeanorland*.

23. Based on administrative data on all defendants diverted in that jurisdiction between 2014 and 2017.

24. In *Bell v. Wolfish*, for instance, the Court ruled that overcrowded and abusive conditions of incarceration did not constitute punishment because officials had not imposed the conditions with punitive intent. Bell v. Wolfish, 441 U.S. 520 (1979).

25. Sheffey v. Greer, 391 F.Supp. 1044 (1975); Johnson v. Glick, 481 F.2d 1028 (1973); Miller v. Hawver, 474 F.Supp. 441 (1979).

26. Mahler v. Eby, 264 U.S. 32 (1924); Bugajewitz v. Adams, 228 U.S. 585 (1913).

27. In *U.S. v. Salerno*, the Supreme Court upheld the preventive detention provision in the Bail Reform Act of 1984. They ruled that pretrial detention is a regulatory act, not a punishment, and as such does not trigger the same level of protection as other forms of incarceration. U.S. v. Salerno, 481 U.S. 739 (1987). For a recent study showing that the experiences of people in pretrial detention do not differ from those of people serving out sentences in jail, see Claudia N. Anderson, Joshua C. Cochran, and Andrea N. Montes, "How Punitive Is Pretrial? Measuring the Relative Pains of Pretrial Detention," *Punishment & Society*, OnlineFirst.

28. Garland, *Punishment and Modern Society*, 17.

29. Nolan, *Reinventing Justice*.

30. Todd R. Clear, *Harm in American Penology: Offenders, Victims and Their Communities* (Albany: State University of New York Press, 1994), 2.

31. Clear, *Harm in American Penology*, 4.

32. Feeley, *The Process Is the Punishment*; Van Cleve, *Crook County*.

33. Digital criminal records are typically available prior to conviction and remain so regardless of the ultimate outcome of the case. The practice of releasing those records is justified by public agencies not as retribution but as transparency or risk management. Lageson, *Digital Punishment*.

34. Clear, *Harm in American Penology*, does not give a specific definition for "harm," but Merriam-Webster defines it as "physical or mental damage." Merriam-Webster, https://www.merriam-webster.com/dictionary/harm#:~:text=%3A%20to%20damage%20or%20injure%20physically,see%20harm%20entry%201)%20to, s.v. "harm."

35. Assari et al., "Discrimination Fully Mediates the Effects of Incarceration History"; Marc Mauer and Meda Chesney-Lind, eds., *Invisible Punishment: The Collateral Consequences of Mass Imprisonment* (New York: The New Press, 2002); Pager, *Marked*; Robert Stewart and Christopher Uggen, "Criminal Records and College Admissions: A Modified Experimental Audit," *Criminology* 58, no. 1 (2020): 156–88; Uggen et al., "The Edge of Stigma."

36. Erving Goffman, *Stigma: Notes on the Management of Spoiled Identity* (Englewood Cliffs, NJ: Prentice-Hall, 1963), 3.

37. See table 4 in methodological appendix A.

38. American Bar Association, "Collateral Consequences of Criminal Convictions."

39. Pager, *Marked*; Pager and Quillian, "Walking the Talk?"; Uggen et al., "The Edge of Stigma"; Richard D. Schwartz and Jerome H. Skolnick, "Two Studies of Legal Stigma," *Social Problems* 10, no. 2 (1962): 133–42.

40. Akhil Gupta, "Narratives of Corruption: Anthropological and Fictional Accounts of the Indian State," *Ethnography* 6, no. 1 (2005): 5–34, at 28; see also Gilbert M. Joseph and Daniel Nugent, *Everyday Forms of State Formation: Revolution and the Negotiation of Rule in Modern Mexico* (Durham, NC: Duke University Press, 1994); Akhil Gupta, "Blurred Boundaries: The Discourse of Corruption, the Culture of Politics, and the Imagined State," *American Ethnologist* 22, no. 2 (1995): 375–402.

41. Javier Auyero, *Patients of the State: The Politics of Waiting in Argentina* (Durham, NC: Duke University Press, 2012).

42. Shoshana V. Aronowitz et al., "Mixed Studies Review of Factors Influencing Receipt of Pain Treatment by Injured Black Patients," *Journal of Advanced Nursing* 76, no. 1 (2020): 34–46; Jooyoung Lee, "The Pill Hustle: Risky Pain Management for a Gunshot Victim," *Social Science and Medicine* 99 (2013): 162–68; Jane Liebschutz et al., "A Chasm Between Injury and Care: Experiences of Black Male Victims of Violence," *Journal of Trauma* 69, no. 6 (2010): 1372–78; Desmond Patton et al., "Post-Discharge Needs of Victims of Gun Violence in Chicago: A Qualitative Study," *Journal of Interpersonal Violence* 34, no. 1 (2019): 135–55; James Dahlhamer et al., "Prevalence of Chronic Pain and High-Impact Chronic Pain Among Adults—United States, 2016," *Center for Disease Control and Prevention, Morbidity and Mortality Weekly Report* 67, no. 36 (September 14, 2018): 1001–6.

43. Boches et al., "Monetary Sanctions and Symbiotic Harms"; Martin et al., "Monetary Sanctions: Legal Financial Obligations"; Pattillo et al., "Monetary Sanctions and Housing Instability"; Harris and Smith, "Monetary Sanctions as Chronic and Acute Health Stressors."

44. Cohen and Kyckelhahn, "State Court Processing Statistics."

45. Curry, Lee, and Rodriguez, "Does Victim Gender Increase Sentence Severity?"; Farrell, "Mandatory Minimum Firearm Penalties"; Kramer and Ulmer, "Downward Departures for Serious Violent Offenders"; Kutateladze et al., "Cumulative Disadvantage"; Kutateladze, Andiloro, and Johnson, "Opening Pandora's Box"; Miethe,

"Charging and Plea Bargaining Practices Under Determinate Sentencing"; Ulmer, Painter-Davis, and Tinik, "Disproportional Imprisonment of Black and Hispanic Males."

46. Kutateladze, Andiloro, and Johnson, "Opening Pandora's Box"; Besiki L. Kutateladze, Victoria Z. Lawson, and Nancy R. Andiloro, "Does Evidence Really Matter? An Exploratory Analysis of the Role of Evidence in Plea Bargaining in Felony Drug Cases," *Law and Human Behavior* 39, no. 5 (2015): 431–42; Miethe, "Charging and Plea Bargaining Practices Under Determinate Sentencing."

47. Rodney F. Kingsnorth and Randall C. MacIntosh, "Intimate Partner Violence: The Role of Suspect Gender in Prosecutorial Decision-Making," *Justice Quarterly* 24, no. 3 (2007): 460–95; Kutateladze, "Tracing Charge Trajectories"; Kutateladze, Andiloro, and Johnson, "Opening Pandora's Box"; Kutateladze et al., "Cumulative Disadvantage."

48. Administrative data on pretrial diversion from four urban jurisdictions (including my field site) shows consistent, large racial inequalities in completion rates. See chapter 5 for more detail. For published studies documenting significant inequalities in drug court completion, see McKean and Warren-Gordon, "Racial Differences in Graduation Rates from Adult Drug Treatment Courts"; DeVall and Lanier, "Successful Completion"; Shah et al., "Addiction Severity Index Scores and Urine Drug Screens at Baseline."

49. Based on administrative data on all defendants diverted in that jurisdiction between 2014 and 2017.

50. Based on analysis of complete docket entries for 394 defendants diverted in that jurisdiction between 2014 and 2017.

51. DeVall and Lanier, "Successful Completion"; McKean and Warren-Gordon, "Racial Differences in Graduation Rates from Adult Drug Treatment Courts"; Butzin, Saum, and Scarpitti, "Factors Associated with Completion of a Drug Treatment Court Diversion Program"; Dannerbeck et al., "Understanding and Responding to Racial Differences in Drug Court Outcomes"; Howard, "Race, Neighborhood, and Drug Court Graduation."

CONCLUSION

1. Harrington, *Mind Fixers*; Fletcher, *Inside Rehab*.

2. National Institute of Mental Health, "Mental Illness," 2019, https://www.nimh.nih.gov/health/statistics/mental-illness.shtml#part_154785; SAMHSA, "Key Substance Use and Mental Health Indicators in the United States."

3. Cha and Cohen, "Demographic Variation in Health Insurance Coverage."

4. Frank, Humphreys, and Pollack, "Our Other Epidemic"; Mark, Dowd, and Council, "Tracking the Quality of Addiction Treatment Over Time and Across States"; Taylor, "The Workforce Shortage in Addiction Care Reaches a Crisis Stage."

5. Andrilla et al., "Geographic Variation in the Supply of Selected Behavioral Health Providers."

6. Strach, Zuber, and Perez-Chiques, "Why Policies Fail."

7. Thornicroft, *Shunned*; Roth, *Insane*; Lara-Millán, *Redistributing the Poor*; Herring, Yarbrough, and Alatorre, "Pervasive Penality"; Stuart, *Down, Out, and Under Arrest*.

8. National Center on Addiction and Substance Abuse at Columbia University, "Behind Bars II."

9. SAMHSA, *Treatment Episode Data Set (TEDS)*. The vast majority of treatment centers receive public funding and are therefore represented in this dataset.

10. Institutional *logics* are the taken-for-granted conventions at the heart of every institution. Those logics operate not only through individual cognition but also through continual social enforcement and reinforcement. See Thornton and Ocasio, "Institutional Logics"; Thornton, Ocasio, and Lounsbury, *The Institutional Logics Perspective*.

11. Foucault, *Discipline and Punish*, 82.

12. See, e.g., Rothman, *Conscience and Convenience*; Cohen, *Visions of Social Control*. On the "problem of the unanticipated consequences of purposive action" more broadly, see Robert K. Merton, "The Unanticipated Consequences of Purposive Social Action," *American Sociological Review* 1, no. 6 (December 1936): 894–904.

13. Berger, Kaba, and Stein, "What Abolitionists Do"; Critical Resistance, "Reformist Reforms vs. Abolitionist Steps in Policing"; Interrupting Criminalization, Project Nia, and Critical Resistance, "So Is This Actually an Abolitionist Proposal or Strategy?"; Kaba, *We Do This 'til We Free Us*.

14. Morgan, "Responding to Abolition Anxieties," 1208.

15. Edelman, "Legal Environments and Organizational Governance"; Edelman, "Legal Ambiguity and Symbolic Structures"; Edelman and Cabrera, "Sex-Based Harassment and Symbolic Compliance"; Meyer and Rowan, "Institutionalized Organizations" (1977); Nonet and Selznick, *Law and Society in Transition*; Edelman, *Working Law: Courts, Corporations, and Symbolic Compliance*; Krieger, Best, and Edelman, "When 'Best Practices' Win, Employees Lose"; Edelman et al., "When Organizations Rule."

16. Davis and Greve, "Corporate Elite Networks and Governance Changes in the 1980s"; DiMaggio and Powell, "The Iron Cage Revisited"; Friedland and Alford, "Bringing Society Back In"; Hannan and Freeman, *Organizational Ecology*; Haveman and Rao, "Structuring a Theory of Moral Sentiments: Institutional and Organizational Coevolution in the Early Thrift Industry"; Johnson, Ridgeway, and Ridgeway, "Legitimacy as a Social Process"; Meyer and Rowan, "Institutionalized Organizations" (1977); Meyer and Rowan, "Institutionalized Organizations" (1991); Strang, *Learning by Example*; Zucker, "Institutional Theories of Organization."

17. Edelman, "Legal Environments and Organizational Governance"; Edelman, "Legal Ambiguity and Symbolic Structures"; Edelman and Cabrera, "Sex-Based Harassment and Symbolic Compliance"; Meyer and Rowan, "Institutionalized Organizations" (1977); Nonet and Selznick, *Law and Society in Transition*; Edelman, *Working Law*; Krieger, Best, and Edelman, "When 'Best Practices' Win, Employees Lose"; Edelman et al., "When Organizations Rule."

18. Gottschalk, *Caught*, 165; see also Katherine Beckett, *Ending Mass Incarceration: Why It Persists and How to Achieve Meaningful Reform* (Oxford and New York: Oxford University Press, 2022); Beckett, Reosti, and Knaphus, "The End of an Era?"; Ruth

Wilson Gilmore, "The Worrying State of the Anti-Prison Movement," *Social Justice*, 2015, http://www.socialjusticejournal.org/the-worrying-state-of-the-anti-prison-movement/; Seeds, "Bifurcation Nation."

19. Seeds, "Bifurcation Nation"; Beckett, *Ending Mass Incarceration*; Beckett, Reosti, and Knaphus, "The End of an Era?"; Michael Campbell, Heather Schoenfeld, and Paige Vaughn, "Same Old Song and Dance? An Analysis of Legislative Activity in a Period of Penal Reform," *Punishment and Society* 22, no. 4 (2020): 389–412; Gottschalk, *Caught*.

20. Cohen, "The Punitive City"; see also Cohen, *Visions of Social Control*.

21. Aebi, Delgrande, and Marguet, "Have Community Sanctions and Measures Widened the Net of the European Criminal Justice Systems?"; Padgett, Bales, and Blomberg, "Under Surveillance"; Lilley, Stewart, and Tucker-Gail, "Drug Courts and Net-Widening in U.S. Cities"; Spaans, "Community Service in the Netherlands"; Daniel P. Mears et al., "Juvenile Court and Contemporary Diversion: Helpful, Harmful, or Both?," *Criminology & Public Policy* 15, no. 3 (2016): 953–81; Blomberg and Lucken, "Stacking the Deck by Piling Up Sanctions"; Blomberg, Bales, and Reed, "Intermediate Punishment."

22. Cohen, *Visions of Social Control*, 822.

23. Phelps, "The Paradox of Probation."

24. Stuart, *Down, Out, and Under Arrest*.

25. Victor Ray, "A Theory of Racialized Organizations," *American Sociological Review* 84, no. 1 (2019): 26–53.

26. M4BL, "The Movement for Black Lives Announces Support for the People's Response Act," June 28, 2021, https://m4bl.org/press/support-for-the-peoples-response-act/; Amistad Law Project, "Philly Rallies for Non-Police Mobile Crisis Response"; Fuller et al., "Overlooked in the Undercounted."

27. Michael S. Rogers, Dale E. McNiel, and Renée L. Binder, "Effectiveness of Police Crisis Intervention Training Programs," *The Journal of the American Academy of Psychiatry and the Law* 47, no. 4 (2019); J. D. Livingston, "Contact Between Police and People with Mental Disorders: A Review of Rates," *Psychiatric Services* 67, no. 8 (2016): 850–57.

28. Community Oriented Policing Services, US Department of Justice, "New Funding Opportunities Open Now!," 2023, https://cops.usdoj.gov/html/dispatch/04-2023/new_funding_opportunities.html; Office of Public Affairs, US Department of Justice, "Justice Department Announces $40 Million in Funding to Advance Community Policing and $5 Million in Funding for the Collaborative Reform Initiative," 2022, https://www.justice.gov/opa/pr/justice-department-announces-40-million-funding-advance-community-policing-and-5-million; Bureau of Justice Assistance, US Department of Justice, "FY 2022 Collaborative Crisis Response and Intervention Training Program," 2022, https://bja.ojp.gov/funding/opportunities/o-bja-2022-171099; Ethan Dewitt, "Sununu Signs Bill to Fund Crisis Intervention Training for Police," July 8, 2022, https://newhampshirebulletin.com/briefs/sununu-signs-bill-to-fund-crisis-intervention-training-for-police/; Sheldon Whitehouse, US Senator for Rhode Island, "Reed & Whitehouse Announce $1.2 Million to Expand Crisis Intervention Training for Police Departments across RI," July 11, 2022, https://

www.whitehouse.senate.gov/news/release/-reed-and-whitehouse-announce-12-million-to-expand-crisis-intervention-training-for-police-departments-across-ri; Norm Ornstein and Steve Leifman, "How Mental-Health Training for Police Can Save Lives—and Taxpayer Dollars," *The Atlantic*, August 11, 2017, https://www.theatlantic.com/politics/archive/2017/08/how-mental-health-training-for-police-can-save-livesand-taxpayer-dollars/536520/; National Alliance on Mental Illness (NAMI), "Crisis Intervention Team (CIT) Programs," https://www.nami.org/Advocacy/Crisis-Intervention/Crisis-Intervention-Team-(CIT)-Programs.

29. Rogers, McNiel, and Binder, "Effectiveness of Police Crisis Intervention Training Programs"; Livingston, "Contact Between Police and People with Mental Disorders."

30. Edelman et al., "When Organizations Rule."

31. Lauren A. Rivera, *Pedigree: How Elite Students Get Elite Jobs* (Princeton, NJ: Princeton University Press, 2015); Frank Dobbin and Alexandra Kalev, *Getting to Diversity: What Works and What Doesn't* (Cambridge, MA: Belknap Press, 2022); Anne S. Tsui and Charles A. O'Reilly, "Beyond Simple Demographic Effects: The Importance of Relational Demography in Superior-Subordinate Dyads," *The Academy of Management Journal* 32, no. 2 (1989): 402–23.

32. Dobbin and Kalev, *Getting to Diversity*; Frank Dobbin, Daniel Schrage, and Alexandra Kalev, "Rage Against the Iron Cage: The Varied Effects of Bureaucratic Personnel Reforms on Diversity," *American Sociological Review* 80, no. 5 (October 2015): 1014–44.

33. Michael Givel, "Motivation of Chemical Industry Social Responsibility through Responsible Care," *Health Policy* 81, no. 1 (April 2007): 85–92.

34. Shanti Gamper-Rabindran and Stephen R. Finger, "Does Industry Self-Regulation Reduce Pollution? Responsible Care in the Chemical Industry," *Journal of Regulatory Economics* 43, no. 1 (January 2013): 1–30; Andrew A. King and Michael J. Lenox, "Industry Self-Regulation Without Sanctions: The Chemical Industry's Responsible Care Program," *The Academy of Management Journal* 43, no. 4 (2000): 698–716; Givel, "Motivation of Chemical Industry Social Responsibility through Responsible Care."

35. Sarah Brayne, *Predict and Surveil: Data, Discretion, and the Future of Policing* (Oxford and New York: Oxford University Press, 2021), 6.

36. Brayne, *Predict and Surveil*; Sarah Brayne, "Big Data Surveillance: The Case of Policing," *American Sociological Review* 82, no. 5 (2017): 977–1008.

37. Gottschalk, *Caught*, 260.

38. Cohen, "The Punitive City"; see also Cohen, *Visions of Social Control*.

39. Frank, Humphreys, and Pollack, "Our Other Epidemic."

40. Strach, Zuber, and Perez-Chiques, "Why Policies Fail."

41. Harrington, *Mind Fixers*; Arthur J. Lurigio, "People with Serious Mental Illness in the Criminal Justice System: Causes, Consequences, and Correctives," *The Prison Journal*, Supplement, no. 3 (2011): 66S–86S.

42. Madhukar H. Trivedi et al., "Bupropion and Naltrexone in Methamphetamine Use Disorder," *New England Journal of Medicine* 384, no. 2 (January 14, 2021): 140–53;

Leshner and Dzau, "Medication-Based Treatment to Address Opioid Use Disorder"; Wakeman et al., "Comparative Effectiveness of Different Treatment Pathways for Opioid Use Disorder"; Fairley et al., "Cost-Effectiveness of Treatments for Opioid Use Disorder."

43. Santo et al., "Association of Opioid Agonist Treatment with All-Cause Mortality"; Long and Gottlieb, "Is Opioid Agonist Treatment Associated with Reduced Risk of Overall and Cause-Specific Mortality in Opioid-Dependent People?"; Sordo et al., "Mortality Risk During and After Opioid Substitution Treatment"; Schottenfeld, Chawarski, and Mazlan, "Maintenance Treatment with Buprenorphine and Naltrexone"; Schuckit, "Treatment of Opioid-Use Disorders"; Leshner and Dzau, "Medication-Based Treatment to Address Opioid Use Disorder"; Kakko et al., "1-Year Retention and Social Function after Buprenorphine-Assisted Relapse Prevention Treatment"; Wakeman et al., "Comparative Effectiveness of Different Treatment Pathways for Opioid Use Disorder"; Fairley et al., "Cost-Effectiveness of Treatments for Opioid Use Disorder."

44. Steven Shoptaw et al., "Behavioral Treatment Approaches for Methamphetamine Dependence and HIV-Related Sexual Risk Behaviors Among Urban Gay and Bisexual Men," *Drug and Alcohol Dependence* 78, no. 2 (May 2005): 125–34; Mark P. McGovern et al., "A Randomized Controlled Trial of Treatments for Co-occurring Substance Use Disorders and Post-Traumatic Stress Disorder," *Addiction* 110, no. 7 (July 2015): 1194–1204; Kathleen M. Carroll et al., "Computer-Assisted Delivery of Cognitive-Behavioral Therapy for Addiction: A Randomized Trial of CBT4CBT," *American Journal of Psychiatry* 165, no. 7 (2008): 881–88.

45. National Harm Reduction Coalition, "Principles of Harm Reduction," 2023, https://harmreduction.org/about-us/principles-of-harm-reduction/.

46. They gave me permission to write about their work here, and I obtained approval from my university's Institutional Review Board before observing them in action.

47. Thomas Kerr et al., "Supervised Injection Facilities in Canada: Past, Present, and Future," *Harm Reduction Journal* 14, no. 1 (December 2017): article no. 28.

48. Ahmed M. Bayoumi and Gregory S. Zaric, "The Cost-Effectiveness of Vancouver's Supervised Injection Facility," *CMAJ* 179, no. 11 (2008): 1143–51; Steven D. Pinkerton, "Is Vancouver Canada's Supervised Injection Facility Cost-Saving? Insite Supervised Injection Facility," *Addiction* 105, no. 8 (July 9, 2010): 1429–36.

49. Thomas Kerr et al., "Safer Injection Facility Use and Syringe Sharing in Injection Drug Users," *The Lancet* 366, no. 9482 (July 2005): 316–18; Bayoumi and Zaric, "The Cost-Effectiveness of Vancouver's Supervised Injection Facility."

50. Brandon D. L. Marshall et al., "Reduction in Overdose Mortality After the Opening of North America's First Medically Supervised Safer Injecting Facility: A Retrospective Population-Based Study," *The Lancet* 377, no. 9775 (April 2011): 1429–37.

51. Evan Wood et al., "Changes in Public Order After the Opening of a Medically Supervised Safer Injecting Facility for Illicit Injection Drug Users," *CMAJ* 171, no. 7 (2004): 731–34.

52. Evan Wood et al., "Impact of a Medically Supervised Safer Injecting Facility on Drug Dealing and Other Drug-Related Crime," *Substance Abuse Treatment, Prevention,*

and Policy 1, no. 1 (December 2006): 13; Thomas Kerr et al., "Circumstances of First Injection Among Illicit Drug Users Accessing a Medically Supervised Safer Injection Facility," *American Journal of Public Health* 97, no. 7 (July 2007): 1228–30.

53. Evan Wood et al., "Rate of Detoxification Service Use and Its Impact Among a Cohort of Supervised Injecting Facility Users," *Addiction* 102, no. 6 (2007): 916–19; Evan Wood et al., "Attendance at Supervised Injecting Facilities and Use of Detoxification Services," *New England Journal of Medicine* 354, no. 23 (June 8, 2006): 2512–14.

54. Kora DeBeck et al., "Injection Drug Use Cessation and Use of North America's First Medically Supervised Safer Injecting Facility," *Drug and Alcohol Dependence* 113, nos. 2–3 (2011): 172–76.

55. European Monitoring Centre for Drugs and Drug Addiction, "Drug Consumption Rooms: An Overview of Provision and Evidence," 2018, https://www.emcdda.europa.eu/system/files/publications/2734/POD_Drug%20consumption%20rooms.pdf; Harm Reduction International, "The Global State of Harm Reduction 2016," https://www.hri.global/files/2016/11/14/GSHR2016_14nov.pdf. The United States has been particularly slow to adopt the model of the safe injection site, but the nation's first just opened in 2021. See Jeffery C. Mays and Andy Newman, "Nation's First Supervised Drug-Injection Sites Open in New York," *The New York Times*, November 30, 2021, https://www.nytimes.com/2021/11/30/nyregion/supervised-injection-sites-nyc.html.

56. National Law Center on Homelessness & Poverty, "Housing Not Handcuffs."

57. Herring, Yarbrough, and Alatorre, "Pervasive Penality."

58. National Law Center on Homelessness & Poverty, "Housing Not Handcuffs."

59. Bureau of Justice Statistics, "Drugs and Crime Facts"; Federal Bureau of Investigation, "Uniform Crime Report: Crime in the United States, 2015," 2015, https://ucr.fbi.gov/crime-in-the-u.s/2015/crime-in-the-u.s.-2015/persons-arrested/persons-arrested.

60. Elderbroom and Durnan, "Reclassified: State Drug Law Reforms."

61. Acker, *Creating the American Junkie*; Alexander Cockburn and Jeffrey St. Clair, *Whiteout: The CIA, Drugs, and the Press* (New York: Verso, 1998).

62. An updated list of all controlled substances is published annually in Title 21 of the Code of Federal Regulations (CFR), §§1308.11–1308.15. Substances are classified into Schedules I–V. Schedule I substances are defined as "drugs with no currently accepted medical use and a high potential for abuse" and include heroin and marijuana. Schedule II substances are defined as "drugs with a high potential for abuse, with use potentially leading to severe psychological or physical dependence" and include oxycodone, fentanyl, cocaine, and methamphetamine. Each of the remaining three categories is considered to have less "potential for abuse" than the last. Schedule III substances include buprenorphine (Suboxone, used to treat heroin use disorders) and products containing small amounts of codeine, such as Tylenol with Codeine. Schedule IV substances include alprazolam (Xanax) and clonazepam (Klonopin). Schedule V substances include medications with an even smaller amount of codeine, such as Robitussin. United States Drug Enforcement Administration, "Drug Scheduling," 2024, https://www.dea.gov/drug-information/drug-scheduling. On the adoption of drug

prohibitions, see Catherine Carstairs, "The Stages of the International Drug Control System," *Drug and Alcohol Review* 24, no. 1 (2005): 57–65.

63. Foster and Hagan, "Punishment Regimes and the Multilevel Effects of Parental Incarceration"; Harding, Morenoff, and Herbert, "Home Is Hard to Find"; David Kirk and Sara Wakefield, "Collateral Consequences of Punishment: A Critical Review and Path Forward," *Annual Review of Criminology* 1 (2018): 171–94; Sugie and Turney, "Beyond Incarceration."

64. Global Financial Integrity, "Transnational Crime and the Developing World," Global Financial Integrity, 2017, https://gfintegrity.org/report/transnational-crime-and-the-developing-world/.

65. Nadelmann and Kleiman, "Should Some Illegal Drugs Be Legalized?," 46.

66. Babu, "What Is Fentanyl and Why Is It Behind the Deadly Surge in US Drug Overdoses?"; Hoffman, "Tranq Dope."

67. Singh, Browne, and Montgomery, "The Emerging Role of Toxic Adulterants in Street Drugs."

68. Maher and Dixon, "Policing and Public Health: Law Enforcement and Harm Minimization in a Street-Level Drug Market"; Maher and Dixon, "The Cost of Crackdowns"; Campbell Aitken et al., "The Impact of a Police Crackdown on a Street Drug Scene: Evidence from the Street," *International Journal of Drug Policy* 13, no. 3 (2002): 193–202.

69. Council on Foreign Relations, "Mexico's Long War: Drugs, Crime, and the Cartels," 2021, https://www.cfr.org/backgrounder/mexicos-long-war-drugs-crime-and-cartels; International Crisis Group, "Drug Trafficking, Violence and Politics in Northern Mali," 2018, https://icg-prod.s3.amazonaws.com/267-drug-trafficking-violence-and-politics-in-northern-mali-english.pdf; Robert Muggah and Katherine Aguirre Tobón, "Citizen Security in Latin America: Facts and Figures" (Igarapé Institute, April 2018), https://igarape.org.br/en/citizen-security-in-latin-america-facts-and-figures/; Harvey Redgrave, "Two Sides of the Same Coin? The Link Between Drug Markets and Serious Violence," 2022, https://institute.global/policy/two-sides-same-coin-link-between-drug-markets-and-serious-violence.

70. Mirella van Dun, "'It's Never a Sure Deal': Drug Trafficking, Violence, and Coping Strategies in a Peruvian Cocaine Enclave (2003–2007)," *Journal of Drug Issues* 44, no. 2 (2014): 180–96; Paul J. Goldstein, "The Drugs/Violence Nexus: A Tripartite Conceptual Framework," *Journal of Drug Issues* 15, no. 4 (1985): 493–506; Angélica Durán-Martínez, *The Politics of Drug Violence: Criminals, Cops and Politicians in Colombia and Mexico* (Oxford and New York: Oxford University Press, 2018).

71. Nicholas Dorn, Karim Murji, and Nigel South, *Traffickers: Drug Markets and Law Enforcement* (London: Routledge, 1992); Durán-Martínez, *The Politics of Drug Violence*; Jeffrey A. Miron, "Violence, Guns, and Drugs: A Cross-Country Analysis," *The Journal of Law and Economics* 44, no. S2 (2001): 615–33; Robert Vargas, "Criminal Group Embeddedness and the Adverse Effects of Arresting a Gang's Leader: A Comparative Case Study," *Criminology* 52, no. 2 (2014): 143–68; Robert Vargas, *Wounded City: Violent Turf Wars in a Chicago Barrio* (Oxford and New York: Oxford University Press, 2016); van Dun, "'It's Never a Sure Deal'"; Mirella van Dun, "Exploring Narco-Sovereignty/Violence: Analyzing Illegal Networks, Crime,

Violence, and Legitimation in a Peruvian Cocaine Enclave (2003–2007)," *Journal of Contemporary Ethnography* 43, no. 4 (2014): 395–418; H. Richard Friman, "Drug Markets and the Selective Use of Violence," *Crime, Law and Social Change* 52 (2009): 285–95; Miron, "Violence, Guns, and Drugs."

72. Ambros Uchtenhagen, "Heroin-Assisted Treatment in Switzerland: A Case Study in Policy Change," *Addiction* 105, no. 1 (2010): 29–37.

73. Uchtenhagen, "Heroin-Assisted Treatment in Switzerland"; Jürgen Rehm et al., "Mortality in Heroin-Assisted Treatment in Switzerland, 1994–2000," *Drug and Alcohol Dependence* 79, no. 2 (August 2005): 137–43; Uwe Verthein et al., "Long-Term Effects of Heroin-Assisted Treatment in Germany," *Addiction* 103, no. 6 (June 2008): 960–66; Rosanna Smart and Peter Reuter, "Does Heroin-Assisted Treatment Reduce Crime? A Review of Randomized-Controlled Trials," *Addiction* 117, no. 3 (March 2022): 518–31.

74. Uchtenhagen, "Heroin-Assisted Treatment in Switzerland," 35.

75. Uchtenhagen, "Heroin-Assisted Treatment in Switzerland."

76. Mary Ellen Stitt and Javier Auyero, "Drug Market Violence Comes Home: Three Sequential Pathways," *Social Forces* 97, no. 2 (2018): 823–40.

77. Bureau of Justice Statistics, "Drug Use, Dependence, and Abuse Among State Prisoners and Jail Inmates, 2007–2009," 2017, https://bjs.ojp.gov/library/publications/drug-use-dependence-and-abuse-among-state-prisoners-and-jail-inmates-2007-2009.

78. Jeffrey A. Miron, "The Budgetary Effects of Ending Drug Prohibition," Cato Institute, 2018.

79. Nora Volkow, "Recent Research Sheds New Light on Why Nicotine Is So Addictive," National Institute on Drug Abuse, 2018, https://nida.nih.gov/about-nida/noras-blog/2018/09/recent-research-sheds-new-light-why-nicotine-so-addictive; UCSF Health, "Nicotine Dependence," 2023, https://www.ucsfhealth.org/conditions/nicotine-dependence.

80. Teresa W. Wang et al., "Tobacco Product Use Among Adults—United States, 2017," *Morbidity and Mortality Weekly Report (MMWR)* 67, no. 44 (November 9, 2018): 1225–32.

81. SAMHSA, "National Survey on Drug Use and Health, 2020," 2020, https://www.samhsa.gov/data/data-we-collect/nsduh-national-survey-drug-use-and-health.

82. Center for Disease Control and Prevention, "Current Cigarette Smoking Among Adults in the United States," 2022, https://www.cdc.gov/tobacco/data_statistics/fact_sheets/adult_data/cig_smoking/index.htm#print.

83. Center for Disease Control and Prevention, "Trends in Tobacco Use Among Youth," 2022, https://www.cdc.gov/tobacco/data_statistics/fact_sheets/fast_facts/trends-in-tobacco-use-among-youth.html#print.

84. Prabhat Jha et al., "Reducing the Burden of Smoking World-Wide: Effectiveness of Interventions and Their Coverage," *Drug and Alcohol Review* 25, no. 6 (November 2006): 597–609; Thomas R. Frieden and Michael R. Bloomberg, "How to Prevent 100 Million Deaths from Tobacco," *The Lancet* 369, no. 9574 (May 2007): 1758–61.

85. Evan T. Stanforth, Marisa Kostiuk, and Patton O. Garriott, "Correlates of Engaging in Drug Distribution in a National Sample," *Psychology of Addictive Behaviors*

30, no. 1 (2016): 138–46; Shirley J. Semple et al., "'High on My Own Supply': Correlates of Drug Dealing Among Heterosexually Identified Methamphetamine Users," *The American Journal on Addictions* 20, no. 6 (2011): 516–24.

86. Brian Mann and Conrad Wilson, "Why Oregon Is Recriminalizing Even Small Amounts of Illicit Drugs," *NPR*, March 5, 2024, https://www.npr.org/2024/03/05/1236075494/why-oregon-is-recriminalizing-even-small-amounts-of-illicit-drugs; Mike Baker, "Oregon Is Recriminalizing Drugs, Dealing Setback to Reform Movement," *The New York Times*, March 1, 2024, https://www.nytimes.com/2024/03/01/us/oregon-drug-decriminalization-rollback-measure-110.html?searchResultPosition=1; Associated Press, "Oregon Governor Signs a Bill Recriminalizing Drug Possession," *PBS News*, April 1, 2024, https://www.pbs.org/newshour/politics/oregon-governor-signs-a-bill-recriminalizing-drug-possession.

87. National Law Center on Homelessness & Poverty, "Housing Not Handcuffs."

88. Marco Venniro et al., "Volitional Social Interaction Prevents Drug Addiction in Rat Models," *Nature Neuroscience* 21, no. 11 (November 2018): 1520–29; Marcello Solinas et al., "Reversal of Cocaine Addiction by Environmental Enrichment," *Proceedings of the National Academy of Sciences* 105, no. 44 (November 4, 2008): 17145–50; Joëlle Nader et al., "Loss of Environmental Enrichment Increases Vulnerability to Cocaine Addiction," *Neuropsychopharmacology* 37, no. 7 (June 2012): 1579–87; Claudia Chauvet et al., "Environmental Enrichment Reduces Cocaine Seeking and Reinstatement Induced by Cues and Stress but Not by Cocaine," *Neuropsychopharmacology* 34, no. 13 (December 2009): 2767–78.

89. E. E. Schattschneider, *The Semisovereign People: A Realist's View of Democracy in America* (New York: Holt, Rinehart, & Winston, 1960), 68.

METHODOLOGICAL APPENDIX A

1. See, e.g., Lepage and May, "The Anchorage, Alaska Municipal Pretrial Diversion Program"; Virginia A. Hiday and Bradley Ray, "Arrests Two Years After Exiting a Well-Established Mental Health Court," *Psychiatric Services* 61, no. 5 (2010): 463–68; Robert C. Davis et al., "A Multisite Evaluation of Prosecutor-Led Pretrial Diversion: Effects on Conviction, Incarceration, and Recidivism," *Criminal Justice Policy Review* 32, no. 8 (October 2021): 890–909.

2. Kelly, *Criminal Justice at the Crossroads*, 172.

3. See, e.g., Henry J. Steadman, Joseph J. Cocozza, and Bonita M. Veysey, "Comparing Outcomes for Diverted and Nondiverted Jail Detainees with Mental Illnesses," *Law and Human Behavior* 23, no. 6 (1999): 615–27; Swaminath et al., "Experiments in Change"; Franklin E. Zimring, "Measuring the Impact of Pretrial Diversion from the Criminal Justice System," *University of Chicago Law Review* 41, no. 2 (1974): 224–41; Steven J. Lamberti et al., "The Mentally Ill in Jails and Prisons: Towards an Integrated Model of Prevention," *Psychiatric Quarterly* 72, no. 1 (2001): 63–77; Lepage and May, "The Anchorage, Alaska Municipal Pretrial Diversion Program"; H. Richard Lamb, Linda E. Weinbergeu, and Cynthia Reston-Parham, "Court Intervention to Address the Mental Health Needs of Mentally Ill Offenders," *Psychiatric Services* 47, no. 3 (1996): 275–81; Rani A. Hoff et al., "The Effects of a Jail Diversion Program on Incarceration: A Retrospective Cohort Study," *Journal of the American Academy of Psychiatry and Law* 27, no. 3 (1999): 377–86; Rafael A. Rivas-Vazquez et al.,

"A Relationship-Based Care Model for Jail Diversion," *Psychiatric Services* 60, no. 6 (2009): 766–71; Hiday and Ray, "Arrests Two Years After Exiting a Well-Established Mental Health Court"; Butler, Goodman-Delahunty, and Lulham, "Effectiveness of Pretrial Community-Based Diversion."

4. National Association of Pretrial Services Agencies, "Performance Standards and Goals for Pretrial Diversion/Intervention."

5. I relied on two publications to identify those common practices: Center for Health and Justice at TASC, "No Entry"; and National Association of Pretrial Services Agencies, "Pretrial Diversion in the 21st Century."

6. Todd D. Minton, Lauren Beatty, and Zhen Zeng, "Correctional Populations in the United States, 2019," Bureau of Justice Statistics, 2021, https://bjs.ojp.gov/library/publications/correctional-populations-united-states-2019-statistical-tables; National Association of Pretrial Services Agencies, "Pretrial Diversion in the 21st Century."

7. See Michèle Lamont and Ann Swidler, "Methodological Pluralism and the Possibilities and Limits of Interviewing," *Qualitative Sociology* 37 (2014): 153–71.

8. Clair, "Being a Disadvantaged Criminal Defendant."

9. Defined by US Census regions.

10. Caroline Wolf Harlow, "Defense Counsel in Criminal Cases: Bureau of Justice Statistics Special Report," 2000, https://bjs.ojp.gov/library/publications/defense-counsel-criminal-cases.

11. Eisenstein and Jacob, *Felony Justice*; Eisenstein, Flemming, and Nardulli, *The Contours of Justice*; Jeffery T. Ulmer, "Criminal Courts as Inhabited Institutions: Making Sense of Difference and Similarity in Sentencing," *Crime and Justice* 48, no. 1 (2019): 483–522.

12. See Lamont and Swidler, "Methodological Pluralism."

13. Eisenstein, Flemming, and Nardulli, *The Contours of Justice*; Eisenstein and Jacob, *Felony Justice*.

14. Robert M. Emerson, Rachel I. Fretz, and Linda L. Shaw, *Writing Ethnographic Fieldnotes* (Chicago: University of Chicago Press, 2011).

15. Howard S. Becker, "Problems of Inference and Proof in Participant Observation," *American Sociological Review* 23, no. 6 (1958): 652–60.

16. Johnson, King, and Spohn, "Sociolegal Approaches to the Study of Guilty Pleas and Prosecution"; Spohn, "Reflections on the Exercise of Prosecutorial Discretion."

17. Frederick and Stemen, "The Anatomy of Discretion."

18. For a complete list of cities included in the sample, see methodological appendix C.

19. Center for Sustainable Systems, University of Michigan, "U.S. Cities Factsheet," 2021, https://css.umich.edu/publications/factsheets/built-environment/us-cities-factsheet#:~:text=It%20is%20estimated%20that%2083,to%20live%20in%20urban%20areas.

METHODOLOGICAL APPENDIX B

1. Russell-Brown, *The Color of Crime*; Beth Richie, *Arrested Justice: Black Women, Violence, and America's Prison Nation* (New York: New York University Press, 2012); Simone Browne, *Dark Matters: On the Surveillance of Blackness* (Durham, NC: Duke University Press, 2015); João H. C. Vargas, *Never Meant to Survive: Genocide and Utopias in Black Diaspora Communities* (Plymouth: Rowman & Littlefield, 2008).

2. Yimeng Guo et al., "Population Survey Features and Response Rates: A Randomized Experiment," *American Journal of Public Health* 106, no. 8 (2016): 1422–26; Martha Sinclair et al., "Comparison of Response Rates and Cost-Effectiveness for a Community-Based Survey: Postal, Internet and Telephone Modes with Generic or Personalised Recruitment Approaches," *BMC Medical Research Methodology* 12, no. 132 (2012): 1–8.

3. Diana C. Mutz, *Population-Based Survey Experiments* (Princeton, NJ: Princeton University Press, 2011).

4. Diana C. Mutz, Robin Pemantle, and Philip Pham, "The Perils of Balance Testing in Experimental Design: Messy Analyses of Clean Data," *The American Statistician* 73, no. 1 (2019): 32–42.

5. Baker and Hassan, "Gender and Prosecutorial Discretion: An Empirical Assessment"; Eric P. Baumer, Steven F. Messner, and Richard B. Felson, "The Role of Victim Characteristics in the Disposition of Murder Cases," *Justice Quarterly* 17, no. 2 (2000): 281–307; Myers and Hagan, "Private and Public Trouble"; Ulmer, Kurlychek, and Kramer, "Prosecutorial Discretion and the Imposition of Mandatory Minimum Sentences"; Hartley, Maddan, and Spohn, "Prosecutorial Discretion: An Examination of Substantial Assistance Departures."

6. Pamela Grimm, "Social Desirability Bias," in *Wiley International Encyclopedia of Marketing*, ed. Jagdish N. Sheth and Naresh K. Malhotra (New York: John Wiley & Sons, 2010), 258.

7. Ivar Krumpal, "Determinants of Social Desirability Bias in Sensitive Surveys: A Literature Review," *Quality and Quantity* 47, no. 4 (2013): 2025–47; Pager and Quillian, "Walking the Talk?."

8. Caravelis, Chiricos, and Bales, "Static and Dynamic Indicators of Minority Threat in Sentencing Outcomes"; Crow and Johnson, "Race, Ethnicity, and Habitual-Offender Sentencing"; Ulmer, Kurlychek, and Kramer, "Prosecutorial Discretion and the Imposition of Mandatory Minimum Sentences"; Kutateladze, Andiloro, and Johnson, "Opening Pandora's Box"; Kutateladze et al., "Cumulative Disadvantage; Wayne McKenzie et al., "Prosecution and Racial Justice: Using Data to Advance Fairness in Criminal Prosecution," Vera Institute of Justice (New York: March 2009).

Index

abortion, 27
acceptance and commitment therapy, 75
ACLU (American Civil Liberties Union), 6
addiction. *See* substance use disorders
Affordable Care Act, 25
Alaska, 215n58
alcohol, 44, 58, 60, 96–98. *See also* breathalyzers
alcoholism, 21
anxiety, 97
Arizona, 62
arrests, 1, 3, 22–24, 34, 43, 79, 100, 114, 116–17, 181n2, 205n20. *See also* policing
assimilation of institutional logics: and control, 55–56, 65–71, 86–87; and public safety discourses, 64–65; punitive, 128, 131. *See also* institutional entrenchment
Auyero, Javier, 120
Aviram, Hadar, 24

bail, 1, 55, 77, 110. *See also* jail; legal system
Bell, Monica, 103
Biden, Joe, 30
Blomberg, Thomas, 7
blood-borne diseases, 137–38
Boudin, Chesa, 27, 31
Brayne, Sarah, 132
breathalyzers, 61–62, 97–98. *See also* alcohol
buprenorphine, 58, 60, 135, 209n13

California, 24, 209n13, 217n6
California District Attorneys' Association, 31
cannabis. *See* marijuana
Challenge of Crime in a Free Society, The (report), 28–29, 198n97
childcare, 99
chronic pain, 12, 92, 120–21. *See also* painkillers
Clair, Matt, 156
Clear, Todd, 116, 166
cocaine, 1, 60, 91, 125, 136
coercion, 13–14, 19, 40, 46, 50, 55–56, 77–78, 86, 114, 127. *See also* governability; punishment
cognitive behavioral therapy, 32, 75
Cohen, Stanley, 7, 48, 51, 130
Color of Change PAC, 169
compliance, 12–14, 19–20, 34, 43, 57–58, 76, 92, 104–5, 108–10, 113–14, 129–30, 164, 223n7, 224n8
confidentiality, 6–7, 58–59, 81–82, 224n8. *See also* therapists; transparency
Connecticut, 215n58
corporate sustainability, 132
courtroom workgroup, 41–45, 47–48, 162–63. *See also* defense attorneys; judges; legal system; prosecutors
courts: expanding role of, 38–39, 44, 50–51; presence of diversion program staff in, 42; as public forum, 105–6; required appearances in, 66, 118–20; working norms of, 42, 48, 77, 162–63. *See also* drug courts; legal system

crisis intervention teams (CITs), 131
Cruikshank, Barbara, 41

defense attorneys, 9, 45, 108, 162. *See also* courtroom workgroup; legal system
"defund the police" movement, 24
Delaware, 215n58
deportation proceedings, 45, 116
depression, 39, 97–98, 115
deprosecution, 27
detox, 58, 126, 136. *See also* substance use disorders; treatment
Dewey, Susan, 71
digital punishment, 116–17, 225n33
district attorneys. *See* prosecutors
diversion programs: completion rates of, 7, 43–44, 147–48, 218n4, 227n48; costs of, 31, 56, 61–64, 91, 99–101, 121–22; effectiveness of, 40, 48, 55–56, 70, 104, 181n2, 211n21, 216n68; expansion of, 11, 20, 28–29, 127, 189n56, 198n94; funding for, 44, 60, 63, 161–62, 181n5; goals of, 1–2, 6, 50, 123; limited transparency of, 32–34, 133, 166; noncompliance with, 12, 14, 19–20, 43, 92, 108–10, 113–14, 164; promotion of, 5, 25–26, 28, 30, 38, 43–44, 107–8; reliance of on prosecutors, 67; requiring guilty pleas, 47, 57, 108; standardization of, 8, 48, 68–70, 109–10, 161, 188n43, 223n7; supervision in, 56–57, 64, 76, 117–18; threats of punishment in, 40–41, 56; as voluntary, 1, 46–47, 77–78, 133–34, 206n29. *See also* inpatient treatment; National Association for Pretrial Services Agencies; reform; treatment
domestic violence charges, 31
drug courts, 29, 38–39, 60, 224n9. *See also* courts; legal system
drug decriminalization, 20, 24, 139–40. *See also* reform
drug legalization, 3, 15, 19–20, 136–39. *See also* reform
drug markets, 34, 137–38
drug possession: and arrest rates, 22–23; decriminalization of, 20, 24, 139–40

drug tests: consequences of failing, 12, 92, 101–2; costs of, 1–2, 61, 91, 133; efficacy of, 210n18; and false positives, 60, 210n17; inconveniences of, 37, 51, 56, 58–60; as practice of control, 67, 118–21
DSM-5, 21–22

Edelman, Lauren, 34, 129
employment discrimination, 4, 22–24, 45, 100, 108, 118
existential therapy, 75

Feeley, Malcolm, 28–29, 116
felony convictions, 45, 91, 100, 108, 110, 115, 117
fentanyl, 137
Ferrell, Jim, 64–65
Florida, 27
Foucault, Michel, 7, 26, 105, 128–29

Garland, David, 66, 116
Goffman, Erving, 117
Gorz, André, 189n50
Gottschalk, Marie, 48, 129, 133
governability, 67, 128–29. *See also* coercion
group therapy, 32, 44, 58–59, 73, 82–83. *See also* psychotherapy; treatment
guilty pleas, 47, 56–57, 108, 207n31. *See also* plea deals
Gupta, Akhil, 120

harm reduction, 135–36, 138. *See also* overdose; reform
Harrison Narcotic Act, 136
heroin, 1, 55, 100, 138
Herring, Chris, 24
HIV, 135, 137–38
homelessness, 3–4, 12, 23, 97–98, 136
housing discrimination, 22, 24
humonetarianism, 24

Illinois, 166
immigration, 45, 116
incarceration: exacerbating mental illness, 23; financial costs of, 4–5; and

growth in prison population, 4, 45, 66, 194n39. *See also* jail
Industrial Revolution, 21
inpatient treatment, 58, 114. *See also* diversion programs; outpatient treatment
institutional entrenchment, 2, 10–12, 15, 51, 55–56, 70–71, 128–32. *See also* assimilation of institutional logics; legal system; legitimation of institutional logics; obfuscation of institutional logics; reform

jail, 1, 47, 55, 78, 80, 91, 110, 125. *See also* bail; incarceration; punishment
judges: election of, 26, 197n79; as mental healthcare providers, 38–39; and plea deals, 110; and referrals to pretrial diversion, 5, 163–64. *See also* courtroom workgroup; legal system

Kaba, Mariame, 7
Kohler-Hausmann, Issa, 67, 104
Krasner, Larry, 27

Lageson, Sarah, 116
legal system: consequences of entanglement with, 1, 4, 45, 116; exit from, 37, 71, 123–24; expansion of, 51, 86–87, 131–32; perceptions of, 86, 103; and responsibility for mental health, 15. *See also* bail; courtroom workgroup; courts; defense attorneys; drug courts; institutional entrenchment; judges; policing; prosecutors; punishment
legitimation of institutional logics: and expanding jurisdiction, 20, 44–45, 50–51; and organizational norms, 65–66; and promises of reform, 26, 34, 129–30; and public concern, 10–11, 127–28. *See also* institutional entrenchment
leniency, 27–28
Louisiana, 166, 210n17

Manion, Leesa, 64
marijuana: arrests for possession of, 80, 92; legalization of, 3, 43; required abstinence from, 60, 120; return to use of, 12; testing for, 39, 60
Medicaid, 44, 61, 99
medication-assisted treatment. *See* buprenorphine; methadone
mental health: best care practices, 11–12, 56, 69–70, 134–35; social construction of, 21, 183n9; underfunded services, 21, 86, 191n15. *See also* social services; treatment
mental illness: contributing factors to, 22–23; definitions of, 12, 21–22, 126, 140, 183n9; punishment as response to, 3–4, 15, 21, 98, 134–35; stigma surrounding, 11, 24. *See also* post-traumatic stress disorder (PTSD); psychiatric medication; substance use disorders
methadone, 55, 58, 60, 135, 209n13
mimetic isomorphism, 69
Missouri, 23
Morgan, Jamelia, 129
Movement for Black Lives, 24
mug shots, 116–17
Mulla, Sameena, 87
Musto, Jennifer, 71

naloxone, 135
Narcotics Anonymous, 32, 76
National Academy of Sciences, 60
National Association for Pretrial Services Agencies, 48, 109, 149, 166. *See also* diversion programs
National Association of Drug Court Professionals, 60
net widening, 48–50, 133
neuroscience, 25
Nevada, 62
New Jersey, 215n58
New York, 166, 224n9
New York Times, 62
Nolan, James, 29, 224n8

obfuscation of institutional logics: and invisibility of punishment, 12, 128; and perceptions of empirical objectivity, 131–32. *See also* institutional entrenchment; transparency

opioid overdose, 4–5, 25, 55, 59, 196n66. *See also* substance use disorders
opioid withdrawal, 135. *See also* buprenorphine; methadone
Oregon, 20, 140
outpatient treatment, 99. *See also* inpatient treatment
overdose: deaths, 4–5, 25, 34, 135, 137, 140; increased risks of, 34, 59, 137–38; opioid, 4–5, 25, 55, 59, 196n66 (*see also* substance use disorders); symptoms of, 210n18. *See also* harm reduction

painkillers, 60, 120. *See also* chronic pain
penal harm, 116–17
Pennsylvania, 27, 166
Pew Research Center, 25
Pfaff, John, 205n23
Phelps, Michelle, 51, 130, 214n47
plea deals, 9, 14, 110. *See also* guilty pleas
policing, 1, 4, 19, 22–24, 27–28, 71, 103–4, 127, 131, 136. *See also* arrests; legal system
possession. *See* drug possession
post-traumatic stress disorder (PTSD), 61, 120, 152. *See also* mental illness; trauma
poverty, 2, 6, 23, 39, 41, 62–63, 71, 80–81, 91–92, 97–98, 100–101, 105, 114–15, 120–22, 127, 152, 156
pretrial diversion. *See* diversion programs
Progressive Era, 29
prosecutors: decision-making processes of, 38, 45–47, 49–51, 110–12, 123–24, 164–65, 171–78, 224n15; discretion of, 5, 9, 31, 45, 108, 205n19, 205n21, 206n25; election of, 26–27, 64, 169–70, 182n7, 197n79; relationship of to police, 27–28. *See also* courtroom workgroup; legal system
psychiatric medication, 22, 25, 134–35. *See also* mental illness; self-medication
psychodynamic therapy, 32
psychotherapy, 32, 76, 79–81, 134. *See also* group therapy; therapists
public defenders. *See* defense attorneys

public housing, 4, 24
public records requests, 148, 154–55, 167
public safety, 32–33, 64–65, 70, 136, 139. *See also* risk
Punishing the Poor (Wacquant), 71
punishment: assignment of, 107–8, 111–13; expansion of, 115, 127, 129, 214n47; legal definitions of, 115–16, 122–23; opposition to, 2, 6, 24–26, 33–34; reinforcement of, 10, 41, 67–68; visibility of, 1–2, 23, 26, 105–6. *See also* coercion; jail; legal system
Punishment and Modern Society (Garland), 116

racial inequality, 4, 7, 22, 104
racism: and anxieties about drug use, 22; criminalization of Blackness, 41, 65, 124; and institutional trust, 102–3; and sentencing, 112–13. *See also* systemic racism
Real Justice, 169
recidivism rates, 40, 44, 55–56, 70, 105, 147–48
reform: backlash against, 27–28; and institutional logics, 50–51, 55–56, 71, 86–87, 105, 128–30; and obfuscation of institutional logics, 108, 124–27; widespread political support for, 4–7, 24–25, 137–38. *See also* diversion programs; drug decriminalization; drug legalization; harm reduction; institutional entrenchment
reformist reforms, 7, 188n50
responsibility: assignment of, 15; judgment of, 99–100; negotiation of, 14, 80–81, 85
Responsible Care program, 132
restorative justice, 68
retributive violence, 26. *See also* punishment
Rhode Island, 215n58
risk, 14, 66, 81–83, 200n115. *See also* public safety
Rothman, David, 7

safe injection facilities (SIFs), 135–36
San Francisco, 24, 27, 31

Satterberg, Dan, 64
Schattschneider, E. E., 141
schizophrenia, 21, 126
Seattle Times, 65
Seeds, Christopher, 24
self-medication, 23, 61, 120. *See also* psychiatric medication
sentencing decisions, 111–12, 193n38, 224n9
sexual abuse, 31, 87
sex work, 71
Singh, Rashmee, 205n18
slavery, 65
social services: decreased availability of, 3, 22, 86; exclusion from, 23, 39–40, 204n7; long waiting lists for, 126–27; underfunding of, 21, 191n15. *See also* mental health; treatment
solitary confinement, 23. *See also* incarceration
Soss, Joe, 41
stacking charges, 108–9, 110
St. Germain, Tonia, 71
stigma, 117–18
Stuart, Forrest, 130
substance use disorders: diagnoses of, 21–22; rates of, 3–4, 140; and relapse temptations, 117; and social disadvantage, 99; variety of treatment approaches for, 32, 134, 209n13. *See also* detox; mental illness; opioid overdose; war on drugs
Surgeon General, 21
surveillance, 64, 75, 129
Sweet, Paige, 87
Switzerland, 138
symbolic compliance, 34, 129–30
systemic racism, 4, 22, 66, 91–92, 99, 104, 124, 132. *See also* racism

Texas, 23
therapists: dual roles as enforcers, 6, 13, 74–75, 78, 128; employment by programs, 63, 149, 161; relationship with clients, 76, 79–81, 84–85, 101–2, 151, 157–58. *See also* confidentiality; psychotherapy; treatment
tobacco, 139
transparency, 6, 32–34, 48, 58–59, 62, 127–28, 133–34, 148, 152, 166–67, 190n64. *See also* confidentiality; obfuscation of institutional logics
transportation: costs of, 6, 99, 114–15; and inconvenient timetables, 73–74; limited access to, 1, 126–27
trauma, 12, 82–83, 92, 99, 125–26. *See also* post-traumatic stress disorder (PTSD)
treatment: and coercion, 5–6, 13–14, 19, 40; costs of, 55; effectiveness of, 30–32; inaccessibility of, 39–40, 126–27; and power disparities, 152; as serving time, 14, 83–85, 115–16, 124; and social connections, 150; widespread support for, 25–26. *See also* detox; diversion programs; group therapy; mental health; social services; therapists
Treatment Advocacy Center, 24
Treatment Assessment Screening Center (TASC), 62–63
2008 fiscal crisis, 24

Van Cleve, Nicole, 116
Vera Institute for Justice, 38

Wacquant, Loïc, 71, 105
war on drugs, 1, 3–4, 29, 193n38. *See also* substance use disorders
Warren, Andrew, 27
Washington State, 19, 35, 64, 166, 209n13
Weaver, Vesla, 103
work schedules, 58, 99
World War I, 137

xylazine, 137